Weather as Medium

Leonardo

Roger F. Malina, Executive Editor

Sean Cubitt, Editor-in-Chief

See http://mitpress.mit.edu for a complete list of titles in this series.

Weather as Medium

Toward a Meteorological Art

Janine Randerson

The MIT Press
Cambridge, Massachusetts
London, England

This book was set in ITC Stone Serif Std by Toppan Best-set Premedia Limited. Printed and bound in the United States of America.

Library of Congress Cataloging-in-Publication Data is available.

Names: Randerson, Janine, author.
Title: Weather as medium : toward a meteorological art / Janine Randerson.
Description: Cambridge, MA : The MIT Press, 2018. | Series: Leonardo book
   series | Includes bibliographical references and index.
Identifiers: LCCN 2017059435 | ISBN 9780262038270 (hardcover : alk. paper)
Subjects: LCSH: Art and meteorology. | Weather in art. | Art and science. |
   Art, Modern--21st century--Themes, motives.
Classification: LCC N72.M48 R36 2018 | DDC 700.4/36--dc23 LC record available at https://lccn
   .loc.gov/2017059435

10 9 8 7 6 5 4 3 2 1

This book is dedicated to my daughter, Hazel Jessie Johnston. Aroha nui.

Contents

Series Foreword

Leonardo/International Society for the Arts, Sciences, and Technology (ISAST)

Leonardo, the International Society for the Arts, Sciences, and Technology, and the affiliated French organization Association Leonardo, have some very simple goals:

1. To advocate, document, and make known the work of artists, researchers, and scholars developing new ways in which contemporary arts interact with science, technology, and society.

2. To create a forum and meeting places where artists, scientists, and engineers can meet, exchange ideas, and, when appropriate, collaborate.

3. To contribute, through the interaction of the arts and sciences, to the creation of the new culture that will be needed to transition to a sustainable planetary society.

When the journal *Leonardo* was started some fifty years ago, these creative disciplines usually existed in segregated institutional and social networks, a situation dramatized at that time by the "Two Cultures" debates initiated by C. P. Snow. Today we live in a different time of cross-disciplinary ferment, collaboration, and intellectual confrontation enabled by new hybrid organizations, new funding sponsors, and the shared tools of computers and the Internet. Sometimes captured in the "STEM to STEAM" movement, new forms of collaboration seem to integrate the arts, humanities, and design with science and engineering practices. Above all, new generations of artist-researchers and researcher-artists are now at work individually and collaboratively bridging the art, science, and technology disciplines. For some of the hard problems in our society, we have no choice but to find new ways to couple the arts and sciences. Perhaps in our lifetime we will see the emergence of "new Leonardos," hybrid creative individuals or teams that will not only develop a meaningful art for our times but also drive new agendas in science and stimulate technological innovation that addresses today's human needs.

For more information on the activities of the Leonardo organizations and networks, please visit our websites at http://www.leonardo.info/ and http://www.olats.org/. Leonardo books and journals are also available on our ARTECA art science technology aggregator: http://arteca.mit.edu/.

Roger F. Malina
Executive Editor, Leonardo Publications

ISAST Governing Board of Directors: Nina Czegledy, Greg Harper, Marc Hebert (Chair), Gordon Knox, Roger Malina, Tami Spector, J. D. Talasek, Darlene Tong, Joel Slayton, John Weber

Leonardo Book Series Editor-in-Chief: Sean Cubitt

Advisory Board: Annick Bureaud, Steve Dietz, Machiko Kusahara, José-Carlos Mariategui, Laura U. Marks, Anna Munster, Monica Narula, Michael Punt, Sundar Sarukkai, Joel Slayton, Mitchell Whitelaw, Zhang Ga

Acknowledgments

I would like to express my deep gratitude to the many artists have given their time and lively thoughts to this research. I have enjoyed the vital conversations with Phil Dadson; David Behrman and Bob Diamond (via Skype); Joyce Hinterding and David Haines; Amy Howden-Chapman and Abby Cunnane of *The Distance Plan*; Natalie Robertson; Tom Corby; Billy Apple and Mary Morrison; Andrea Polli; Thorbjørn Lausten; Zune Lee; Bjarki Bragason (via Skype); and Sue Jowsey of F4; who have all helped to shape this manuscript. I also extend my thanks to all the artists who have given images for this book, and particularly to Ursula Biemann for the videos to view and the parts of narration that I have transcribed. I am profoundly grateful to climate scientist Dr. Jim Salinger and urban meteorologist Dr. Jennifer Salmond for their insights.

I am indebted to the eyes of many colleagues at AUT University who have given me feedback on my draft, including Professor Tina Engels-Schwarzpaul, Professor Chris Braddock, Professor Welby Ings, and Dr Maria O'Connor. I have been fortunate for the steady support of my research assistant, Lucy Meyle: a colossal thank you for all your work. Thanks also to Paul Barrett for proofing and Rumen Rachev for referencing assistance. I owe many of my students for the creative impetus for this project. I am also thankful for the funding given by the AUT School of Art and Design and the Faculty of Design and Creative Technologies. In addition, I am grateful to Doug Sery and the editorial team at the MIT Press and to Kathleen Caruso in particular for her care and patience, and the opportunities provided for research with the Leonardo network.

My reflections on Māori ecological paradigms developed from generous conversations with artists and academics Amanda Yates (Ngāti Rangiwewehi, Ngāti Whakaue, Te Aitanga ā Māhaki, Rongowhakāta), Natalie Robertson (Ngāti Porou, Ngāti Puai, Clann Dhònnchaidh), Rachel Shearer (Te Aitanga ā Māhaki, Rongowhakaata, Ngāti Kahungunu), and Tracey Tawhiao (Ngai Te Rangi, Whakatohea, Tuwharetoa). I thank Jason De Santolo for his insight into the Garrwa weather world. This project began with my PhD research at the University of Melbourne, and I owe a great deal to my former supervisors, Professor Sean Cubitt and Professor Scott McQuire, for their expansive outlook and many conversations. This book is also inspired by the memory of my colleague, Dr. Paul Cullen—an "ambidextrous" thinker who energized me with his ecological curiosity across art and environmental science.

Finally, my research could not have been carried out without the support of my immediate family, and my parents. When my eight-year old daughter Hazel asks me what my story is about, I explain that it is about the weather as best as I can tell it. The deepest of thanks goes to them for their patience and love; as my husband Jason well knows, I could not have done this without him.

Illustrations

Introduction: Weather as Media

Every day we hear of the desperation for rain, the terrors of flood, or the approach of cyclones along with alarming future climate projections. We read the local signs—and we learn from scientists that the climate is changing: so why is it so difficult to act on this knowledge? As we face irreversible change in the earth's atmosphere, new demands are made for science, politicians, and the arts to do something, anything. Contemporary artists are rising to this call by joining forces with both local communities and environmental scientists. This book suggests that when we feel demoralized or unwilling to hear any more about climate change (some call this *climate fatigue*), art has agency. Meteorological art acts as an alternative to anxiety-fueling news reports or weighty climate reports as a site of dialogue and agitation. I treat the weather as a lively provocateur, collaborator, and catalyst for vital ecocritical conversations. Artists offer moments of release, while holding the new weather in the political spotlight.

For all the gathering interest in art-science-community-nonhuman relations, there is a dearth of critical reflection on their mutual salience in written form. Meteorological art is important to mobilize our passions directly, as opposed to the high degree of specialization and knowledge of numerical data that is often needed to understand scientific language. In recent years, cultural theorists and artists have returned to science as a tangible connection to the "real," material world. Now, even though we have trepidations, we need scientists' ability to produce details about the physical world, particularly about the effects of climate change. We know about weather because we can feel it in a sudden shower or shift in temperature. Increasingly, however, atmospheric knowledge is a vast dataset that is too large and long historically to be experienced as individuals. We rely on science therefore to provide an overall account of climate change as something we can know. Artists, scientists, and community groups depend on each other to rally against a model of consumption that is unsustainable for the earth's atmosphere.

Meteorological art, as I see it, refers not only to artworks themselves, but to our social encounters with live weather. The weather is a co-performer in my art making, and writing, along with meteorological scientists, activists, and Indigenous stakeholders. Many accounts of artwork in this book are based on my conversations with artists, environmental scientists, and agitators from my immediate community in light of the changing climate. This book sustains an inter- and intradisciplinary perspective in which art is infused with atmospheric science and social politics. Artists began to work directly with weather-driven sculpture and performance in the 1960s to explore liveness, the active audience, systems-based science and new electronic technologies. Contemporary meteorological art still operates at the collision of disciplines and cultures, where generative platforms for ecological change flourish.

Many of the artworks included in this book hail from the Global South, Te Moana nui a Kiwa (the Pacific diaspora), particularly Aotearoa New Zealand, from where I write. Aotearoa is often translated as "the land of long white cloud," a name given by early Māori navigators on the *waka* (canoes) who first glimpsed our volcanic North island, swathed in dense cloud. These narrow isles have always weathered the storms, and now the tropical cyclones that afflict our Pacific island neighbors in higher latitudes (Tonga, Samoa, and the Cook Islands) are altering our weatherscape in the 40th parallel south. This vantage offers a direct connection to artists concerned with our new, more turbulent weather, who bring Indigenous values, environmental science, and activism together in energetic constellations. My narrative roves between hemispheres also stitching together artworks from Asia, Europe, and the Americas. Many artists, each with their own distinct cultural milieu, are brought together contingently, rather than in an attempt to pin down a new typology, art movement, or complete survey of weather in art. Instead, I hone in on modern and contemporary artworks in which meteorological strategies can be found. Weather as media is approached as a vibrant site of exchange, rather than through the modernist frame of medium specificity. Although there is no singular means to solve complex ecological problems, I will argue that meteorological art has a situated, local value and global online distribution that keeps weather politics in circulation.

In the process of writing this book, I have tested whether a low-carbon mode of research is possible. On this island, I live at a physical distance from many of the artists in the Northern Hemisphere. My conversations with many of the contemporary artists and environmental scientists take advantage of Skype, email dialogues, the sharing of video files, and online discussion networks. I have visited museums in Australasia that house significant international artworks from Alan Sonfist's *Crystal Enclosure* and David Medalla's *Cloud Canyons* at Auckland Art Gallery (AAG) to John Constable's

Clouds at the National Gallery of Victoria (NGV) Melbourne to Jean Dubuffet's meteorological lithographs and Fujiko Nakaya's *Fog Sculpture #94925: Foggy Wake in a Desert: An Ecosphere* at the National Gallery of Australia (NGA) Canberra. I have also curated international artworks into venues in Auckland to reach an audience in this part of the world. The global flows of contemporary art mean that artists are increasingly in dialogue with each other, and with invested communities, beyond arbitrary national borders— much like the circulation of weather. Before I trace specific moments in an eccentric prehistory of meteorological art, I probe the idea of weather as a form of media, along with the postanthropocentric currents of thought that orient the book.

Weather as Media

Everyday weather is part of the atmospheric envelope in which we sustain our lives, providing the circumstances for our survival. If we describe weather *as* media, then atmospheric phenomena are foregrounded, rather than understood as a given. The term *media*, when set in relation to weather, can be understood technologically as data, as well as culturally as part of our environment. Weather as an artist's medium can be an input in a process-based meteorological artwork, in the sense of a constitutive "material," like clay or paint. As a medium, weather connects us to the world and to each other through the rain, wind, and sunlight that carry sensations to our human and machinic receptors. Air and water might be the primary "media" for life, but, as Peter Sloterdijk (2009) reminds us, we are condemned to "being in" these atmospheric containers, even when they can no longer be taken for granted as good.

Weather exists in the media in the familiar context of *weather as news*, in which the forecasting of weather through maps and broadcasts structures our daily activities. Artists respond to the instant informatics of everyday practices of weather reporting, weather mapping, or lay observations of weather and climate in online media. However, the term *meteorology* originally suggested "meteors," or the extraordinary event in the sky. There is a tradition of meteoric reportage in painting, private diaries, chronicles, newspapers, and sermons from when the principles of modern meteorology were still in negotiation. Contemporary global media reportage of cyclones, drought, hurricanes, and tsunamis communicate warnings or dramatize the spectacle of weather. Televised satellite maps build tension as they track the path of cyclones, as they approach landfall with necessary yet often sensationalized storm warnings. Several of the artworks discussed in this book, including New Zealand artist Billy Apple's *Severe Tropical Storm 9301 Irma* (2002–2015) and Belgian artist Francis Alÿs's *Tornado* (2000–2010), reinterpret the dramatic narrative of a violent storm.

Contemporary artworks are also embedded in a politics of institutional critique and societal turmoil.

This book engages with weather as media through art practices that draw on the data sets used by meteorological scientists. Artists now occupy the same locations as meteorologists, from urban weather stations to remote fieldwork at glaciers and poles. Since the mid-twentieth century, however, the prime loci of climate and weather "media" are supercomputers and complex informational networks. The weather is dispersed through satellite information systems and climate is mediated and tracked by advanced instrumentation. Environmental sensors magnify our own perceptions of the weather. Meteorological and climate scientists work with data in ever-expanding variables, mathematical modeling, and data visualizations of predictive behavior. These computational forms have changed the communication of meteorological data in science, and they are rerouted again when harnessed by artists. Throughout this book, I show how meteorological art politicizes and contests the same weather data that drives the technosciences. Weather data becomes an affective, often charged material in the hands of artists.

The definition of media itself has been enlarged beyond its conventional usage as the technical reproducibility of visual, acoustic, and textual phenomena. The idea of media as technology has expanded to media *as environment*. Marshall McLuhan once compared the social habits created in early electronic environments to the natural environment: "An environment is naturally of low intensity or low definition. That is why it escapes observation. Anything that raises the environment to high intensity, whether it be a storm in nature or violent change resulting from a new technology, turns the environment into an object of attention" (1997b, 114). Today, we are at a phase of high intensity in which networked online culture and the new weather are equally sensitive to our collective actions. Artists, as argued by McLuhan, often show us where transformations in the social and natural environments occur. For John Durham Peters (2015), contemporary digital media are more than substrates that carry messages: they are "containers of possibility" in which nature and human invention meet. We exist in a swirl of "elemental media" that compose and recompose our world, from data clouds to celestial navigation. The medium of cinema has also been investigated through a meteorological lens *as weather* (McKim 2012). Meteorological art, like such expanded definitions of media, is considered here as both natural and cultural.

Artists interpret the aesthetics of weather phenomena through experiments with media technologies. The unexpected aesthetic effects when natural phenomena fuse with technical objects are studied closely by media historian Douglas Kahn. The aesthetics of sferics and whistlers, for instance, produced by lightning in the magnetosphere,

circulated through telegraph wires that were first enjoyed by long-distance phone oper-
ators last century. Contemporary artists such as Joyce Hinterding and David Haines
create encounters with little-known atmospheric phenomena to harness their sonic
and haptic affects (chapter 4). Rosi Braidotti (2016) offers the concept of *medianatu-
recultures*, which fuses the *medianatures* of Jussi Parikka (2011c) and the *naturecultures*
of Donna Haraway (2003) to frame the coincidence of a high level of technological
mediation with the planetary political era of the "Anthropocene." Braidotti's media-
naturecultures concept displaces the centrality of human life (bios) in the Humanities,
and shifts the focus to nonhuman "nature" and technology. This postanthropocentric
approach still remains committed to social justice and ethical accountability. Many
meteorological art practices also dwell less on human subjectivities, or the "structural
anthropomorphism" and "in-built Eurocentrism," critiqued by Braidotti, than on the
intricate web of relations with our shared atmosphere.

Meteorological Art and the Postanthropocentric Turn

Meteorological art sits within a lively philosophical tradition that displaces the human
subject—from Lucretius to Spinoza, critical philosophy to process-based ontologies and
the environmental posthumanities. In this book, I situate art practices among Indigenous cosmologies, social activism, scientific modes of knowing, and the philosophers
of the "postanthropocentric" turn. First, from a Māori cosmopolitical position in my
immediate referential framework in Aotearoa New Zealand, atmosphere *is* ancestor.
All things have *mauri* (life force), from flora and fauna, artworks and technologies to
Te Reo (the Māori language). When weather systems, mountains, and rivers are understood as ancestors, the spiritual and psychological impact of environmental degradation, such as the erosion of coastline caused by increasingly severe storms and floods,
compounds the losses to livelihood. A critical challenge to the British colonial model
is mounted in Aotearoa New Zealand by the commitment of *tangata whenua* (people of
the land) to a shared ecology, despite the traumatic history of colonization and resource
exploitation.

   Meteorological art extends out to an ontology of the elements, as I have found
in in my conversations, writing or art collaborations with Indigenous researchers Tru
Paraha, Tracey Tawhiao, Natalie Robertson, Amanda Yates, and Rachel Shearer. Māori
knowledge processes advocate slowing down, listening, and more openly contesting
the pace of neocolonial development through the platform of the *hui* (public forum). I
situate the current sociopolitical order, dominated by neoliberal interests, as a precarious set of contingent practices, to make room for Indigenous values. Specific challenges

to objective, scientific understandings of our physical world are framed by Hawaiian philosopher Manulani Aluli-Meyer (2006). For Aluli-Meyer, the objectivity found in scientific measurement and the positing of "facts" is only part of the picture we are looking at when coming to understandings of knowledge and value. She writes that in our current time of "*ike kai hohonu*, of searching and deep knowing" (264), mind, body and spiritual knowledge within should be valued together with scientific environmental knowledge. This worldview is a prompt to reassess the fissure between subject and object, human and nonhuman, long before the postanthropocentric turn in Euro-American thought. In the Māori cosmos we can listen to and speak with the elements, and the weather in turn empathizes with our human circumstances.

Indigenous art emerges from communities with a strong sense of connectedness to ancestors, an ecological paradigm that is often misunderstood or sidelined in academia. Recent Indigenous feminist scholarship in North America and Canada accompanies my understanding of Māori ecological knowledge. Indigenous "cosmovisions" across cultures draw on the past to confront the politics of the contemporary and future eco-crisis (Adamson and Monani 2016, 14). Mohawk and Anishnaabe academic Vanessa Watts describes Indigenous "Place-Thought," in which place, the elements, and thought "never could or can be separated" (2013, 21). To decolonize, she argues that Indigenous histories of elemental goddesses, such as the Sky Woman, should be understood in the context in which they were intended, as a world view, rather than positioned as "dangerously essentializing" folklore, legend, or superstition (Watts 2013, 33). Indigenous histories fuse the feminine, the spiritual, and the coming together of animal, water, and atmosphere prior to human existence. Humans are latecomers to this world of meteorological flux.

Indigenous artists and authors are joined by a growing number of nonindigenous writers who critique the dominance of specific academic voices in the environmental humanities. T. J. Demos (2016) calls for a decolonization of nature to recognize the resurgence of Indigenous cosmopolitics and environmental activism. Demos advocates a strengthening of ethicopolitical solidarity among the historically oppressed. In the same vein, for Isabelle Stengers (2010), science is less a transcendent "truth" than a body of competing interests that are constantly in negotiation. A more widely defined sense of values, she suggests, such as a sense of spirituality, also should be taken seriously by scientists, not merely "tolerated." The approach of this book is to position weather and climate realities as enacted by different entities, including the nonhuman the and spirit world.

From the actor-network theory (ANT) of the 1990s to more-than-human research methods (Whatmore 2006) to speculative philosophy and debate about the

Anthropocene, many authors strive for a reorientation towards "things". Bruno Latour calls on us to overcome the weight of knowledge divides in fresh assemblages around shared matters of concern, where the nonhuman also has agency. Meteorological art unsettles divisions between science and the social world, along with the separation of nature and culture, subject and object. In advance of COP21, for example, in *Make It Work/Le théâtre des négotiations* (2015), spearheaded by Latour and Sciences Po Experimentation in Arts and Politics program (SPEAP), two hundred students simulated a "parliament of things" to negotiate the future climate by adopting the voices of the air, the water, and the cryosphere along with other nonhuman elements.

This book travels still further back to pursue an more-than-human framework for meteorological art, through critical theorists Theodor W. Adorno and Hannah Arendt. Although Arendt is better known for her diagnosis of the human condition, I am interested in her less examined reflections on nature, history, and technology. While reflecting on the space age and its accompanying shift for human thought and for science, Arendt presciently comments, "To understand physical reality seems to demand not only a renunciation of an anthropocentric or geocentric world view, but also a radical elimination of all anthropomorphic elements and principles, as they arise either from the world given to the human five senses or from the categories inherent in the human mind" (Arendt 2006, 260). The Greco-Roman notion of man as the highest being, which later permeated modern science, is explicitly resisted. Following Arendt, we confront our bias toward a utilitarian view of the nonhuman world as a resource. The obsession with single entities and solutions, individual occurrences, and separate causation is rejected in favor of an ecologically oriented understanding of nature and history as a process.

The discourse of mastery continues in Big Science solutions to stave off global warming, while the meteorological turn in art often refuses any positivist escape routes. Through a study of the dynamic, and potentially catastrophic, interaction between nature and history, Adorno also critiques Enlightenment attempts to master nature. He lobbies against the coercive nature of human processes of identification that would turn nature into "second nature" (Adorno 2006b, 121). The tyranny of identification, with an exclusively human agenda, stifles our ability to recognize other-than-human lifeworlds. Adorno proposes that we may never reconcile the divergence of concept and thing, subject and object, or, in our case, human and weather system. How to avoid the reductive trap of naming, identifying and representing, in a time of climate crisis, is a question that contemporary artists need to confront. For this book, specific concepts of Adorno's, rather than the dialectical method per se, provide a relevant critique of the fetish of scientific positivism and regimes of the quantitative. The theorization of

relations between human and nonhuman, following Adorno, emerges from a philosophical position "not *about* concrete details but from *within* them, by assembling concepts around them" (Adorno 2008, 146; emphasis in original). Artists today engage
directly with "real" elemental phenomena from a position wrapped within the atmospheric system, just as they have in the deep history of the meteorological art to which
we now turn.

A Brief History of Meteorological Art: An Art and Science of Clouds, Deluges, and Rainbows

The forces of weather are woven into our material narratives. This brief history swerves
through moments that inform my sense of a meteorological art. The weather appears
as an intermediary for the spirits in the artifacts, rituals, and performances of many
ancient cultures. *Ngabaya* is a powerful songline saga that traverses the Australian continent, connecting all beings to place, and to the weather, through stories told within
a relational ontology. The *Ngabaya walaba* (spirit being public songline) is a multisensory enactment of ancient laws and practices that takes place through performance
for the Garrwa people. Performers wear *markirra* (white ocher) and co-perform with
the elements of fire, lightning, mist, and rain. These rites continue from deep time to
contemporary forms of Garrwa musical expression that resist colonization. Garrwa and
Barunggam researcher Jason De Santolo (2018) writes, "Just as we immerse ourselves
in the beauty of sun showers, the resonant marking of markirra expresses the living
energy of the Yigan, our dreaming."

Weather-borne spatial analogues for currents and divine communication are also
present in the Māori art of *manu tukutuku* (kites) in human or *manaia* (bird/dragon)
shapes. *Manu* means both kite and bird and *tuku tuku* refers to the winding out of the
thread. The art of kite-making and flying involves a sensitive interplay of the human
operator and the currents of wind. Manu tukutuku made of *harakeke* (flax fiber) were
also used to indicate wind strength and direction, as well as to speak to the Gods as a
form of spiritual medium. In the Māori cosmos, humans and all other biotic and abiotic
life are the progeny of Papatūānuku, the Earth mother. Tāwhirimātea, one of her children, is the disruptive god of wind and storms who did not want to separate from his
mother. Tāwhirimātea in turn sent away his wind children: one to the north (Tūāraki),
one to the south (Tonga), one to the east (Marangai), and one to the west (Hauāuru).
The direction to which each child was sent became the name of that wind. Sometimes
kites were used for divination; people would release a kite and follow it, claiming and
occupying the place where it landed. One oral history suggests that when a founding

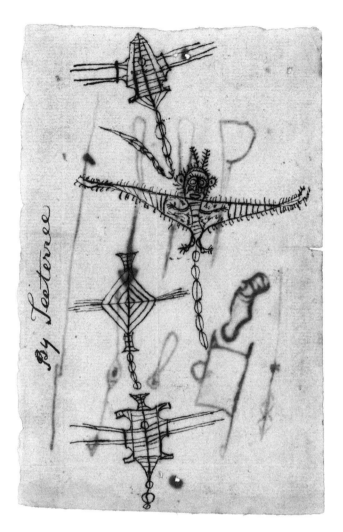

Figure 0.1
Titiri and Tui (Ngāpuhi). *Manu Tukutuku (Māori Kites)*. Ca. 1800. Sir George Grey Special Collections, Auckland Libraries. 7-A3168.

ancestor of the Ngāti Porou iwi (tribe), Porourangi, died in Whāngārā, on the East Coast of Aotearoa New Zealand, a kite was flown, and his brother, Tahu, the founding ancestor of Ngāi Tahu, was able to see it from the South Island.

A technique of simulating the weather's dissipative effects in artworks using air, ink, and silk emerged in the Chinese Tang dynasty. *Chui yun* (the blowing of clouds) is an artform of breath and ink in which ink is blown by mouth onto silk to form aerated cloudscapes. Cloud painters were divided into two groups: those who blew clouds and those who painted them. In Shitao's *Comments on Painting* (1710–1717), he declares that cloud in landscape painting is a means of understanding the universe (Damisch 2002, 213). Shitao would paint with wet ink onto wet paper to create mist and cloud effects that approximated weather. In *Mists on Mountain* (1656–1707), Shitao broke the rules of earlier styles of landscape painting to approximate the hazy Yangzhou mists by allowing the ink to wash into the paper and large sections of the mountain to dematerialize into nothingness. The play of ink was synonymous with invention and transformation; the chance landing of ink droplets suggests the unpredictability and creativity inspired by weather phenomena.

Euro-American art and scientific knowledge evolve from similar foundations in natural philosophy. Yet in the European Enlightenment, science began to separate from cultural life as people made nature the object of study. The title of *scientist* only emerged in the early nineteenth century to delineate, and privilege, the professional pursuit of knowledge of the physical world. The scientific account of nature often is characterized as rationalist, positivist, and detached. Artists, on the other hand, are given the task of providing a subjective, or affecting account of sensorial nature. Yet representations of the sublime turbulence or picturesque and calm weatherscapes laid out before an omniscient spectator have undoubtedly played a part in the estrangement of nature from ourselves. In central European art, when Aristotle's *Meteorologica* dominated meteorological knowledge, artists separated the heavens from the earth by walled gardens in Gothic altarpieces. The divided cosmos of the painters recalls Aristotle's sectioning of the universe into two spheres: the outer heaven made up of pure invisible fire called *aether*, which acts as the physical conduit of light and air, and the inner, earthly sphere. Yet artworks are not merely the byproduct of natural philosophers' ideas; they also generate the cultural conditions for knowledge about the atmosphere to take hold. In an art-mirrors-science model, the movement is largely in one direction, from scientific idea to embodiment of that idea in artwork. This book, however, shows that the movement of ideas between art and meteorology flows in multiple directions.

In the European Renaissance, the artist and natural philosopher merged in pursuit of a classically inspired naturalism. Leonardo da Vinci's studies of hydrology and

Figure 0.2
Leonardo Da Vinci. *A deluge*. Ca. 1517–1518. Black chalk on paper, 16.3 × 21 cm. Royal Collection Trust/© Her Majesty Queen Elizabeth II 2018. RCIN 912380.

aerology, such as eddies of swirling water, are observations of nature rather than the medieval, hierarchical *scala naturae* with God at the apex. *A deluge* (1517) is da Vinci's visual treatise on the flux of a dynamic system of clouds and water. Caught up in this turbulent schema are the shattered blocks of a mountain arch thrown apart by an intense swirl of water. Leonardo da Vinci painted many black chalk and ink deluges in this period during the last couple of years of his life, when he was living in France at the court of Francis I. These drawings imagine a cataclysmic visual spectacle, yet da Vinci's faithful scientific observation is apparent in the instructional inscription buried among the clouds at the top, which reads: "Of rain. You will show the degrees of falling rain at various distances and of varying degrees of obscurity, and let the darkest part be closest to the middle of its thickness" (Clayton 2004, 36).

In the same century, Giorgione's mysterious *La Tempesta* (1506–1508) and Spanish artist El Greco's tempestuous skies have been connected to phrases from Pliny's natural history. Rather than seeking tight equivalence or a deferral to scientific authority, the "allusions" of the European painters to science were also suffused with their own intense visions, as Gillian Beer (1990) has later shown. Vitz and Glimcher's (1984) "conceptual parallelism model" on the other hand, maps paradigmatic shifts between art history and the development of science, yet omits the simultaneous coexistence of other understandings of the weather world and the universe beyond. The illusionism and dynamism of the clouds in Correggio's Italian Baroque cupolas opens out to infinite and open-ended space, rather than working on the contemporary scientific model of the mechanical universe as an orderly clock, as Hugo Damisch (2002) has observed. Neither does a parallel model fit with Indigenous cultural forms or the development of art outside Euro-American frameworks. The complex mathematics of Islamic geometries, the gradual evolution of Chinese landscape painting, and the socially integrated natural philosophy of *Toi Māori* (Māori art) are just a few alternative models to a discourse of revolutionary moments, breaks, and ruptures in which art reflects scientific paradigms.

Rather than a narrative of direct influence between atmospheric science and painting, such exchanges are positioned as part of a shared cultural milieu in which each shapes cultural life. The Enlightenment in Europe placed new demands on the artist as a recording witness to the new empirical basis for experimental science. British painter Joseph Wright of Derby, active in the late eighteenth century, documented science and technology, including the iron forges altering the air quality in the Industrial Revolution. Wright's interest in atmospheric optics in *Landscape with Rainbow* (1795) is reflected in the detailed study of how primary and secondary colors are formed in rainbows. His darkened gray clouds and lighter sky within the arch of the rainbow reveal a meticulous environmental observation. The optics of the rainbow had been carefully described in René Descartes *Les Météores*, an essay in *Discours de la méthode* (1637), still in circulation as a theory of light. The rainbow is also an exuberant symbol of the painter's art in Swiss-born painter Angelica Kaufmann's painting *Colour* (1779), on the entrance hall ceiling of the Royal Academy of Arts. A chameleon sits at the foot of the powerful female muse of painting. The swooping arch of the rainbow she paints displays the Newtonian prismatic primaries of red, yellow, and blue fading into the four other colors of the spectrum. In an earlier version of this painting, a commentator noted that the muse held a prism, in reference to Isaac Newton's seven-color spectrum, although this object was later overpainted (Fraser and Lee 2001, 79). In the catalog of icons, *Iconologia* (1758–1760), popular among painters of this period, the rainbow appears as a symbol of divine benevolence, grace, peace, and air.

In the colonial era, the meteorological artist-observer would bear witness to the "discovery" and subsequent collection of territories and distant weathers. On Captain James Cook's second southern voyage, painter William Hodges recorded extraordinary phenomena off the coast of Aotearoa New Zealand in the tradition of meteoric reporting. In *A View of Cape Stephens with Water Spouts* (1776; figure 0.3), Hodges paints a scientifically accurate account of the tubular water flow of a large foreground spout of seawater with three spouts behind. Yet he heightens the emotive nature of this weather event by setting it against a storm-darkened sky, and the *pā* (fortified village) on the rear cliff is ablaze after a lightning strike. A classically garbed, ostensibly Māori family watch as the ship makes its perilous journey toward them. As reporter, Hodges works in the service of science and Empire; but as entertainer, he provides a sublime thrill for a precinematic audience pitting the sailors against water, wind, and fire.

The emergent science of meteorology was closely reflected in Romantic poetry and painting by the nineteenth century. The interdisciplinary circulation of practices and

Figure 0.3
William Hodges. *A View of Cape Stephens with Water Spouts*. 1776. Oil on canvas, 135.9 × 193cm. Image © Ministry of Defence, Crown Copyright 2018. [See color plate 1]

techniques of cloud observation is discernible in both the freshly minted science of meteorology and landscape painting. In 1802, the British chemist Luke Howard presented the first classification system of clouds, "On the Modification of Clouds," to a small, enthusiastic audience. Drawing on early meteorological knowledge such as Howard's findings, British art theorist John Ruskin's *Modern Painters* treatise contains specific instructions for painters in "Of Truth of Skies" and "Of Truth of Clouds." His quasi-mathematical treatise for professional painters of his day codified clouds into perspective schemas (Ruskin 1846, 89). Yet Ruskin also encouraged artists to negotiate the boundary between the scientific "truth" of weather phenomena and their psychological and imaginative effects.

British painter John Constable's practice of "skying," or cloud painting outdoors, became increasingly based on scientific principles of field observation, as Ruskin encouraged. The painter once stated to a group of scientists at the Royal Society, "Painting is a science, and should be pursued as an inquiry into the laws of nature ... of which paintings are but experiments" (Abraham 2000, 49). *Clouds* (1822; figure 0.4) is one of hundreds of cloud studies Constable made at his "weather station" at Hampstead Heath in London. Such a practice of systematic observing might seem controlled, yet

Figure 0.4
John Constable. *Clouds*. 1822. Oil on paper on cardboard, 30 × 38 cm. National Gallery of Victoria, Melbourne. Felton Bequest, 1938. [See color plate 2]

recording the weather, while immersed in the weather, is a lively experience that is subject to chance, movement, heat and cold, as fieldwork is for the scientist. There is a common intimacy with the elements that both artists and meteorologists share through observational experiments outside. The contemporary artists included in this book have material and compositional habits that often are the result of close encounters with weather in situ, just as Constable pioneered.

Weather is a highly affective phenomenon that can evoke a strong sense of wonder, delight, or terror, as well as a myriad of minor perceptions every moment. Still, in the nineteenth century, the spiritual lens of the poet and painter and the increasingly ordered image of nature of the natural philosophers began to separate further. Romantic William Turner freed himself from Ruskin's prescriptive "truthful" geometries to attune to weather phenomena as an expressive form. Turner fused his optical experiences of weather with Goethe's color theory and the theories of light of the Scottish scientist David Brewster. Turner's painting *Light and Color (Goethe's Theory)—The Morning after the Deluge—Moses Writing the Book of Genesis* (1843) binds art, science and the spiritual realm. Although the story that Turner roped himself to a ship's mast to experience a storm at sea is apocryphal, he did stare at the sun to experiment with the effects of solar afterimages so that he could physically understand vision. The sun is painted as an effect on the eye itself in such canvases from the 1840s, a searing heliotrope (Crary 2006) that is mirrored in Mieko Shiomi's experiments with sunlight in her Fluxus event scores in chapter 2.

Meteorological artists have always experimented with emergent media. The medium of photography first relied on the benevolence of weather. Joseph Nicéphore Niépce's *heliography* (1826–1827), literally "sun-writing," enables images to form through the exposure of sensitive, pewter surfaces to the sun. Then, in 1839, Henry Fox Talbot's photogenic drawings were printed from negatives made with his "solar microscope." Fox Talbot placed objects such as insect wings on top of photosensitized paper and exposed them to the sun to reveal their delineations. The science and the sunlight as a medium for making artwork through live processes reflected a growing reciprocal relation between artist and the elements. Through material experimentation, the creative capacities of unlikely conjunctions of natural phenomena and photographic techniques emerged. Over time, paper, canvas, and nitrate film stock and many other forms evolve, along with atmospheric humidity and their chemical makeup, to include the imprints of microbacteria. The permeation of weather and other agents produced by humidity into such art forms are positioned as "non-human forms of mediation" (Cubitt 2017, 2), as opposed to deterioration, inseparable from their material substrates and their aesthetic value.

Figure 0.5
Marcel Duchamp. *Readymade Malheureux (Unhappy Readymade)*. 1919. Printed in 1958 for *Box in a Valise (from or by Marcel Duchamp or Rrose Sélavy)*. Series C collotype with pochoir coloring on tinted card, 16.2 × 10.5 cm. © Succession Marcel Duchamp/ADAGP, licensed by Viscopy, 2017.

Meteorological art often is "made" by the weather itself. In the twentieth century, Marcel Duchamp offered a set of instructions to orchestrate a weathering process for an artwork-cum-ecological artifact. In 1919, he gifted *Unhappy Readymade* to his sister Suzanne Duchamp on her marriage to his friend Jean Crotti, in the form of a letter, containing instructions for the making of a readymade. Duchamp instructed Crotti to hang a geometry textbook by strings on the balcony of the couple's apartment in the Rue La Condamine in Paris. The book should be hung in such a way that "the wind had to go through the book, choose its own problems, turn and tear out the pages" (Naumann 1982, 13). The textbook disintegrated when left to the elements, although it was documented in a photograph and in a painting by Suzanne Duchamp. The erratic effects of rain, sunshine, and wind dissolved the laws of mathematics formerly enshrined in the geometry text.

The coincidence of weather with art and military affairs is the subject of lighthearted irony in Frank O'Hara's poem *Naphtha* (1959). The poem opens:

Ah Jean Dubuffet
when you think of him
doing his military service in the Eiffel Tower
as a meteorologist
in 1922
you know how wonderful the 20th Century
can be ...
(O'Hara 1995)

The poem's title suggests the volatility of this period: naphtha is a flammable liquid mixture of hydrocarbons. Although better known for his figurative painting, artist Jean Dubuffet's cycle of *Phénomènes* (1958–1960), including the *Sols, Terre* series (1959), are material experiments involving spraying, irrigation, and liquid emulsion directly on a lithographic stone. *Vie Diffuse* and *Alluvions* (1959) are abstract lithographs in this series that evoke the texture of rain tunneling down a window or the ground pounded by rain drops. Dubuffet was an artist with the sensibility of a meteorologist, producing medianature chemical fusions to suggest the vagaries of weather. He was privy to the technical advances in meteorology that were produced in wartime, with its omniscient perspectives. The language of weather forecasting in this period became laden with military terminology, such as *fronts* and *masses*. Critics of scientific positivism draw attention to the fact that many sciences, such as oceanography, seismography, micro-electronics, and meteorology, evolved from military requirements. As Sloterdijk (2009) suggests, terrorism and humanism are bound in new ways by a "black meteorology" that emerged in World War I as the result of "atmotechnic" inventions, such as clouds of mustard gas. This nonobjective warfare no longer targeted the enemy's body but the enemy's environment.

The trauma of the two world wars was the backdrop to more formalized art-science alliances later in the twentieth century. In the postwar period in America, it seemed urgent to bridge the divergent paths of artists and scientists to "humanize" the sciences. The Experiments in Art and Technology (EAT) workshops in 1961 in America were politically timely art-science collaborations that extended to an international network of more than two thousand artists. Fujiko Nakaya's practice of making fog gardens that started with an EAT project is a turning point toward a dematerialized art of weather, as I discuss in chapter 2. Yet the EAT collaborations were fraught due to conflicting expectations of the scientists to produce a commercial outcome and of the artists' desire for creative independence. The EAT encounters underscore the sensitive nature of the collaboration between scientists and artists and the countercultural

Figure 0.6
Phil Dadson. *Hoop Flags*. 1970. Grafton Gully, Auckland. Ten cotton flags on metal hoops with plastic bags of colored ink.

nervousness about collusion with state interests. EAT aimed to overcome the reciprocal suspicion between art and science made explicit in C. P. Snow's 1959 essay on the Two Cultures separation. Questions of technoscientific power continue to hover in artists' collaborations with meteorological scientists.

On the other side of the world, the forces of live weather were also harnessed by New Zealand artist Phil Dadson in an early weather-driven installation. The large-scale installation work *Hoop Flags* (1970) was made of ten two-meter cotton forms sewn over wire hoops. The forms inflated like large wind socks and raced up and down wires across Auckland's Grafton Gully beside a newly constructed motorway. Bags of colored ink hung on wires that would explode over the flags. The political context for the work arose from a new motorway that cut through a cemetery and forced the removal of housing, including Dadson's own house. The displacement of people by the "intrusion" of the motorway was countered by the lively irreverence to rules of the weather-borne objects (Dadson 2017). The *Hoop Flags* were left to the wind and ultimate disintegration. Dadson visited the United Kingdom from 1968 to 1970, during which time he visited the *Cybernetic Serendipity* exhibition at the Institute of Contemporary Arts (ICA) and became interested in the radically transient nature of emergent, process-based art. A black-and-white film was made of the *Hoop Flags* in action by Dadson's colleague, now-well-known cinematographer Leon Narby.

Weather in art has culturally distinct meanings: consider the audience for the painting *Papatūānuku*, a narrative with a very different political agenda from Hodges' *A View of Cape Stephens with Water Spouts* a century before. In the 1980s, during the political renaissance of Māori art, leading artist Robyn Kahukiwa painted the earth and the elements to reconnect to cosmological narratives. In the painting *Papatūānuku* (1983) in the book *Wahine Toa: Women of Māori Myth* with a text by author Patricia Grace, a radiant sun and earth is framed by Māori *pou* (totems) rising from the sea and land to the sky. Papatūānuku, lying on her side, is the earth mother who gave birth to all things. The radiant sun signifies cultural resilience. Papatūānuku's morning mists are her sighs or tears as she weeps for her separated husband, the sky. Kahukiwa used a rainbow to represent each of Papatūānuku's six sons, including Tāwhirimātea, spirit of the wind. The rainbow in later paintings by Kahukiwa evokes the sinking of the Greenpeace ship the *Rainbow Warrior* in a bombing operation by French foreign intelligence services in 1985. The ship was berthed in Auckland harbor, en route to protest French nuclear testing in Mururoa Atoll. The rainbow became a localized symbol of Aotearoa New Zealand's nuclear-free stance and the Peace movement, and Indigenous self-determination. Internationally, the rainbow is still a symbol for gay rights, and acceptance of diversity, in resistance to discrimination. In a fusion of both narratives,

Auckland's sixth annual gay pride parade (2018) was themed "Rainbow Warriors: Pride and Peace."

Contemporary Meteorological Art and Science

Digitality in art has opened the creative playing field with weather materials still further. We may be distant from the physical location of a weather event, yet we know about it almost instantly through our networked culture. Meteorological art often breaks into the global circulation of data and takes advantage of the meteorological instrumentation that tells us about our atmosphere. Weather *as media* in contemporary art can perform complex functions based on algorithmic codes and climate models, while extreme weather is shared through social media by storm chasers with GoPro cameras. Twenty-first century meteorological art makes the most of the capacity, in Roger Malina's words, to "toggle" between the "big picture systems view" and the ground-based perspective, called *ground truth* by scientists. Artists often exploit the perceptual gap between the remote satellite transmission of large meteorological data sets and the immediacy of earthly weather experiences.

Yet artists do more than play with digital possibilities; we are bound by our common inheritance of a warming climate that fuels a growing number of art projects. The climate system is an intricate web of interactions between the atmosphere, the hydrosphere, the cryosphere, the lithosphere, and the biosphere. Climate evolves over time, both internally and because of external pressures such as volcanic eruptions, solar variations, and now—of course—anthropogenic forcings. Artists often attune to the local sites where material evidence of climate change manifests. The difference between weather and climate is simply a measure of time. Weather is the condition of the atmosphere over a short period of time, our daily rhythms of sun, cloud, and rain, whereas the climate is how the atmosphere behaves over much longer periods. For artists, the politics of climate change at the level of consciousness raising often is no longer adequate, in part because the scale of the phenomena involved is no longer that of ordinary human experience. We are no longer dealing with information scarcity, but with voicing the hopes and anxieties that come with a crisis that is scarcely representable.

Both contemporary meteorological art and science deal in the doubts and constraints imposed by uncertainty in atmospheric politics, but they do so differently. Rationalist science tends to ally with technology, establishing the warming climate, for instance, as a problem to which technology will provide solutions. Art tends to dissolve solutions, create problems, or find problems in solutions, particularly in the case of Big

Science ambitions. Science and state are contested, or equally environmental scientists and certain politicians can become strategic allies. Meteorological art is produced by artists in collaboration with many areas of the atmospheric sciences, including air pollution meteorology, climate change science, weather modification, atmospheric optics, and satellite remote sensing.

Art residencies in science institutions have been arranged by Artists-in-Labs (Switzerland), the Synapse residencies in Australia, the Wellcome Trust and Arts Catalyst in the United Kingdom, and Leonardo's Scientific Delirium Madness residency program in Djerassi. In the United Kingdom, David Buckland's Cape Farewell project is one of the most well-known in a wave of art-science field projects focused on the climate crisis after the turn of the millennium. The ARTCOP21 projects in 2015, at the time of the United Nations (UN) Convention on Climate Change enabled new art and science collaborations including Anaïs Tondeur's *The Eophone's Whistle* (2015), discussed in chapter four and *Ice Watch* (2015), a collaboration between artist Olafur Eliasson and geologist Minik Rosing (chapter 7). TEMP in Auckland (2017) brokered relationships between artists and scientists including F4 and NIWA (New Zealand's Institute of Air and Water Research), discussed in chapter 4. Cyfest-11, *Weather Forecast: Digital Cloudiness* (2018), curated by Anna Frants and Elena Gubanova in St Petersburg, Russia, was a ten-day festival where artists, scientists and technology designers convened in a series of workshops and art exhibitions to explore the co-existence of digital and physical realities in the era of cloud-based computing.

In Lucy Lippard's curatorial introduction to the catalogue for *Weather Report: The Art of Climate Change* (2007), at the Boulder Museum of Contemporary Art, Colorado, she hones in on the primary challenges for curators, artists, and scientists working collaboratively to communicate the effects of climate change. She asks: How can an exhibition on the topic of climate "be alarming but not alarmist," "political but not didactic," "aesthetic enough to communicate," and reducible neither to art nor merely to science (Lippard, Smith, and Revkin 2007, 5–6)? There is also some trepidation among artists about aligning with the sciences at all under late neoliberalism, in our epoch, just as with the EAT collaborations last century. Public confidence in scientists' ability to create technological solutions and to convince politicians to regulate industry has diminished. Art practice is frequently framed in terms of détournement or resistance to scientific power mechanisms, but implicitly technoindustrial forces also move through art-science collaborations.

International exhibitions in the Global South—from *The End of the World Biennial* in Tierra Del Fuego (2007–2016) to *The Trouble with the Weather: A Southern Response* at UTS Gallery in Sydney to the data-based meteorological art of the *Weather Tunnel* in Beijing

(2011) to the Melbourne-based Climarte: Arts for a Safe Climate and Vitalstatistix in Adelaide's *Climate Century* (2014–2018)—reflect the intensifying activity in response to the climate crisis. Climarte's *ART+CLIMATE=CHANGE* 2017 event was promoted as a festival of climate change–related arts and ideas from Australian and international artists. Yet in addition to Lippard's quandaries, a reassessment of simple formulations of climate plus art is taking place. Curators often try to imaginatively circumvent the fatigue associated with the use of "climate change" in their exhibition titling. Yet at a time when federal agencies in the USA have been advised to avoid use of the words climate change, to keep this terminology in circulation now seems urgent.

Reviewers and audiences are also becoming cautious about the blind optimism of some curatorial premises. The Serpentine Gallery's *Today We Reboot the Planet* (2013) and The Hague's *Yes Naturally: How Art Saves the World* (2013) are examples that over-promise on solutions to change the world simply through recycling and cooperative methods (Anderson 2015, 342). Amy Howden-Chapman and Abby Cunnane's *Imagine the Present* (2016), at ST PAUL St Gallery, and the Oceanic Performance Biennials directed by Māori curator Amanda Yates (2013–2017) locate climate change as part of a social complex that is already evidencing itself. The second Oceanic Performance Biennial, *Sea-Change: Performing a Fluid Continent*, held in Rarotonga, and the third biennial, *Heat: Solar Revolutions* (2017), held in Auckland, brought performance artists, environmental scientists, and future-oriented speculative design together on the subject of climate-related ecological action. The activist orientation of *ArchipelaGO* (2017), held in Sydney and curated by Latai Taumoepeau, enabled dialogue between artists and community groups—such as the Pacific Sisters and Pacific Climate Warriors. These events focus on establishing a locally situated exchange between cultures, communities, and discipline fields.

A Map of the Book

The scope of Meteorological art magnified when systems theory, cybernetics, and live weather fuse in sculpture, performance, and video in the 1960s and early 1970s. Chapter 1 focuses on artworks fueled by lightning, wind, and condensation and infused with the new sciences of chaos and indeterminacy. My entry point to the art of this period is through Len Lye, a New Zealand–born kinetic sculptor and direct filmmaker who lived in New York when process-based art took hold. Lye's wind wands continue to arch and bend around our coastline, some carried out posthumously according to the artist's design. Hans Haacke's *Weather Cube* (1963–1965), Philippine artist David Medalla's transformative *Cloud Canyons*, and De Maria's *The Lightning Field* use weather as a vehicle of transformation. In parallel with the new attention to the observer in science, and the nonlinear dynamics inherent in chance appearances of weather, the audience-participant became central to the artwork. Politically, these works signal resistance to institutional fixity in an art that drifts, freezes, and evaporates.

In chapter 2, I delve into the affects of live experience in art and Fluxus performance. Fluxus event scores by Yoko Ono and Mieko Shiomi revel in haptic, aural, and televisual sensations. Fujiko Nakaya's fog experiments with the sensory qualities of weather are meditations on time, experience, and event. Artworks are connected to the new sciences of indeterminism, along with Marshall McLuhan and Victor J. Papanek's writings on the senses and technology and Gregory Bateson's ecological approach to systems. I position *Cloud Music* (1974–1979) at the fulcrum of late modern meteorological art and the contemporary digital developments. The lyrical sounds of *Cloud Music* were produced by a protocomputer machine triggered by the passing clouds, developed by Fluxus artist Robert Watts, musician David Behrman, and engineer Bob Diamond.

Contemporary art that adopts, or adapts, meteorological data streams and software is the focus of chapter 3. Weather sensations are directly felt by the body and the nervous system when we are outside, but the communication of temperature measurements or barometric pressure, for instance, involves translation. The first part of the chapter considers a brief history of mapping and visualization in the science of meteorology as a background for the artworks under discussion. In digital culture, such processes of translation are governed by rules and generative calculations that are written into technological codes. Technologies such as the remote earth-observing meteorological satellite surpass the spatiotemporal and sensory limits of the body. The perceptual extensions implicit in instruments and maps are not politically neutral; instead, they actively frame and formulate our understanding of weather data and, hence, nature. In the second part, artists Thorbjørn Lausten, Billy Apple, Lise Autogena and Josh Portway, and Zune Lee are positioned as "hitch-hikers" on existing meteorological data streams. I inquire into the culturally charged atmosphere of the art-science collaboration *O-Tū-Kapua (What Clouds See)* (2016–2017) that intermingles air quality data, augmented reality, and Māori waiata.

In chapter 4, invented or repurposed meteorological instruments, the weather, and the audience converge to produce affective atmospheres in sound art. Distant instruments "sense" phenomena by digital means, and are made visible or audible in art practice. The highly contingent qualities of the live weather source are manifest in Phil Dadson and Andrea Polli's sonic repurposing of sonic anemometers, mobile phones, and wind turbines and other devices. The powerful affects of the sun are brought home with invented instruments such as the hydrogen-alpha telescope or very low frequency (VLF) radio antennae in Joyce Hinterding and David Haines's sound and video work

Earthstar. Through instruments we experience simulated and real meteorological events as sensations, yet ambiguity exists in the question of *where* the art apparatus ends in relation to its sensate operator and the phenomena measured. Through environmental sensing, scientific instruments are argued to increasingly "automate" sensation (Gabrys 2007), although, like artworks they also create human shifts in feeling. The mournful cries across time of Anaïs Tondeur's *The Eophone's Whistle* (2015), a fictional instrument, explores the affective complexities of instrument-agents.

The greater part of the book focuses on the warming climate through the lens of art practice. Willingly, or unwillingly, we are all connected through the ecological crisis we face. Public understanding of weather and climate is increasingly reliant on scientific, transgovernmental, or multinational expertise. Yet Indigenous, community-based, microsocial knowledge needs to be heard in the development agendas that circulate in global politics. In this context, there is an urgent role for artists to voice an array of community issues about atmosphere. Chapter 5 focuses on online projects, installations, and participatory performances of artists, including the Out-of-Sync collective, theweathergroup_U, Leon Cmielewski and Josephine Starrs, and British artists Corby and Baily, who create a "social meteorology" (Ross 1991). Such meteorological artworks have the expansive capacity to bring activist, economic, and postcolonial concerns to bear on weather and climate science. I discuss a series of meteorological artworks by Indigenous Māori artists Natalie Robertson and Rachel Shearer that pass on ancestral knowledge through video and sound works.

It is not an overstatement to say that the Intergovernmental Panel on Climate Change (IPCC) reports are the defining documents of our epoch. Chapter 6 examines how artists negotiate the findings of IPCC in unexpected ways through language and performance. I gather artworks that offer playful strategies to deal with the weight of information about climate change without raising the levels of social anxiety. This chapter considers the art projects of Amy Balkin, Amy Howden-Chapman, and the *Dear Climate*, as well as Mark Harvey's *Political Climate Wrestle* (part of Søren Dahlgaard's *Maldives Exodus Caravan Show*), in light of the critical positions of Arendt and Adorno. Many of these artworks use language to understand, and sometimes to reimagine how climate change can be understood beyond scientific or political discourse. These artists offer alternative routes to climate politics through performance and the distribution of agency to community participants.

Chapter 7 focuses on art-activist engagement with the earth's diminishing cryosphere. When protest was curtailed at COP15 in Paris by the threat of terrorist attack, I marched in Auckland along with millions of other protestors around the world, to pressure the high profile politicians in Paris to make strong commitments to reducing

greenhouse gas emissions. Protest actions are needed, but it is also a time for mediation in words, creative works, or any other kind of communication that we can muster.
Ice is a tangible connection to climate change, and the artists considered in chapter
7 work with its material potency. I am compelled by Tongan/Australian artist Latai
Taumoepeau's work *i-Land X-ile* (2012–2013), in which she publicly suspends her body
beneath a melting block of ice to draw attention to the sea-level rise in our Pacific
neighborhood. In the North, performative events focus on the melting and evaporation of Arctic ice, such as Eliasson and Rosing's *Ice Watch* (2015), Liberate Tate's *Floe
Piece* (2012), and Icelandic artist Bjarki Bragason's *That in Which It* (2013), become a
structuring absence, as our natural heritage diminishes and the larger picture of a col-
lapsing ecosystem emerges.

The final chapter (chapter 8) asks: What happens when we reimagine our meteorological future? Our anterior responsibility for a world is brought into the public domain
by speculative meteorological art. In the last decade, art projects that engage with
weather politics often have aligned with speculative realism; they ask us to imagine
the wider universe beyond our own existence and return to scientific understandings
of the cosmos. The speculative turn presents a challenge to correlationism (the correlation between thinking and being—never to be considered apart) that would trap us in
our human frame of reference (Brassier 2007; Meillassoux 2008). Yet the encourage-
ment to act in an interdisciplinary mode across art and science isn't coming just from
philosophers and artists, but also from neoliberal forces in the "creative industries."
Artists often work independently to make their own quasi-scientific experiments: from
the cosmic clouds in Ursula Biemann's video essays to the cloud-busting machines
and weather balloon–driven launches of instruments into the stratosphere by Joyce
Hinterding and David Haines. The speculative aerial living systems of Tomás Saraceno
unsettle the imperatives of Big Science projects.

Also in chapter 8, I repurpose Elizabeth Povinelli's (2016) notion of "meteorontological power" to express the power formations between the nonhuman atmosphere and
human interests under the conditions of late liberalism. Povinelli riffs on the Foucaul-
dian analysis of state-controlled "biopower," which supplanted the sovereign power
over life and death. She offers "Geontopower" in part to make visible the relations
between the lively and the inert, nonlife (*geos*), in the current conditions of late liberalism (2016, 9). Povinelli's brief mention of meteorontological power concerns the relations between human life and climate change, the byproduct of "fossil fuel–burning"
human enterprise that is bringing about new weather. A web of meteorontological
concerns for Indigenous agendas, for the noncitizen (the climate refugee), and for the
nonhuman atmosphere urgently need to be addressed. To combine the meteorological

with ontology and contemporary artwork positions the weather as embedded in the very nature of being and creating.

Artwork enacts a form of diagnosis of the present state of meteorological and climate knowledge and speculates on what could be. Artist Karolina Sobecka's practice, for instance, brings us into sensorial correlation with cloud by ingesting it in liquid form at both scientific conferences and art events. Her fostering of interdisciplinary dialogue with the sciences is a deliberate provocation to think about the atmosphere's future shape. This book gathers many kinds of voices, in resistance to a hegemonic response to the warming world. The weather knowledge of artists, scientists, and community groups is not assumed to be coherent; rather, we collectively coexist with our differences. This is not just the difference between local, situated experience and the so-called objective view of the environmental scientist: storm chasers, amateur weather enthusiasts, meteorologists, navigators, kite flyers, Indigenous tangata whenua, citizen activists, and farmers have wildly different relationships with our shared weather system.

The chapter framings of artworks as live, sensational, informational, instrumental, socially orientated, Indigenous, materialist, or speculative are not mutually exclusive. The proposition that artworks operate in many spheres is part of the larger argument in the book. To think about atmosphere seems to require a flyover of all the interdependent factors of a highly dynamic system. Inevitably, our atmosphere shrouds us inside, despite the persistent exterior perspective that we try to occupy. I speculate that art's eddies of activity around the weather perturb the scientific hold on facts and offers questions of value in their place. The art-meteorological science encounter might start as a momentary irruption to the flow, yet artists can offer a sustained perturbation to fixed, disciplinary knowledge. The pressing need for dialogue between the sciences, the arts, Indigenous peoples, and every community (human and nonhuman), as the former continues to dominate discourse on climate, underlies the specificity of a book that turns toward a meteorological art.

1   Live Weather, Systems, and Science

Weather acts through multiple registers: the sound of rain, a light breeze, or subtle shifts in temperature. Like many living beings, we anticipate the onset of a storm through smell and scent, or involuntarily react to the colors generated by the sun's light. The wildness of wind or the warmth of solar radiation generates the affects and energies that make weather compelling for artists. Prior to the mid-twentieth century, private experiments in the artist's studio or plein air sketches captured the weather and sun's light in painted form. By the 1960s and 1970s, art embraced the dynamic patterns of weather as a direct feed in kinetic, systems-based, and changeable forms. The liveness of weather became a driver in real-time systems and a chaotic agent to shake up social and artistic vocabulary. Artists working with live weather media, I will argue, model inventive routes between the physical atmosphere and social life. This chapter traces specific moments in meteorological art of this period: Hans Haacke's systems art, Len Lye's *Wind Wands*, Walter De Maria's *The Lightning Field*, and Philippine artist David Medalla's autocreative systems. Weather is treated as a medium in itself, as well as an ahuman participant and creative force.

In 1960s art, a democratization of the audience unsettled the standalone art object. The passive beholder was recast as an active participant, radically changing the nature of art. In science also, the participant-observer began to count as a material force in experimental outcomes. In the predictive science of meteorology, the effect of every element, even human activity, was found to influence the nonlinear dynamics of weather. The excitement among artists about developments in science and technology often has been underplayed in prevailing art histories about the 1960s, in favor of readings that emphasize language, or identity politics for instance. Instead, I set particular artworks in relation to indeterminacy, complexity, and the role of the observer-participant in meteorological and systems science. I maintain that energetic flows between art and science allowed for meteorological thinking to thrive in both fields.

An art of openness, chance, and free play reflected a cultural rethinking of cause and effect in social systems and political hierarchies in the 1960s. The nascent theory of systems fueled creative experiments with liveness, real time, and feedback loops. In second-order cybernetics, exemplified in the work of Heinz von Foerster, Humberto Maturana, and Gordon Pask, among others, the observer in a living system is part of the cycle of information exchange, rather than a one-way model of transmission. The observer does not just monitor preexisting systems, but creates them through the very act of observation. In the *Artforum* essay "Systems Esthetics" (Burnham 1968b), art writer Jack Burnham presciently argues that art resides not in material entities, but in relations between people and between people and their environment. Burnham popularized systems theory in the cultural sphere by theorizing the role of systems in the art of Hans Haacke, Len Lye, Robert Smithson, Allan Kaprow, and other postformalist artists. The aleatory effects of weather imbued 1960s art systems with liveness: live in the sense of being there, as an audience feeling wind in Lye's *Wind Wands* or at the immediate moment of a lightning strike in De Maria's *The Lightning Field* or the slow scrutiny of rain forming in Haacke's *Condensation Cube*. Haacke referred to his 1960s projects as *real-time systems* in which the audience spends time with the work as part of a durational encounter with atmospheric conditions.

The movement of ideas across continents is reflected in the geographic fluidity of these traveling artists. Len Lye made work in the Pacific, as well as America and Britain. Hans Haacke operates chiefly in Germany and New York. David Medalla's career spans Manila, New York, London, and Paris. Lye spent time with local communities in Australia and Samoa, and was even expelled from Samoa by the New Zealand colonial administration for living in the Samoan way, together with the elements. In Indigenous cosmologies, the sense of interconnectedness "discovered" in late modern meteorological science merely described what many cultures already sensed and encoded in social and environmental lore. This chapter also probes the terms *freedom* and *openness*, common to art and philosophy, in light of the emergent sciences and prevailing cultural values. I examine how Marcuse and Adorno used the concept of second nature to critique the pursuit of capital as the status quo. Just as artists designed open systems, Adorno calls for "an open philosophy" in contrast to Kant's "restricted number of theorems" in his "system of principles" (2008, 80). In Adorno's words, however, even infinite openness must avoid the "mollusc-like" tendency to become attached to any and every conceivable object without any form of critical thought (ibid.). This critical philosophical milieu, the artists' own cultural backgrounds, and the new sciences of open systems and nonlinearity inflected the art of live weather of this period.

The Emergent Meteorology

Post–World War II meteorology and systems theory fueled the cultural atmosphere of early meteorological art. The recognition of the sensitivity to minute differences in conditions in meteorological systems and the emergence of process-based art forms occurred in parallel. The appearance of rain, wind, and clouds as live and tactile matter in artworks shared a conceptual basis with mathematician and meteorologist Edward Lorenz's study of nonlinear dynamics. In artworks of Haacke, Lye, Medalla, and De Maria, as we will see, disorder and random movement became productive of change, rather than an aberration in cultural forms. As a means of cultural politics, malleable art processes in response to chaotic factors—like a sudden gust of wind—aimed to perturb the stability of powerful institutional orders.

The shift in both the physical sciences and the social sciences from ontology (what things are) to ontogenesis (how things emerge) in systems far from equilibrium, exemplified by Prigogine and Stengers (1984), held creative potential for artists beyond the static art object as endpoint. By the 1970s, Stengers and Prigogine note, neither artists nor scientists could retreat from the potential and threat that we are living within a biosphere that is highly sensitive to small fluctuations (ibid.). Complex systems and the chaotic have been the subject of thought and scientific investigation since Lucretius or earlier, and certainly since the French mathematician-philosopher Henri Poincaré. By the mid-twentieth century, the connections forged between computers and weather during World War II enabled meteorologists to increase the accuracy of weather prediction. The study of complexity in meteorology intensified when systems theorist Norbert Wiener delivered his "Nonlinear Prediction and Dynamics" paper at Berkeley (1956). Wiener's theory introduced a mathematical model in which the coordinates would constantly fluctuate. Several meteorologists at Massachusetts Institute of Technology (MIT) used Wiener's nonlinear dynamics to reinforce their current statistical forecasting methods.

Further development of computers in the postwar period helped to prove that weather prediction was incompatible with any linear set of components from a fixed set of rules. Formulas emerged with the capacity to embrace a spectrum of changing factors such as humidity, wind speed, or the temperatures of a neighboring city. The meteorologist Lorenz built on Wiener's theories by selecting a nonlinear, hypothetical set of weather-driven equations based on the various interactions of twelve variables (Lorenz 1993, 131). He charted how the weather changed in each scenario through these nonlinear differentials. At that point, the story goes, Lorenz was excited to find more unpredictability than he had bargained for. His numerical experiments revealed the "sensitive dependence of the initial conditions" (Lorenz 1993, 8), where the amplification of an initial discrepancy could produce a weather pattern that was quite different from an earlier weather forecast. This realization would radically shift the nature of weather prediction. Lorenz's rethinking of linear statistical models in meteorology culminated in "Deterministic Periodic Flow" (1963). Mathematicians much later realized the importance of the "strange attractor" diagram in "Deterministic Periodic Flow" for many chaotic structures, from flu epidemics to commodity prices.

Artists' experiments with chance events that could alter the shape of an artwork took hold at the same time as Lorenz's notion that "certain fluctuations produce a higher order through complex relationships" (Lorenz 1993). In the cultural moment at which the principles of orderly disorder in science were recognized, music developed a nonvisual, nonverbal paradigm for "feeling chaos" as a bodily resonance. Interpretations of disorder, order, probability, randomness, freedom, and indeterminacy can be found in compositions by Pierre Boulez, Steve Reich, and John Cage. Cage's influential book of essays and lectures called *Silence* (1961) includes a chapter on indeterminacy, in which he discusses the time object, in close reference to science. Umberto Eco ([1962] 1989) was equally enthusiastic about artists' translation of terms from physics, either literally or in spirit, as an elegiac expansion of science into the open work in the arts, literature, and information theory. The new paradigm of *chaotics*, a term coined by N. Katherine Hayles (1990), was later used to describe complex dynamics and unstable narrative forms in literature. The pursuit of a chaotics of weather as a form generator in avant-garde music, art, and literature attempted to break away from institutionalized stasis without resorting to a reductive dichotomy of order and disorder. Lye, as we see next, designed a sculptural language of wind-driven kineticism, offering freedom of movement to counter cultural inertia.

Live Weather in Len Lye's Kinetic Art

I place New Zealander Len Lye at the beginning of this trajectory of meteorological art, with a series of artworks that concentrate on weather as a live, energetic force. In 1958, Lye began to transfer some of the moving motifs from his experimental films into kinetic sculpture. Lye made his first *Wind Wand* site installations in 1960 in New York. Eight poles made of hollow aluminum rods rose forty feet in the air from a metal base. Although much of Lye's sculpture consisted of motorized stainless steel, the poles of the *Wind Wands* were activated by the forces of weather. In a strong wind, the poles spring or sway from side to side, exploiting the flexible quality of metal. In an iteration

Figure 1.1
Len Lye. *Wind Wand*. 1960. New York. Len Lye raises a wand, assisted by Robert Graves. Aluminum with metal base. Len Lye Foundation Collection, Govett-Brewster Art Gallery/Len Lye Centre. Photograph: Maurie Logue.

on the Taranaki coastline of Aotearoa New Zealand, opened in the year 2000, made to Lye's original specifications, a red ball inside a clear plexiglass sphere is suspended on top of a 48 metre high pole. Lye intended the design of the wands to be "so finely balanced that if a bumblebee stood on the ball at the top it would dip a bit" (Horrocks 2001, 283). He termed his form of kinetic art *tangible motion sculpture*.

Lye's sound and moving sculptures are a mix of engineering, meteorological systems, and the Indigenous cosmologies and forms he encountered in Samoa and in Australia. The word *wand* in the title suggests the ancient rites of magicians or artist-shamans. Lye's sound sculptures and the soundtracks of many of his films are explicitly linked to a rich cultural history of weather music and weather noise. In Pacific culture, the artist may be a *tohunga*, or spiritual leader. The kinesthetic effects of drumming and instruments for calling rain in Te Moana nui a Kiwa (the Pacific diaspora), such as the Māori *purerehua* (a wood or bone blade whirled on a cord), make deep vibrations with air currents. These instruments produce physical sensations as they reverberate through the bodies of musician and listeners, as encountered by Lye as a young man. Lye's vibrating sculpture *Storm King* (1968), made from a sheet of steel, connects to a rich global history of sound-producing meteorological instruments. The title refers to the thunderous voice of Shango, the Yoruba tribe of West Africa's storm god. Noise has also been used in European culture since classical antiquity to drive storms away by banging on drums, crashing cymbals, blowing woodwind instruments, or ringing consecrated bells. As theatrical devices, thunder and lightning machines have made appearances in history from the pebbles in copper pots of Greek and Roman theater to Victorian phantasmagoria to continental son et lumière. Lye's sculptures resonate with the power of these ancient forms.

Lye's *Wind Wands* assembles the audience, the artist, a site, and the weather system in a new set of social relations. The first site chosen for the installation of the steel wands was a vacant lot on the corner of Horatio and Hudson Streets in 1960. A *Village Voice* journalist recorded one viewer's comment: "They're as graceful as dancers, it's like making the motion of the wind visible." The light afternoon breeze, which made the poles nod and sway rhythmically, was compared to "beings from another planet conversing with each other" (Horrocks 2001, 284). The journalist also noted that children ran between the poles, while Lye wandered around nervously with his wrenches, adjusting the sculptures as he went. Lye was a presence, if not a performer, in his installations, tending to the technology, rather than separating himself from the finished work. The wind itself was made tangible by the visible movement of the poles at the same time as it was felt on the skin. The *Wind Wands* were re-exhibited in 1961 as part of an exhibition organized by the Committee to Save West Village. Lye's wife, Ann, was an active member of this civic project designed to draw attention to the demolition of an historic area in New York, where many artists had studios. The *Village Voice* framed the work with the headline "Swaying Mobile Is Art's Ode to West Village Battle" when the works were exhibited in the playground of St. Luke's school. The sculptural object materialized a heated political debate.

In 1960s' sculptural language, industrial materials were often deployed for their specific or material qualities, rather than as signifiers of a higher meaning. Engineer Maurice Gross collaborated with Lye on the production of the smooth aluminum poles of the wands, yet in *Wind Wands* the weather becomes a medium for Lye as much as the metal poles. Lye's central aesthetic concern was for movement and change rather than fixity. Reviewer Stewart Kranz (1974) wrote that an "observer-participant" engages with the *Wind Wands* artwork in a space of encounter, rather than as a passive viewer. Each of our perceptual encounters with the moving *Wind Wands* must be different as the wind is a randomizing element. Lye's own concept of *bodily empathy* refers to energetic transfer between elemental energies, the metal forms, and the audience in the moment of perceiving the sculpture's movement. Lye's contemporary Jack Burnham praised Lye's sculpture for generating "a feeling of barely harnessed physical power— half material and half pure energy" (1968a, 269). Although Lye resisted the prevailing scientific language that many kinetic artists exhibited at the time, his artwork became representative of Burnham's discursive study of systems. Writing in response to Lye's kinetic sculpture, Burnham described weather as a disruptive force that resets the system; "wind destroys the self-contained stability of the sculpture" because any system desires a return to equilibrium (1968a, 234). Burnham delighted in kinetic sculpture's changeable aesthetics of free play, randomization, and instability.

In his own writing, Lye emphasizes the embodiment of sensations in his continuously moving forms. The search for patterns, or "figures of motion," and the question of "how to get bodily senses into the act" are vital to Lye's practice. Lye describes how, as a fifteen-year-old student, he became fascinated by movement in the natural world (Horrocks 2001, 12–13). He watched clouds rolling through the sky and was reminded of Constable's oil paintings of cloud movement. Lye writes (narrating his life in the third person): "Then it hit him: why not make cloud shapes that actually moved instead of simulating their motion? But then he saw that cloud movements were fairly limited. Why not make his own shapes and compose his own motion? And that was it" (Lye 1984, 81). Lye's intuitive practice of sensory self-experiment found a home in the growing kinetic art discourse in New York in the 1960s. He became familiar with the early twentieth-century kinetic sculpture in Naum Gabo's rotating constructions and Alexander Calder's gently floating mobiles, which were sometimes meteorologically themed, such as *Snow Flurry I* (1948). Lye reached New York in 1943, informed by his travels through the Pacific and the United Kingdom.

Of the kinetic mobiles of Calder, Eco writes: "Theoretically, work and viewer should never be able to confront each other twice in precisely the same way. Here there is no suggestion of movement: the movement is real, and the work of art is a field of open possibilities" ([1962] 1989, 86). Lye's *Wind Wands* also operates as an open system, with endlessly variable movements possible in the bending poles. Although Lye's practice makes physical forces tangible, unlike many postwar kineticists Lye was wary of progressivist science. Lye was aware of creative interpretations of cybernetics, but he generally avoided direct scientific terminology in relation to his own work. This differed from the attitudes of the Parisian kineticists, such as members of the GRAV (Groupe de recherche d'art visual) collective. Le Parc of GRAV, for instance, made a series of mobiles called *Determinism and Indeterminism* (1962) made of hanging plastic squares illuminated by light. Lye describes his work as a "homage to energy" yet he finds the discourse of cybernetics as distancing, commenting that cybernetic theory does not give much "emotional satisfaction." He uses the term *negative feedback* in relation to his sculpture *Rotating Harmonic* (1959), while qualifying his usage by explaining that he is not particularly interested in the of a "brain machine" of nascent computing (Lye 1984).

Lye's self-described "old brain" is the biological, deep-embodied knowledge that he contrasts with "learned" knowledge, the "new brain of the intellect" (Lye 1984, 90). The immediate sensations of the audience produced by his sculptures are, for Lye, both culturally learned and spontaneous. In philosophy, Lye's contemporary Maurice Merleau-Ponty speculates on whether a "return to the immediate" is possible; distinguishing between "perception fashioned by culture" and "brute" or "wild" perception (Merleau-Ponty and Lefort 1968). How does one undo thinking to return to lived experience, the phenomenal (ibid., 212)? In Lye's (1984) own account of childhood "sense games," he would attempt to repeat movements in nature inside himself as a bodily "inner echo." He writes: "I got so I could feel myself into the shoes of anything that moved, from a grasshopper to a hawk, a fish to a yacht, from a cloud to a shimmering rustle of ivy on a brick wall" (ibid., 82–83). He created his own language of the body through observing and imagining movement.

For Lye, empathy with the motion of the wind in kinetic art frees human beings from the anatomical limits of the body in a way that exceeds earlier art forms such as dance (1984, 81). Our ability to empathize with his sculptures depends on a bodily act of attunement with the elements. Empathetic tension increases with scale. In a radio interview, Lye describes empathy for the waves as follows: "The difference that you feel in empathy for this little furling wave—so minute that you hardly notice it—and the empathy that you feel when you are watching a huge comber—a 15 or 25 foot comber—is increased in ratio to the size of the thing, the energy involved in it" (Horrocks 2001, 284). However, Michael Fried—an art critic at the time—challenged the minimalist group of sculptors, including Robert Morris, Carl Andre, and Tony Smith, on the "theatrical" choice of an installation site that demands such empathetic participation. In his essay "Art and Objecthood," Fried writes that in the theatrical situation, the "beholder" is necessarily included in the situation that the artist creates. The quality of the new sculpture that Clement Greenberg identified as "presence," Fried considered to be a theatrical effect or mere "*stage* presence" ([1967] 1998, 155). Fried worried about the animate sensibility of site-specific art in relation to the human viewer: " [the literalist sculpture] depends on the beholder, is incomplete without him, it *has* been waiting for him. And once he is in the room the work refuses, obstinately, to let him alone—which is to say, it refuses to stop confronting him, distancing him, isolating him" (ibid., 163–164).

From a contemporary perspective, Fried's critique of the active role for the participant in the artwork reads as a positive trope. Lye's choice of an abandoned lot as the location for the first *Wind Wand* assembles people in a built environment, rather than a gallery, in open air. Lye locates a feeling for wind as a common experience, creating space for the audience to feel the chaotic dynamics of a shared ecology. The new version of Lye's *Wind Wand*, installed on the coastal walkway in New Plymouth, Taranaki, as the city's turn of the millennium project by The Len Lye Foundation, followed Lye's original instructions for an increase in scale of the wand. The wand uses yacht-mast materials to allow it to bend up to twenty meters in the strong prevailing wind coming from the Tasman sea. The red sphere on the top contains 1,296 light-emitting diodes (LEDs) that light up at night. The dynamic bends and arcs of the wand chart the movements of the wind. When I visit the Taranaki coast, I feel the same wind that moves the sculpture on my skin. When the gusts subside and the sculpture is becalmed, I wait impatiently for any motion at all to register. Lye wrote: "Just as silence emphasizes sound, motion enhances the perception of stillness after the interaction is over" (1961, 227). The wind wands at rest are full of latent potential.

Walter De Maria's *The Lightning Field*

If we compare Lye's *Wind Wands* to Walter De Maria's later and better-known artwork *The Lightning Field* (1971–1977), radically different approaches to site and participation become apparent. Both works used metal poles to conduct the weather to produce specific sensations, and both works engage energetic forces. Yet *The Lightning Field* is situated far from urban life in Quemado, New Mexico. No one gives a more detailed account of the formal arrangement of the poles, their construction, and the details of the site than Walter De Maria himself. De Maria's formal statement (1980) about *The Lightning Field*, published in *Artforum*, is the key document and an extension of the work itself. The text is a mix of dry scientific facts and sudden statements about De Maria's aesthetic concepts. The bureaucratic language of science and industry is explicit in De Maria's statement, whereas the engagement with the physical sciences is immanent in Lye's *Wind Wands*.

The title of De Maria's statement about the work—"Some Facts, Notes, Data, Information, Statistics and Statements"—borrows from the language of scientific fieldwork. The desirable qualities of the desert location are its "flatness, high lightning activity, and isolation." He tells us that *The Lightning Field* is located 7,200 feet above sea level and 11.5 miles east of the Continental Divide. The lightning field has four hundred highly polished stainless steel poles with solid, pointed tips, each an average height of twenty feet. The poles are arranged in a grid array (sixteen wide by 25 long) and are spaced 220 feet apart. A walk around the perimeter of the poles takes more than two hours. Each pole was "triple checked for accuracy" to make sure that the poles were all of equal height above the ground, based on a land survey that took points from four positions around each pole. Because of differences in ground level at different parts of the site, the height of the poles is subtly different, yet a continuous flat plane is formed by the level of the pole tips. An imaginary plane is created over the tips of the poles, which could "support a sheet of glass" (De Maria 1980). The factual nature of this statement could be a technical description from an engineer. Yet De Maria once wrote in his essay "On the Importance of Natural Disasters" more emotively: "I like natural disasters and I think they may be the highest form of art possible to experience" ([1960] 1995, 630). He describes tornadoes, floods, and sandstorms as rare forms of art that we should be thankful for.

In *The Lightning Field*, however, De Maria removed both his own physical body and the audience from the published images of the work, unlike Lye. De Maria provides a script for interaction with the work, and access to the site is highly controlled. The artwork has been infamously challenged due to its so-called authoritarian stance (Beardsley 1981). Visitors must apply individually to view the field in the remote Nevada desert by reservation, for only six people at once. The work is a contemporary homage to the "medium" of lightning, but the poles stand sentinel for a strictly limited audience and the rare visitations of lightning. The chance appearance of lightning is set against the precise numerical structuring arrangement of the poles, yet as Harris

Dimítropouios (1985) suggests, this arrangement can be linked to the numerology of the Buddhist *I Ching* as much as to science.

The energetic and potentially destructive qualities of *The Lightning Field* and the role of the series of images De Maria released in *Artforum* in April 1980, are part of the narrative of the artwork. The photographs engaged a wider public and were integral to the circulation of lightning as art media. Art writer James Nisbet situates *The Lightning Field* as "a brief moment in the history of photo-energy," to show how De Maria's work internalizes a conflicted moment in ecology. Nisbet addresses what he considers the "persisting problem" of histories of land art that tend to focus on the land, rather than other atmospheres or energies. He writes: "By rendering energy flow itself as a series of constants—poles and sky, object and camera—the photographic *Lightning Field* maintains a sense of ecology that forecloses subjective presence or influence" (Nisbet 2013, 78). De Maria's attention to the properties of lightning and his extension of "site" to a spread of photographs challenges the limited readings of the work as interventionist and highly controlled "land" art (Nisbet 2013, 84). With Nisbet, my focus on meteorological media suggests an expanded ecological vista beyond the land itself.

Natural phenomena are part of a social system in Lye's *Wind Wand* in Taranaki, where it can be found on a coastal walkway. Walkers can interact freely with the swaying pole that amplifies and embodies the effects of weather. The restricted access to *The Lightning Field* in Quemado, on the other hand, limits the participation of human visitors. Yet De Maria's (1980) expansion of the installation into a series of lightning-animated photographs in *Artforum* situates his work in the social realm. From a postanthropocentric perspective, *The Lightning Field* is open to the natural energies of lightning as media for contemporary art.

Hans Haacke's Weather Systems

… make something, which experiences, reacts to its environment, changes, is nonstable …

… make something indeterminate, which always looks different, the shape of which cannot be predicted precisely …

… make something, which cannot "perform" without the assistance of its environment …

… make something, which reacts to light and temperature changes, is subject to air currents and depends, in its functioning, on the forces of gravity …

… make something which the "spectator" handles, with which he plays and thus animates it …

… make something that lives in time and makes the 'spectator' experience time …

… articulate something natural …

Figure 1.2
Hans Haacke. *Condensation Cube*, also known as *Weather Cube*. 1963–1965. Plexiglass and water,
76 × 76 × 76 cm. © Hans Haacke. VG Bild-Kunst, licensed by Viscopy, 2017.

This statement was originally written by Hans Haacke to accompany an exhibition in
Cologne in 1965 (Haacke and Alberro 2016, 5). They represent critical tropes in his
practice: mutability, temporality, and audience experience. The imperative, "make,"
consciously sets out a new paradigm for art, wherein the static nature of traditional
painting and sculpture gives way to mutable "system artworks" (Burnham and Haacke
1967). Air currents, temperature, gravity, and environmental reactions over time are
also the stuff of a quasi-meteorological enquiry.

Haacke's institutional and political critique has occupied most of the scholarship on
his practice. Recently, however, there has been a growing interest in the early phase of
Haacke's career, during which he manufactured systems as enquiries into physical processes. Haacke has been called a systems artist, a term that embraces his engagement with

physical, biological, and social systems at once. Haacke's plexiglass boxes from 1963 to 1965, often regarded as parodies of the minimalist cube, are given a more layered interpretation by Pamela Lee (2004). *Grass Cube* (1967), for example, a growing piece of grass sod on an acrylic box, is described as a "self-generating work about self-generation" that reflects a study of mutual causation in both the social and the biological realms (Lee 2004, 80–81). In addition, a reframing of Haacke's practice in light of Jack Burnham's "Systems Aesthetics" has been offered by Luke Skrebowski "as a productive methodological framework for considering post-formalist art as a whole" (2008, 58–59).

The physical system of meteorology that pervaded Haacke's oeuvre from 1963–1968, however, has garnered less critical attention, though in the late 1960s art writer Jack Burnham devoted an entire book, with Haacke, entitled *Hans Haacke: Wind and Water Sculpture* (1967), to the meteorological aspect of his practice. Haacke himself writes, while reflecting on this series in 1971: "I was very excited about the subtle communication with a seemingly sealed off environment and the complexity of interrelated conditions determining a meteorological process" (2016, 48). Haacke's *Condensation Cube*, also known as *Weather Cube* (1963–1965), engages experimentally with the physical transformation of water. According to Haacke, a meteorological process produces in the viewer's mind a conceptual oscillation, in dialectical conflict with both traditional art and the hierarchical organization of physical relationships. In this new set of relations, the audience and the atmospheric conditions each play a part in making the artwork.

Systems Theory Meets Art

An enthusiasm for emergence, ontogenesis, and how randomness and chance might produce higher forms of order suffuse Burnham's writing. Haacke credits Burnham with introducing systems theory to the New York art world (Skrebowski 2008). His lens on art acknowledged complexity theory and an emergent "systems consciousness" as opposed to the "cultural obsession with the art object" (Burnham 1968a, 369). Much of the language Burnham uses is developed from Austrian biologist Ludwig von Bertalanffy, author of *General System Theory* (1968), with whom he shared a publisher. Burnham locates both Lye and Haacke as "systems" artists. He draws on the interdisciplinary nature of systems theory to counteract the search for an irreducible essence in separate arts of his contemporaries, most notably art critic Clement Greenberg.

Lorenz's discoveries in meteorology are closely aligned with the emergent systems theory that fascinated Haacke. One of the seductions of the complex science of meteorology for postformalist artists was the idea of the open system. Von Bertalanffy analyzed the dynamics of complex systems in response to the perceived fragmentation and technologically enhanced pace of social life. In the preface to *General System Theory*, he comments on the ubiquity of the word *system* as a fashionable catchword in science, sociology, and mass media in the 1960s. New jobs were emerging as a result, such as systems designer, systems analyst, and systems engineer (von Bertalanffy 1968, 3). He proposed that the complexity of social life means the modern subject is forced to deal with wholes, or the system overview, in all fields of knowledge. Stable modes of categorizing natural and biological phenomena began to give way to a discourse of nonlinearity and complexity.

Von Bertalanffy's *General System Theory* (1968) refers to *The Organismic Conception in Meteorology* (1961) by J. W. Thompson to draw a detailed comparison of "modern meteorological concepts" and Thompson's organic understanding in biology and open systems in the modern world. He notes that, in *Thermodynamic Studies and Irreversible Phenomena* (1947), Prigogine pinpointed meteorology as a field in which open systems theory could be applied. Open systems are characterized by a time-independent steady state, but they are not in equilibrium, or homeostasis. An open system may or may not reach a steady state; its development is independent of the initial conditions (von Bertalanffy 1968, 141–143). Architect Buckminster Fuller also wrote a chapter called "General Systems Theory" in his small book *Operating Manual for Spaceship Earth* (1969). He warns against the exhaustion of essential resources on our fragile planet as the "cushion for error" for humanity's survival and growth diminishes. Von Bertalanffy, Fuller, and Burnham's exchanges revitalized communications between science and cultural life after the media-hyped "two cultures" split (Snow 1959). An interdisciplinary and open model of relations seemed urgent in the years following the cataclysmic results of technological warfare.

Haccke's Weather Systems

In the 1960s, Haacke simulated meteorological effects using water vapor, air currents with free-floating balloons, sails, and freezing constructions. His experiments with air currents and fine mists began prior to his arrival in New York from Germany. Particular works of Haacke's are framed here as a meteorological interpretation of his oeuvre. These artworks are natureculture systems energized by processes of drift, flow, and transformation. I put forward links between Haacke's weather-infused works and early meteorological instruments. In 1962, for instance, Haacke produced *Rain Tower*, a small, oblong-shaped tower of clear acrylic divided into ten floors. Water drips through the holes between the floors of the structure. The work has a formal relation to the metered measurements of the glass rain gauge instrument in meteorology. Haacke's

Rain Tower was designed to be flipped vertically to reverse the flow of water in either direction. The handling of the tower by the audience adds an unpredictable element to the system. According to museum administrators, when the work was exhibited later in 1962 at the Museum of Modern Art (MoMA) in New York, museum staff "played with the artwork for days," delighting at the tactile interaction invited by water and gravity (Burnham and Haacke 1967, 282).

Rain Tower was a precursor to Haacke's *Condensation Cube* (1963–1965), in which he developed his interest in the self-regulating system of atmosphere. The *Condensation Cube* (30 × 30 × 30 cm) is a single clear acrylic cube, placed on the floor. A small quantity of water is introduced to the cube's floor, which slowly evaporates, forms droplets on the roof and sides of the cube, reaches a critical mass, then drops down like rain. There are various openings within the cube via which air can enter and leave to assist the condensation process. The rate of evaporation or condensation depends on the air temperature and sunlight conditions outside the cube. The climate of the gallery becomes an important condition of the work's responsivity; a cold room that quickly warms with the sun creates greater condensing of droplets for instance. The mutable process of condensation never repeats itself, simulating the atmospheric cycle at micro scale. The relatively new material of plexiglass allows a visual flow from the outside to the experimental interior. Haacke describes the function of the cube, disclosing the length of time required for the work to be apprehended: "The drops grow hour by hour; small ones combine with larger ones. The speed of their growth depends on the intensity and the angle of the intruding light. After a day, a dense cover of clearly defined drops has developed and they all reflect light. With continuing condensation, some drops reach such a size that their weight overcomes the forces of adhesion and they run down along the walls, leaving a trail" (2003, 265).

The activity of Haacke's *Condensation Cube* is reminiscent of early cloud chamber experiments. In 1894, Victorian meteorologist C. T. R. Wilson tried to simulate optical weather phenomena from the Scottish mountain Ben Nevis in glass vessels in his laboratory. The particles became visible as tracks in condensation. When Wilson expanded the air in the cloud chamber, he found that the vapor in the chamber was not forming drops on dust, as with clouds, but rather was forming on invisible, charged ions that he did not recognize. By 1912, Wilson introduced a radioactive source and found that he could photograph long lines of subatomic particles. This radical shift in method from imitating nature to taking it apart—or, as philosopher of science Peter Galison describes it, from "mimetic experimentation (simulating clouds) to analytic experimentation (detecting 'real' sub atomic particles)"—is played out within the narrative of the cloud chamber (1997, 75). Cloud chamber photography became widely known to artists in America through MIT professor Gyorgy Kepes's exhibition and catalog *The New Landscape in Art and Science* (1956).

Haacke's mimesis of physical systems of condensation, wind, or rain are cultural analogues for systems of control and release. For Haacke, the condensation is a free, animate agent. He writes, "The conditions are comparable to those of a living organism that reacts in a flexible manner to its surroundings. The image of condensation cannot be precisely predicted. It is changing freely, bound only by statistical limits. I like this freedom" (Haacke 2003, 265). The *Condensation Cube* has been positioned as a dialogue between the museum and architecture (Jarzombek 2005); I see the atmospheric conditions in the art gallery and the developing veil of condensation as co-performers. The activity of the water vapor even reflects the warmth of human bodies passing through the gallery. The cube is less a minimalist thing in itself than a functioning environmental and social ecology.

The *Condensation Cube* was understood by Burnham as a process of metabolic exchange between system and environment. Haacke's weather work sometimes uses catalyzers, such as incubators, electric fans, and refrigeration units, to accelerate processes of change and amplify natural processes. Before Haacke met Burnham in 1965, cybernetic systems were part of Haacke's creative milieu. Haacke exhibited with the German art collective Group Zero (1956–1968). He was also associated with the cyberneticist artmakers in GRAV. Later, von Bertalanffy's open conception of a system would become of particular importance to Haacke. By 1967, Haacke explicitly describes his artworks as a self-regulating "open system," in von Bertalanffy's terms, rather than as sculpture. State changes in Haacke's physical systems allude to the experimental materiality of meteorological science. In *Water in Wind* (1968), for instance, two purpose-built spray nozzles generated a fine mist on the rooftop of his studio at 95 East Houston Street in New York. The water vapor produced rainbow effects when the sun shone through the fine spray. This art event was as ephemeral as a naturally occurring rainbow, affecting the participant for only the briefest moment of time.

As well as the freezing and condensation of water vapor, Haacke also made use of the wind in several works, sometimes using outdoor air currents, and sometimes using electric fans blowing material sails in works such as *Wind Room* (1968–1969). *Sky Line* (1967) is the most visually spectacular of these, in which several hundred white balloons were used to visualize air currents in a public event in Central Park in New York. White helium-filled balloons drift according to the wind patterns to form a line in the sky, tethered together by fishing line. Haacke also made indoor works with electric fans to keep balloons and cloth buoyant in the air. Since the late nineteenth century, weather balloons (or sounding balloons) have been employed to monitor wind direction and later to carry instruments, such as the radiosonde, to send back atmospheric, temperature, and humidity data. The fluctuations of wind sensed by the parkgoers on the ground also propelled the floating system of balloons in a transmission of subtle informational patterns. Burnham notes that in Haacke's sail pieces and outdoor balloon lines, "the decision to allow natural entities to organise themselves began" (1969, 52). Haacke's attention to the subtleties of currents suggests a sensory language beyond institutional constraints—the same freedom that he enjoyed in his statement about *Condensation Cube*. This project resonates with Phil Dadson's wind-inflated *Hoop Flags* (1970) described in the introduction and anticipates Joyce Hinterding and David Haines *Soundship (descender 1)*, in which a weather balloon and custom-made instruments reach the stratosphere.

Like Haacke's *Condensation Cube*, Alan Sonfist's artwork *Crystal Enclosure* (1965; figure 1.3) also suggests an early meteorological instrument. A glass sphere is filled with natural mineral crystals, which convert to a gas in reaction to atmospheric conditions. As the atmospheric heat and light fluctuates, the crystals make patterns on the surface of the glass. The functioning system of this sculpture recalls the Victorian storm glass, a type of barometer, once used by navigators such as Admiral Fitzroy on the *Beagle* (1834–1836). The growth of the crystals in the storm glass was used in marine weather forecasting; rapid advance of the crystals indicated a storm was brewing at sea. Sonfist, Haacke, and Philippine artist David Medalla mimetically engage with physical phenomena by creating isolated conditions for artificial reactions, just as scientists do. They playfully experimented with the materiality and formal language of the dominant "superscientific culture" (Burnham 1968a).

The artificial enclosure of industrialized life is captured in the Hegelian term *second nature*. This term surfaces in the writing of Adorno and Marcuse in the late 1960s, while artists such as Sonfist also searched for metaphors for the earth's delicate ecosystem. Adorno problematizes the vain attempt to try to know a thing through processes of mediation, or the "capture" of nature into "second nature" (Adorno 2006b, 121). By *primary nature*, Adorno means "no more than the elements, the objective elements that the experiencing consciousness encounters without his experiencing them as things he has himself mediated." He characterizes the transformation of primary to secondary nature as follows: "Nothing that is outside appears to me to be outside—thanks to the total mediation that transforms even the elements of nature into elements of second nature" (Adorno 2006b, 121–122). In Marcuse's view (1969), the work of art has no means of circumventing humankind's repressive second nature so long as it still exists within it.

In the sealed containers of Haacke and Sonfist, there is a sense of an enclosed second nature that is offset by the free process of material transformation and dissipation

Figure 1.3
Alan Sonfist. *Crystal Enclosure*. 1965. Photograph courtesy of the artist. [See color plate 3]

inside. As Nisbet (2013) points out, in the 1960s and 1970s, artists' understanding of ecological systems was tied to a critique of capitalist consumption. In *An Essay on Liberation* (1969), Marcuse connects the related capitalist desires of "possessing, consuming, handling, and constantly renewing" with a "second nature of man which ties him libidinally and aggressively to the commodity form" (1969, 10). For Adorno, citing Marx, the law of capitalist accumulation has been metamorphosed by economists into "a pretended law of Nature." In Adorno's two lectures titled "The History of Nature (I)" (2006a) and "The History of Nature (II)" (2006b), he sketches a world where we have become so completely trapped by social and rational mechanisms that first and second nature cannot be distinguished between each other. Nature is suppressed by the global

Figure 1.4
David Medalla. *Cloud Canyons*. 1967. Installation view at Auckland Art Gallery Toi o Tāmaki. Plastic tubing, aquarium, pump, pipe, 400 × 300 cm.

events of world history in Hegel, yet Adorno goes a step further to argue that second nature becomes the only reality. Capitalism becomes naturalized to the extent that, Adorno writes, "the organic nature of capitalist society is both an actuality and at the same time a socially necessary illusion" (Adorno 2006a, 118). To bring the commodity trap of second nature to light, condensation, melting, and freezing in artworks of this period politicized the shape-shifting qualities of environmental media.

Social Climates in the 1960s: Medalla and Haacke

In 1962, Medalla exhibited *Ice Melting Sculpture* at the Signals gallery in London, in which blocks of ice were literally allowed to melt in the gallery space at a speed determined by atmospheric conditions. When I first encountered a version of Medalla's sculpture *Cloud Canyons* (1967) at Auckland Art Gallery at a crowded opening, I remember the bubbles frothing over the trough and seeping all over the gallery floor. I was struck by irreverence of this antimachine that joyously ignores the laws of the gallery situation. *Cloud Canyons* (1967) is made from plastic tubes, pumps, and pipes that froth bubbles like an out-of-control scientific experiment. Water is recycled through the lower half of the mechanical sculpture, which pushes the bubbles up in piles of cloud-like forms through the columns; they then slowly slide down into a rubber trough that can barely contain their exuberance. The lively, techno-organicist fusion of materials reflects Medalla's observations of the gentle buildup and decay of cloud phenomena.

Medalla's first bubble machine was exhibited in a solo show at the Signals gallery in London in 1964, cofounded by Paul Keeler and Medalla himself. Burnham describes Medalla's artworks as producing "thermal walls with mutable mist and frost patterns" that would "sweat and perspire" (Burnham 1968a, 344–346). As an early artist-run space, there was freedom to experiment wildly without fear of a gallerist's demand for pristine white walls and saleable work. According to Burnham, Medalla described his world view as *hylozoist* in the 1960s, comparing himself to the pre-Socratic philosopher who believes matter is animate. Philosopher of arts and sciences Michel Serres often cites a hylozoist text, *La Mer*, written by the natural historian Jules Michelet in the late nineteenth century, in which the sea and earth are constantly in "a labour of metamorphosis, transformation, production, generation" (Serres 1982a, 33); these phase changes of physical state are connected to a political state of unrest. For Serres, the abstract ideal of a steady state is unreachable and contrary to history.

Haacke and Medalla's transformations of matter had political implications for the restless culture of the late 1960s. They were experiencing historically turbulent times; Burnham attests that Haacke was profoundly troubled by the continuing Vietnam war and the effects of May 1968 in Paris. Signals produced a gallery news bulletin edited by Medalla that acted as a conduit among art, politics, and the new sciences. Medalla published Lewis Mumford's speech at the American Academy of Science condemning the US role in the Vietnam war; articles by the physicist Werner Heisenberg on indeterminacy; and writings of Professor J. D. Bernal, a crystallographer who was involved in the development of holograms. Medalla's aleatory forms are vital, as Jun Terra argues, because they touch on "the most basic law that governs the individual, the world, and the universe; that is, that the only immutable and changeless law is the law of change" (1995, 98). Haacke also condemned the art object in "inert, static" conditions as a "politically dangerous" illusion of timeless stability (Bijvoet 1997, 84).

At a more personal level, Medalla's autocreative machines reflect his own history and sensory memories from Manila, a city ravaged by war in his early childhood during the Japanese occupation and bloody recapture by American and Philippine troops. The bubbles recall his encounter with a dying soldier foaming from the mouth, memories of his mother's bubbling cream of coconut soup, and later experiences of canyons of clouds in formation by airplane. Medalla now sees himself as a "citizen of the world"; like clouds in their unpredicatable movement, he is at home anywhere (Tate 2012). Haacke and Medalla's artworks contributed to a cultural "dialectics of transformation" (Burnham and Haacke 1975, 131) in which art became integral to the political landscape.

Like Medalla, Haacke avoided the categorization of his practice into social, meteorological, biological, or behavioral systems. The foregrounding of systems theory is deployed here as a counterpoint to art historians, such as Benjamin Buchloch, who have had less interest in Haacke's early, more scientific, work. Buchloch separates Haacke's political work from his investigations of biological and physical systems, suggesting that only his explicitly political work is "mature" (Skrebowski 2008, 74). Yet Haacke's *Recording of Climate in an Art Exhibition* (1970), for instance, engages on several intersecting registers. This work featured in the *Conceptual Art and Conceptual Aspects* exhibition curated by Joseph Kosuth at the New York Cultural Center (1970). Haacke displayed three functioning instruments—a barograph, a thermograph, and a hydrograph—while recording live shifts in humidity and temperature within the gallery. The unaltered display of meteorological instruments in *Recording of Climate in an Art Exhibition* suggest a Duchampian readymade, although there is no disjunctive jolt as these devices generally are to be found sitting unobtrusively in any major gallery.

The movement of the stylus on the barograph in *Recording of Climate in an Art Exhibition* charts the microclimate of institutional spaces and registers human presence. The work operates within the social system at play in the rarefied gallery environment and jabs at the institutional values that preserve artworks in climate-controlled environments as commodities. The instruments are presented as anonymous social mediators in a *real-time system*, as Haacke calls it, linking human and nonhuman, atmospheric and machinic. In computing, real time is a constraint, with operational deadlines from event to system response; for artists, real time suggests immediacy and accessibility. In Burnham's 1969 article entitled "Real Time Systems" in *Artforum*, he quotes Haacke as follows: "The artist's business requires his involvement in practically everything. … An artist is not an isolated system" (Burnham 1969, 52). The cultural impact of the so-called rediscovery of time in science, to include irreversibility, randomness, and fluctuation (Prigogine and Stengers 1984, xxvii), manifests physically in Haacke's meteorological oeuvre. At the same time, Haacke's real-time instruments connect the gallery's physical atmosphere to the ideological climate of the art world.

The weather as a new medium for art catalyzed multidirectional flows between atmospheric science and systems theory within the cultural milieu of Lye, Haacke, De Maria, and Medalla. Artworks verged on the function of scientific instruments, such as weather balloons or cloud chambers, and reimagined the scientific language of openness. In the influential chapter in which von Bertalanffy describes a model of an open system, he writes, "An open system is defined as a system in exchange of matter with its environment, presenting import and export, building up and breaking down of its material components" (1968, 141). Live weather sources generate and decay, ebb and flow, as social systems do. Systems thinking, in art of the 1960s, evolved into an ecological perspective. Serres's writing also draws on systems theory in his chaotic fusion of disciplines, proposing that "noise, chance, rain, a circumstance" may produce a small fluctuation, a contradiction, or an inversion that creates a new system that "could be entirely different from the one that was interrupted" (1982b, 18).

The open dynamics in 1960s autocreative art are precursors to open-source programming, open architecture, and participatory art. Environmental activism rose out of the counterculture, yet at the time, artists involved in these subcultures still depended on the infrastructure of the gallery and art world. Paradoxically, countercultural figure Stewart Brand's early ecopolitical manual, *The Whole Earth Catalogue* (1968), later became an Internet-based bulletin board that facilitated the smooth integration of computing technology and associated work styles into American life (Lash 2010). The artists discussed in this chapter struggled against the workings of capitalism and the distance from real experience implied by *second nature*, by confounding gallery norms or finding sites outdoors, in free exchange with the elements.

Meteorological artworks may not always promote or reflect "ethico-aesthetic rupture" (Guattari 1995) simply by virtue of their choices of media, yet they convene vital forums for ecological debate and specific local resistance. Lye's *Wind Wands* (1961), for instance, became a focal point for the civic unrest surrounding the demolition of parts of New York's West Village. Haacke used the open system to counteract the hierarchical organization of physical relationships, which he believed operated within formalist art and systems of capital. The remote site of large-scale land art is often contrasted with the social engagement of contemporary ecological art, yet De Maria's *The Lightning Field* pervaded the social environment through its circulation in *Artforum*. Medalla, Haacke, and Lye's work called on audience-performers, attuned to atmospheric nuances in artwork that is relational, rather than sealed off from the physical world.

As barometers of feeling and catalysts for political action, 1960s meteorological art objects continue to engage audiences. With Latour, I see art objects as more than discrete "matters of fact"; rather, they are "matters of concern," open entities that provoke perplexity and productive dialogue among those who gather around them (Latour 2004b, 66). As a symbolic matter of concern, Lye's revived *Wind Wand* (opened in 2000), installed on the Taranaki foreshore, continues to play a part in social and meteorological narratives. Like Walter De Maria's poles, the wand is sometimes struck by lightning. A story of the Te Atiawa *iwi* (tribe) of the region traces a drop of rain from the top of Mount Taranaki, the high mountain that overshadows the town, through rivers, to the seabed, where condensation rises again to the sky as clouds. The intergenerational retelling of the connective cycle of weather, land, and sea at Waitara marae (communal meeting house) is a politicized message to the New Zealand government as it moves slowly on Te Atiawa land claims to the seabed and foreshore to honor the Treaty of Waitangi (1840). Lye's *Wind Wand*, positioned prominently among the elements on the shore, signifies the complexities of human-weather relations.

2 Sensing the Weather

In the 1960s and 1970s, Fluxus and early televisual and technology-based artists reveled in the production of intimate weather sensations. The New York avant-garde artworld and the Japanese experimental music scene are the milieu for the meteorological art practices detailed in this chapter, yet Fluxus event scores can be reperformed across geographic and temporal divides in response to any weather. Clouds, wind, and sunlight are the primary media for Japanese artist Mieko Shiomi's performance event *Wind Music* (1963) and Yoko Ono's *Sky TV* (1966)—one mediated by the skin of the body, the other a closed-circuit television loop. Imperceptible changes in the breeze are registered by vapor in Fujiko Nakaya's *Fog Gardens* (1970–present), made possible through agricultural engineering technology. *Cloud Music* (1974–1979) by Fluxus artist Robert Watts, David Behrman, and Bob Diamond is a musical score activated by cloud movement via a custom-built synthesizer. Each of these artworks amplifies the effects of the weather as sensory stimuli through performative and often technical means. As much as electronics or early transmission technologies become part of the system of art of many of these works, so too does the weather's constant mutability.

The artists in this chapter flout discipline boundaries to delve into human-technology-nature relations. They play with scientific and cybernetic concepts in which water vapor piping, cameras, video analyzers, and circuitry are freed from their predetermined uses. Mieko Shiomi's compositions reframe concepts from physics and information theory, just as the *flux* in George Macunias's *Fluxus Manifesto* (1963) is in part a reference to a term in chemistry. Watts, Behrman, and Diamond's *Cloud Music* grew out of Fluxus in New York, has been exhibited across America and in Berlin, and is now archived in the Smithsonian American Art Museum as a significant precursor to technology-based art. Hierarchies among engineers, artists and audiences, human and machine are called into question in pursuit of the open weather system.

Shiomi's event scores, Nakaya's *Fog Gardens*, the live cloud feed in Ono's *Sky TV*, and *Cloud Music* operate as ecological systems rather than as autonomous art objects.

The science of circular, causal mechanisms, indeterminacy and feedback loops of all kinds, caught the imagination of artists and composers in this period. I suggest that British cyberneticist Gregory Bateson's connected sense of systems, across biological and technical realms, spills into avant-garde art. Cybernetics is concerned with differential relations between and across systems, whether they be environmental, social, or technological, rather than with any one system in isolation. This chapter finds an emergent ecopolitics in these artworks, via which we coexist in constant exchange with the weather through our senses.

Mieko Shiomi: Music of Sun and Winds

In 1963 in Japan, Mieko Shiomi (also known as Chieko Shiomi in New York in the 1960s) made the following event score for *Wind Music* and sent it to her Fluxus colleagues:

1 Raise wind.

2 Be blown by wind.

3 Wind at the beach,

     wind in the street,

     wind passing by a car.

     Typhoon.

(Friedman 2002, 94)

To activate the event score, we call the wind, acquiesce to it, and recall the wind. The awakening power of a typhoon ends the event. Shiomi invites us to feel the weather and, at a different register, the passage of life plays out. The economy of expression of Japanese poetry based on nature, such as haiku, or Zen koans, and Shiomi's desire to "grasp natural phenomena" have been autobiographically connected to the artist's childhood intimacy with the environment in a seaside village near the Seto Inland Sea (Yoshimoto 2005, 141). In this chapter, I also take the connections between contemporary science and systems theory in Shiomi's compositions into account.

The instructions of a Fluxus event score can be picked up and performed at any time or any place. We feel the event time of a weather system, as well as inner time in Shiomi's event scores. *Event for the Midday in Sunlight* (1963) instructs us to open and close our eyes once each minute during the seven minutes after noon. The final time we open our eyes, we must look at our hands. The scores were first published in Fluxus newspapers, but they can be reperformed at any time. I tried out *Event for the Midday in Sunlight* on a summer day with a group of my students. The warmth of sunlight on the skin canceled out our visual senses. In the moment of reopening our eyes, the reflected light from our hands produced a blinding effect on the retina. The heightened sensory experience in *Event for the Midday in Sunlight* comes from a consciousness of the body as a weather barometer, in a direct experience of the elements.

The enigmatic or absurdist event score form evolved through the practices of John Cage, Yoko Ono, George Brecht, and La Monte Young. Although the weather in art historically has been the scene of painted spectacle, the visual is often suppressed in Fluxus event scores in place of written instructions. Attention was directed to senses other than sight, such as smell, hearing, or thermoception (heat, cold). Fluxus event scores instructed the audience to perform by using words to evoke a mental image in which text supplants image. In 1953 in New York, Yoko Ono developed her first "word-score" composition, *Secret Piece*, in which she inserted words into a music score, instructing a musician to "decide on one note that you want to play" with the accompaniment of "the woods from 5am to 8 am in summer" (Yoshimoto 2005, 82). Shiomi evolved her scores from her experimental music practice. *Wind Music*, *Event for the Midday in Sunlight*, and other event scores, composed in Tokyo, were translated into English and sent to Maciunas in New York through contact with a Japanese member of Fluxus, Ay-o. In his excitement, Maciunas had already assembled Shiomi's "complete" works into a Flux Kit of event scores when she came to New York from 1964 to 1965. Shiomi spent only one year with Fluxus, although she continued to correspond with the group after her return to Japan.

Ono called this new kind of practice *idea art*. In 1966 for a show at Indica gallery, she wrote: "Idea is what the artist gives, like a stone thrown in the water for ripples to be made. Idea is the air or the sun, anybody can use it and fill themselves according to their own size or shape of body" (Munroe et al. 2000). As well as the analogy with imagination, air and sunlight are also recurrent motifs in traditional Zen koans. Koans from the fifth or sixth centuries are short cryptic statements or puzzles designed to be used as philosophical thinking tools to disrupt habits of thought. Like the koan, Fluxus artworks transform the mundane into the resonant through attuning to incidental moments in the everyday. Event scores offer an availability to direct experience in which art and life, ancient traditions, and the new sciences meet.

Shiomi and Ono's language of an *event* was informed by John Cage. In the 1950s, Cage borrowed the word "event" from physics, where it is used to describe a set of particle interactions in space-time, a four-dimensional continuum in which events occur. Cage experimented with a textual form of musical notation with the composition *4'33"* (1952), which directs a performer to remain silent during three movements of undetermined time. In this piece, a conventional score is replaced by a short set of typewritten numbers and words. The observer's (listener's) decision about whether this is music or noise infamously comes to the fore. For Cage, *event* meant individuated "sounds in themselves"; Fluxus artist George Brecht reinterpreted *event* much more broadly as "everything that happens" (Kotz 2001, 70–71).

The participatory Fluxus event scores emerged in a cultural period of renewed attention to the observer in science and second-wave cybernetics. In *Order out of Chaos*, Stengers and Prigogine describe the time-orientated activity of preparing for a scientific experiment in which the scientist is an active performer during the experimental event. The scientific observer becomes a macroscopic agent "in a world far from equilibrium" (Prigogine and Stengers 1984, 300). In the 1960s and 1970s, contributors to the Macy conferences, particularly Bateson, Margaret Mead, and Heinz von Foerster, began to recognize the observer as an influential agent in a system. Cybernetics can be understood as a model of an ecology, as Bateson makes explicit. He posits that cybernetics is a means to think through the problem of "relations between an organism and its environment" when faced with the destruction of the world's environment (1973, 454). He warns, however, that if you "arrogate all mind to yourself, you will see the world around you as mindless and therefore not entitled to moral or ethical consideration. The environment will seem to be yours to exploit" (1973, 468). Mind, for Bateson, is immanent in pathways and messages outside the body in the structural organization of systems.

Shiomi described sound as four-dimensional in her event scores based on chance, time, and space. The nod to the modern sciences is clear in her compositions with the avant-garde music ensemble Group Ongaku, cofounded in 1960 in Tokyo. Her composition *Mobile I, II, III* for Group Ongaku is described in program notes entitled "Music of Centrifugal Space and Indeterminate Time." Ono also performed the series of Fluxus compositions *Works of Yoko Ono* (1962) with Group Ongaku at the Sogetsu Art Centre. One of the works she played was *AOS-To David Tudor*, an opera of "blue chaos," made of a cacophony of recorded and live speech in different languages. In Japanese, *ao* is the word for blue; the *os* comes from chaos. Together with Cage, electronic music pioneer and pianist David Tudor had explored indeterminacy in performance in the 1950s. Like Tudor, Shiomi and Ono also came to equate the chance element in the observer/audience encounter with the indeterminate in physics.

Tensions exist about the unruly interchange of terminology between art, information theory, and physics in this period. Physicist Richard Bright argues that the language of physics can be misleading for general purposes. He points out that in physics, chaos does not mean randomness, relativity does not mean that "anything goes," and the uncertainty principle does not mean that "everything is uncertain" (Ede 2000,

139). On the other hand, Umberto Eco challenges the defenders of "the purity of aesthetic discourse," arguing that words such as form, power, and germ, once belonging to physics and cosmology, now have wider, productive applications ([1962] 1989, 88). I maintain that the eccentric translation of scientific terms by Fluxus and other artists generates new ecoaesthetic experiences and social allegiances.

Shiomi's compositions with Group Ongaku engaged with emergent electronic technology, imbuing her simple recursive loops with the sensibility of the cybernetic age. She developed nontraditional instruments or radically altered methods of playing violins or pianos. In 1961, Shiomi performed in the protocomputer piece *IBM—Happening and Music Concrète*, composed by Ono's husband Toshi Ichiyanagi with Group Ongaku. As the title suggests, the performance also paid homage to Pierre Shaeffer's *Music Concrète*, in which electroacoustic compositions were arranged with environmental sounds, sometimes made with everyday objects. Each of the eight performers of Group Ongaku created random compositions using an arbitrary set of IBM computer punch cards as scores. Shiomi played an electric wave instrument, similar to a theremin, and later blew bubbles that drifted through the air currents of the auditorium of a packed Sogetsu Art Centre. The other performers played noninstrumental tools, such as drills and saws, furniture, grinding bowls, and winding a reel of paper tape over the stage and through the audience, accompanied by a piano (Yoshimoto 2005, 144). This absurd entwining of computer-like number systems, electronic instruments, and chance elements reflects the flow of cybernetic concepts into avant-garde music.

Shiomi's meteorological compositions transformed physical systems such as states of water into event scores. A growing fascination with turbulent flow, movement, and liquescence in twentieth-century physics parallels a growing feminist concern with fluidity within systems. Feminist philosopher Luce Irigaray (1999) suggests that the historically masculine bias of science resulted in the late development of fluid dynamics (associated with the feminine body) in a gendered preference for the solidity of Newtonian mechanics. The feminist performance art developed by Yvonne Rainer, Shigeko Kubota, Ono, and others explicitly challenged the privileging of looking, replacing visualism with sensory concern for interior bodily and exterior elemental media. Erotic or gendered associations with storms persist in many cultures, such as the naming of cyclones after women. The erotic dimension of fog as part of the medieval Japanese aesthetics of Yūgen is explored by Rurihiko Hara (2016) in relation to Fujiko Nakaya's oeuvre. Hara suggests that the word fog (*kiri*) is prefered by Nakaya rather than cloud, as fog is a female element in Yūgen aesthetics. Fog reflects a profound or indescribable feeling inspired by meteorological phenomena in the natural landscape. A Yūgen sensibility manifests in Shiomi's practice through her desire to merge with natural phenomena. When the body is enshrouded by the elements, we move past the mere beholding of a weatherscape to become an active participant. In another mode of feminist operation, Ono's *Sky TV* (1966) opens out to the clouds and disrupts the rational (masculine-oriented) system of televised weather, presented by the "weather lady."

Yoko Ono's Sky TV: Cloud Feedbacks

Sky TV is Ono's only video work, first exhibited at Indica Gallery in the exhibition *Yoko at Indica: Unfinished Paintings and Objects* by Yoko Ono in 1966. In *Sky TV*, cloud or cloudless sky, depending on the weather, becomes an informational pattern materialized on a consumer television set. A closed-circuit camera on the gallery roof transmits a live feed onto the television in the middle of an otherwise empty room, as a closed-circuit loop. When, at the same instant, the sky outside the window appears on the screen, the gap between the televisual and the "real" is closed, and a weather experience becomes intimate. The uncanny proximity of the sky in a live transmission, from just outside the gallery, accrues affective power through the surprise of simultaneity. At a time when video images were largely controlled by television broadcasters, live-transmitted weather offered a radical mode of direct access for viewers.

In 1963, the first consumer video recorder had become available; by 1965, Korean artist Nam June Paik introduced video to the Fluxus artists with his Sony Portapak video camera. Video as an alternative to the expensive developing costs of photochemical film processing was attractive to artists. Ono's understanding of real-time video complimented Paik's belief that the live, moving image would diversify global culture. Paik speculates that the appeal of liveness in video is "the uniqueness, the spontaneity, the virginity" of the image (Kellein and Stoss 1993, 125). The liveliness of weather combined with the "live" system of real-time video offered the possibility of a continuous cybernetic loop between video and the elements. By 1960, the concept of *homeostasis* (the ability of organisms to maintain steady states in information theory in any environment), in which the output feeds back into the system, became relevant to artists' experiments with feedback mechanisms. The observer in the second phase of cybernetics and the audience in a gallery, or a video loop, were now conceived as agents in process-based activity.

At the same time that Paik and Ono were experimenting with television sets as a sculptural element, McLuhan and Papanek wrote, "With the TV you are the screen. And TV is two-dimensional and sculptural in its tactile contours" (1962, 39). In *Verbi-Voco-Visual Explorations*, published in Fluxus's *Something Else Press*, McLuhan and Papanek (1967) observe that in Western culture the visual sense is "intensely separated" from the other senses in the performance of tasks and in the formation of psychological states.

Counterintuitively, they describe the television as *audile-tactile*, rather than visual, and speculate that this new technology will allow the "ratio of the senses" to be altered. In 1969, Ono reversed McLuhan's well-known formulation by pronouncing that "the message is the medium," to foreground the aesthetic and political implications of new televisual technologies.

Closed-circuit practices in early televisual art bridge the common separation of material reality—in this case, the cloud system—from the apparent abstraction of television broadcasting networks. Although cloud phenomena appear as informational patterns in *Sky TV*, the artwork still takes material form in the solid weight of the television set and the wires and the camera on the roof of Indica Gallery. The system has a tactile, sensation-producing presence. Event scores often produced other residual materials that could be exhibited as objects. *Sky TV* is a tangible product of Ono's earlier cloud-based event scores in which "art as idea" takes form.

Sky TV was part of a suite of weather works in Ono's practice. In one version of *Cloud Piece* (1963), the viewer is given a template with a dotted circle in the middle and instructed to "cut along dotted line and look at the sky through the hole" (Ono 1966, 16). While in another version of *Cloud Piece*, we are instructed to "Imagine the clouds dripping. Dig a hole in the garden to put them into" (Ono 1970). In the same year as *Sky TV*, Ono also made small cardboard cards inscribed with the word *SKY* in pencil, produced by the *Sky Dispenser* (1966, no. 17). *Sky TV* acts as a similar, televisual method of framing pieces of sky as a small pocket of imaginative potential. The motif of the open sky has been positioned as an analogue for unlimited possibility, individual freedom, women's liberation, and antiwar protest (MacDonald 1989, 12), recurrent themes of Ono's work in the late 1960s. In 1968, Ono dedicated a more personal instructional work to "John Lennon as a Young Cloud," which included instructions to "Open and close inside John's head" (Ono 1970).

In addition, *Sky TV* and the event scores of Ono and Shiomi invite an intensified experience of time, rather than time by the clock. The framing of a piece of sky suggests a duration of idle looking—waiting for the sky to change, or our habitual glances at the weather out of the window. Our daily lives are tied to many different circadian rhythms; night and day, growth and decay, and seasonal changes in weather from warm to cold or wet to dry. Ono's *Sky Event* (1968) instructs, "Wait until a cloud appears and comes above your head." (Ono 1970) The instruction to gaze at clouds insists that we do very little at all—signaling a countercultural resistance to the capitalist work ethic. The limit of my patience determines the duration of this event, even as my body registers subtle weather changes and the chance to rest. A sense of weather's periodicity in the gentle ebb and flow of fog is also found in Nakaya's *Fog Gardens*.

Figure 2.1
Fujiko Nakaya. *Cloud Shroud*. 1970. Part of EAT's Pepsi Pavilion at Expo '70, Osaka, Japan, March 18. Photograph: Shunk-Kender. © J. Paul Getty Trust. Getty Research Institute, Los Angeles, California.

Fujiko Nakaya: Gardening in the Atmosphere

In the desert climate of the sculpture garden of Australia's National Gallery in Canberra, Japanese artist Fujiko Nakaya's artwork *Fog Sculpture #94925: Foggy Wake in a Desert: An Ecosphere* (1976) lies in wait. A fine mist dampens my skin as I walk along a path between leaning trees and hardy desert shrubs, and the fog settles low over the plants and the marsh pond behind. When I look closely along the side of the garden path, an array of nozzles on an aged, red metal grid reveals the simple mechanism that creates this cinematic atmosphere. A fine, artificial vapor drifts with the updrafts of "real" weather, and the ephemeral installation also functions to keep the plants alive. The artworks nearby are infused by the fog, including the Pukumani poles of the Tiwi people, which were installed in Nakaya's garden in the mid-eighties. As other people join me on the path, the low-lying fog parts in response to our movements.

The sculpture now operates from 12:30 p.m. to 2:00 p.m. only, reflecting the imperative to conserve the resource of water in the Australian climate. The system depends on precious water sourced from Canberra's Cotter Dam. When Nakaya embarks on a fog sculpture, she measures the behavior of the atmospheric microclimate, including the prevailing wind direction and rainfall levels. She carefully attends to the topography of the ground of the fog garden; even the amount of heat produced by stones that causes the fog to hover or disperse is taken into account. Like a scientist, Nakaya measures and thoroughly calculates the environmental system, yet she also has an animist sense of the interaction between atmosphere, stones, plants, and her role as a gardener. She regards even the stones as "adjusting themselves to the breathing of fog" (Morioka, n.d.).

Nakaya's first experiment with the meteorological element of fog was part of an initiative by the Experiments in Art and Technology (EAT) group to create a low-lying fog over the entire Pepsi Pavilion at the Osaka World's Fair (1970). Nakaya, who was raised in Tokyo, first began to investigate the "echo-state of the cloud" as a "vehicle of correspondence and reverberation with nature" when she shifted from her art school studies in Illinois to New York in the mid-1960s (Morioka, n.d.). She was thinking about creating an artwork informed by temperature differences and "organic decomposition" when she volunteered to help with the research for the Pepsi Pavilion in 1968. When core EAT member Billy Klüver discovered Nakaya's father was a scientist with extensive connections in Japan, he asked Nakaya to oversee a meteorological project. The Pepsi Pavilion was dominated by white sculptures by artist Robert Breer, which moved slowly around the plaza at less than two feet per minute while emitting sounds. Tall black towers housed xenon lights, which created a frame of light around the pavilion at night. Nakaya's task was to compose a sensitive system of swathes of generated and natural fog that would soften the pavilion's architecture.

The Pepsi Pavilion project developed from orchestrated ventures between artists and scientists in the postwar period. Nakaya was one of two thousand artists and engineers invited to work with EAT. Founded in 1966, EAT's core members evolved to include Bell Labs engineers Klüver and Fred Waldhauer, artist Robert Rauschenberg, sound artist David Tudor, and performance artist/filmmaker Robert Whitman. The EAT venture aspired to ameliorate a state of internal tension among the counterculture movement, science, and industry. In a period when military researchers in the United States were conducting experiments in cloud seeding and weather modification over Cuba, to work on the aesthetics of fog generation was implicitly a political, metacritical endeavor.

Haacke also sent five proposals to EAT, including a meteorological simulation of a wind and cold-warm environment, but he was unable to raise a corporate sponsor to support his collaboration.

Fog is technically defined as low-lying clouds that obscure visibility, forming on small particles of dust, soot, sea salt, or other airborne elements called *cloud-condensation nuclei*. When air cools, relative humidity increases and water molecules in the atmosphere condense onto these small particles. The onset of a fog is heavily influenced by nearby bodies of water, topography, and wind conditions. Nakaya's nascent interest in ecology convinced her of the need to invent a water-based technique, rather than a chemical system, to create "a more people-friendly environment for the E.A.T. Pavilion" (McDougall 2013, 15). Prior to the Osaka World's Fair at the close of the 1960s, Nakaya tracked down research scientist Tom Mee in Pasadena to design a nozzle system for a programmed water-vapor control system. Although Mee had once experimented with the production of water-based fog, the research scientist was now relying on chemically produced fog in his agricultural research. Nakaya persuaded Mee to return to his earlier system; together, they produced the first water-generated fog. The small openings of the nozzles, designed by Mee, are fitted with tiny pins that disperse the water into billions of ultra-fine fog droplets measuring between fifteen and twenty microns in diameter. Thirty years after her physicist father, Dr. Ukichiro Nakaya, discovered the phases of snow crystal growth and made the first scientific photographic studies of simulated snow crystals, Nakaya collaborated on an equally ephemeral weather form.

Art world excitement about Nakaya's dematerialized environmental artwork rapidly sprung up. In 1976, Nakaya's *Fog Sculpture #94768: Earth Talk* was exhibited in the second Sydney Biennale opposite the Art Gallery of New South Wales. Bateson's notion of "organism plus environment" (1973) is important to Nakaya's sensitivity to environmental feedbacks. Nakaya developed the work *Opal Loop/Cloud Installation # 72503* (1980) with the Trisha Brown Dance Company to include the fluid movements of performers in the environmental system. The dancers literally rehearsed with fog as a co-performer. Installations as well as performances, such as *Fog Sculpture #94925: Foggy Wake in a Desert: An Ecosphere* (1976), create open-ended environmental feedback loops between inanimate things and human participants.

Nearly twenty-five years after her first fog pavilion, Nakaya was sponsored once again by EAT for her *Greenland Glacial Moraine Garden* (1994) designed for the Ukichiro Nakaya Museum of Snow and Ice, in Kaga, Japan. She traveled to Greenland, assisted by EAT staff, to collect sixty tons of ancient glacial moraine stones from the Thule-Qaanaaq area in Northwest Greenland. The *Greenland Glacial Moraine Garden* incorporated the stones and fog to honor her father, who had passed away. As a pioneer in low-temperature physics, Uchikiro had spent summers in Northwest Greenland working with ice-core samples from the glaciers to study the viscoelastic properties of snow and ice. The garden conjoins the glacial stones from Greenland and the fog in Japan with the spirit of Nakaya's father.

Over the years, the fog-producing system Nakaya developed with Mee for the Pepsi Pavilion has remained technically much the same for all the (carefully numbered) fog gardens she has designed. The installation *Fog Chamber—Riga #26422* (2005) created for the *Conversations with Snow and Ice* exhibition at the Natural History Museum of Latvia in Riga pays homage to the cloud chamber in physics, marking Nakaya's enduring connection to science. Artists Anthony Gormley (United Kingdom) and Ann Veronica Janssens (Belgium) also manufacture fogs that permeate interior spaces of galleries to explore their sensory and perceptual effects. Gormley calls *Blind Light* (2007) his "cloud chamber" (Evening Standard 2007). *Cloud Music*, the last artwork I consider in detail in this chapter, represents a technological turning point between 1960s live weather, emergent televisual art, and the digital media art of the latter part of the book.

Cloud Music and the Cloud Machine

Cloud Music (1974–1979) is a collaboration between the artist Robert Watts, well-known for his work in Fluxus; David Behrman, experimental composer of electronic music; and Robert (Bob) Diamond, systems engineer and video designer. An account of the development of *Cloud Music* was relayed to me in a Skype interview in May 2013 with David Behrman and Bob Diamond; Robert Watts passed away in 1988. Central to *Cloud Music* (1974–1979) are, of course, the clouds themselves, a highly dynamic physical system. Even now, scientists still struggle to understand the complex set of drivers that determine the height, density, composition, and color of clouds; clouds remain one of the more mysterious aspects of the weather system.

To realize Fluxus artist Robert Watt's whimsical idea of listening to the clouds, Behrman and Diamond designed a whole audio and video system from scratch, dubbed the "Cloud Machine." The video analyzer, designed by Bob Diamond, linked six cross hairs on a monitor positioned toward a particular set of clouds, to six control voltages. As the light values of the moving clouds changed as they passed across the cross hairs, the voltages changed and were converted into triggered progressions of pitched sounds, made by a music synthesizer. Diamond explained, "The whole idea of it was to almost be able to feel the shape of the clouds. ... depending on the shape of the cloud different parts of the screen will be activated at different sensitive points" (Behrman

Figure 2.2a, b
Robert Watts, David Behrman, and Bob Diamond. *Cloud Music.* 1974–1979. From the *Canadian/ American Sky* installation at Electric Gallery, Toronto, Canada, 1974. Photograph: Robert Watts, © Robert Watts Estate, 1974/2017.

and Diamond 2013). Behrman regarded each of the six cross hairs as possessing a musical personality.

The artists worked together over a two-year period from 1972 to 1974 to develop *Cloud Music* in a remote cabin in Montrose, Pennsylvania. The egalitarian nature of this collaboration was unusual for the 1970s, when electronic art often was promoted as the work of a single well-known artist, supported by unnamed assistants. Bob Diamond traveled between Montrose and his job developing video synthesizers and video circuitry for popular shows such as *Sesame Street* and *The Electric Company* (1971–1979) at the experimental WNET TV-Lab in New York. He also custom-designed video switchers for Nam June Paik during this busy period. In the cabin, over ten months, the six circuit boards for each cross-hair of the video analyzer were soldered together by Diamond's wife, Pat, in a small version of a "Model-T- Ford" style production line, as Diamond quipped (2013). Diamond's method of responding to the clouds relied on the time-base or sync signal of the video. This video signal synchronizes the sweeping movement of the electron beam in a television tube with the Sony video camera in the artwork.

Watts would journey to the cabin in Montrose to exchange ideas with Diamond on the artwork, then drive back to New York. Watts was primarily responsible for the installation design and, like Hans Haacke's *Condensation Cube* (1963–1965), he made a plexiglass box on top of a steel box to house the circuit boards. The interior workings of Diamond and Behrman's intricate electronics were open to view through the clear casing of the Cloud Machine. To reveal the interior of the technological black box was important to the *Cloud Music* collaborators (Behrman and Diamond 2013). Open or closed boxes that revealed or hid their structural workings were objects of interest among avant-garde artists, as well as a key motif in cybernetics (Wiener 1948). In 1964, the Dwan Gallery staged the show *Boxes*, which included Robert Watts's earlier artwork, *Three Clouds* (1965). Photographs of clouds and human skin were applied to three box-shaped plastic-laminated pedestals in this work.

Behrman's wiry, custom-built audio generator included both analog and digital chips. In 1975, Behrman was acting director at the Center for Contemporary Music at Mills College, in Oakland, California. A small community of artists was working there with emergent digital technology. Diamond described Behrman's music generator in reverential terms: "It actually had AI [artificial intelligence] and a temporal memory. It could remember sequences that happened in the past. This was before computers had hard-drives and memories" (Behrman and Diamond 2013). Behrman explained further: "The synthesizer had counters and adders that could mark and count the light-change events as they came in. It had six banks of three oscillators; each one could run backwards to replay what just happened, on a simple level. The history of light change-caused changes was recorded. Voltages from the video analyzer were changed into digits 0 to 7, and these integers determined the audio output tunings" (Behrman and Diamond 2013). In addition to having a temporal memory, environmental responsiveness was a central trope in *Cloud Music*. Behrman notes:

If you think of a conventional composition as an object that is fixed from beginning to end, [instead] we were creating a situation to be explored by musicians. So that situation where the musician would play and trigger things is analogous to what happens in *Cloud Music* where the clouds could randomly trigger things. So these ideas of interactivity were in the air then, and they were related to Cage. Where you would leave in elements that you can't predict and it keeps it lively that way. You try and get rid of your own clichés. Cage used chance, he used the I-Ching to open up a situation. And, in a way, the clouds moving across the sky is like the I-Ching. (Behrman and Diamond 2013)

Taoist philosophy informs the aesthetics of *Cloud Music*. Behrman refers to Cagean aesthetics and the 1960s countercultural talisman the *I Ching*, or the *Book of Changes* (3000 BC–2000 BC). The *I Ching* provides a framework for the relations among people, matter, and nature (the Tao). Three cognitive capacities for human perception of the world are posited in the Tao: sensation, intuition, and intellect. Equilibrium can be found in an ethics of balance between human beings and the natural world.

At the same time, Behrman affirms that Watts was aware of cybernetic concepts through his involvement in Fluxus at the time of making *Cloud Music*. A cultural aesthetic responsive to nature's chaotic factors was prompted in resistance to the technological determinism of twentieth-century militarism. In our interview, Behrman employed cybernetic notions of "self- regulating systems that feed back on themselves" and drift. *Drift* is a term used by linguists and in cyberneticist Wiener's pure mathematics. In audio composition, drift is produced by "cumulative changes in the articulation of sounds that can be related in turn to the interferences that distort any audible communication" (George Kubler, cited in Lee 2004, 233).

Behrman experimented with harmonic tonal compositions in which frequencies would develop randomly and the sequences would eventually drift. In *Cloud Music*, however, the system was intended for a long-term, unmanned installation, so it was not allowed to drift indefinitely, to ensure that the oscillators didn't go out of tune. Behrman explains: "There was a finite set of pitch possibilities derived from one Master oscillator, using digital dividers and multipliers. This gave the sound of *Cloud Music* a slightly colder feeling than earlier pieces that were allowed to drift. [Yet even] on a day with a plain blue or grey sky, some little change will happen in the sky once in a while, causing a voltage to cross over a threshold in the synth, resulting in a harmonic change" (Behrman and Diamond 2013). The tendency toward random harmonics in the Cloud Machine mechanism was restrained by a return to a core family of harmonic tones. Behrman notes that a listener can always recognize the sounds in the installation as *Cloud Music*.

Cloud Ecologies

The process of sensing the differences in clouds in *Cloud Music* relies on an analysis of pixel coordinates. Diamond professes to seeing the sky in terms of equations, saying, "I see a mesh of two-dimensional points with depth and magnitude" (Behrman and Diamond 2013). There are parallels with Diamond's practical knowledge of feedback systems from his training in electro-engineering, Watts's Fluxus-infused idea of a cloud-produced music, and cybernetic theory. For a cyberneticist, Bateson writes, "formal processes of mapping, translation or transformation are, in principle, imputed to every step of any sequence of phenomena which the cyberneticist is attempting to explain" (1973, 454). In Bateson's analysis, substance devolves to the information "carried" by the events and objects in the circuit, just as the physical movements of the clouds devolve to audio signals in the artwork.

Bateson describes systems as always open, in which "the circuit is energized from some external source" or "events within the circuit may be influenced from the outside or may influence outside events," yet the system itself is a restraint mechanism in cybernetic theory (1973, 410). Mechanisms in the circuit of *Cloud Music* restrain the constant variation of the clouds to produce harmonic changes. Aesthetic restraint is also apparent in the minimal harmonics that the clouds trigger.

Bateson asks us to entertain the following idea: "Consider a variable in the circuit at any position and suppose this variable subject to random change in value (the change perhaps being imposed by impact of some event external to the circuit). We now ask how this change will affect the value of this variable at that later time when the sequence of effects has come around the circuit. Clearly the answer to this last question will depend on the characteristics of the circuit and will therefore, be not random" (1973, 410). The notion of randomness as part of a greater pattern can also be understood as a larger relational nexus, or ecology, beyond the confines of the box. If *pattern* was initially a privileged term among the electrical engineers developing information theory, then *randomness* became increasingly understood as the creative ground from which new forms can emerge (Hayles 1999, 285–286). Pattern is understood as the realization of a certain set of possibilities, whereas, randomness is "the much, much larger set of everything else, from phenomena that cannot be rendered coherent by a given system's organization to those the system cannot perceive at all" (Hayles 1999, 286). In the case of *Cloud Music*, the chance occurrence of cloud movement or the timing of an encounter of a listener with the sound may be part of a higher order, or, part of an unknowable complexity.

Diamond's professional experience in the space-research environment translates to his willingness to experiment with the chaotic problem of sensing the clouds. He reflects:

For two years I was working for NASA, working on Project Apollo. And one of the problems was that the engines kept exploding. And I was working on a way of determining by analyzing the engines to figure out why they were failing. Part of that problem was chaos; where the engine was acting like a whistle and it was blowing itself up because of the vibrations. ... This experience influenced me a lot in thinking about interactivity and designing an artwork that was interactive. Because depending on what that engine was sensing it would react in an interactive way; you could have blown on the exhaust and cause an oscillation that could explode it. ... The work with systems in *Cloud Music* was actually some kind of closure of this period of NASA research, where a concept that was causing so much pain could actually be resolved into a pleasurable experience. (Behrman and Diamond 2013)

Diamond also noted that the video analyzer for *Cloud Music* was made from military-grade parts that could withstand up to 100°C and work in a radioactive environment or on a spacecraft. The cross hairs on the monitor that sense the difference in the light of a passing cloud use similar technology to the marking of a target in ground-based artillery. Such technologies, redeployed in an art context, were understood by artists and technologists as a resistance to their intended use in warfare. The military origins of cybernetic ontology, including Wiener's development of war machines such as the Antiaircraft AA Predictor, form part of the political backdrop of *Cloud Music*.

Bateson's version of cybernetics is ethical in reach. If the mind expands beyond the ego, he writes, then "a certain humility becomes appropriate, tempered by the dignity or joy of being part of something much bigger" (Bateson 1973, 467–468). To watch the sky and listen to weather patterns creates immediate affects that exist beyond the self. In *Cloud Music*, we find an assemblage of cloud-machine-observer or -listener. To attend to both the clouds and the machine at once extends creativity to the nonhuman physical world. Instead of controlling machinery and nature, we experience the gentle chaos of clouds along with the imperceptible workings of the machine's inner circuitry. *Cloud Music* is ecological in the sense that the audience listens intently to the vagaries of the clouds, relayed through nascent computer technology.

The flux of ideas among art, science, and cybernetics in the 1960s and 1970s transpired from both deliberately orchestrated ventures, such as the EAT collaborations, and the spontaneous exchange that simply happens in a shared cultural climate.

Meteorological aesthetics express a yearning for openness and free space when, in the political context of the draft for the Vietnam war in America, young lives were becoming increasingly unfree. For Marcuse, "Capitalist progress not only reduces the environment of freedom, the 'open space' of the human existence, but also the 'longing', the need for such an environment" (1969, 18). Early weather-based artworks offer space for inward reflection while oriented toward the sky.

Marcuse finds that freedom and "a new sensibility" can be found in both art and science. On art, he writes: "The term 'aesthetic,' in its dual connotation of 'pertaining to the senses' and 'pertaining to art,' may serve to designate the quality of the productive-creative process in an environment of freedom" (Marcuse 1969, 24). As for science, he argues that to become "vehicles of freedom," science and technology "would have to change their present direction and goals; they would have to be reconstructed in accord with a new sensibility—the demands of the life instincts" (1969, 19). In Marcusean terms, only a technology and science of liberation and imagination will be free to project and design the forms of the human universe without exploitation. Yet there is a difference between *inner freedom*, in which we *feel* free, and the problematic

Figure 2.3
Random International. *Rain Room*. 2012–2013. Installation view at MoMA, New York, 2013.

separation of social politics from the concept of freedom as Arendt points out (2006, 149–150).

Marcuse's "new sensibility" can be detected in *Cloud Music*—an artwork driven by the radical submission to chance that characterizes the Fluxus movement, yet only realizable through the rapid advance of computer science and televisual technology. For Behrman, the art-making process acts as a release mechanism from the destructive extremes of space science, yet implicitly technoindustrial forces also move through the materials and operating system of the Cloud Machine itself. The collective principles of the *I Ching*, however, bring a different lens to the artwork of this period. By adopting a Taoist ethic of natural balance joined by a delight in physics and open systems, the Cloud Machine, Shiomi's event scores and the animist spirit in Nakaya's *Fog Gardens* attend to the nonhuman biota that surround us, beyond Marcuse's *human* universe.

The live, sensory experiences first made available through early technological experiments in meteorological art intensify with the digital encoding of weather as medium in software. The delight of immersion in simulated weather continues in Random International's *Rain Room* (2012), a widely exhibited assemblage of live weather and digital technology. The experience of rain indoors is joyous, just as Nakaya's simulated fogs have enchanted audiences for over forty years. The *Rain Room* is a complex open system made from custom software, 3-D tracking cameras, solenoid values, pressure regulators, and custom-designed tiles designed to envelop us in rain. As we enter the gallery space, we are at once exposed to and protected from the water. Although the sensations produced by the sound and smell of rain are overwhelming, we stay disconcertingly dry within the downpour, in a communal moment of reprieve from the everyday.

3   Weather Envisioning: Visualization and Mapping

Digital culture opens out to the weather, forging new alliances among art, science, social life, and the physical world to predict the weather to come and to model change over time. Our desire for an instant daily weather report calls for new imaging processes, and techniques of disseminating information. With new media art, the difference between creative and scientific means of meteorological representation has diminished; artists use the same tools and meteorological data streams as scientists to gather digital weather media for their practice. In the age of big data, dense tracts of information from remote-sensing satellites is plumbed by supercomputers and classified weather knowledge is held in powerful international conglomerates to be bought and sold. Under these conditions, artists' resourcefulness in accessing weather media becomes critical. Artists conjure representations of weather from contingent, confounding, and often difficult to access data sets to sensory and political effect.

Meteorological scientists and visualization experts turn the numerical data from instruments into recognizable visual schemas, whereas artists look for gaps in these maps. I begin by charting some conventions of meteorological data visualization, from hand-drawn notations to satellite meteorology, before turning to artists' aberrant mappings. The repurposing of digitized weather for art is described here as *data hitchhiking* to draw out the complex relations between artists and scientific information. In *Most Blue Skies* (2006–2009), British artists Lise Autogena and Josh Portway hitchhike on existing data streams controlled by a network of governmental meteorological agencies to speculate on how we perceive. Entirely new weather schemas emerge in installations by Thorbjørn Lausten (Denmark) and Billy Apple (Aotearoa New Zealand). Korean artist Zune Lee's game *Weather Pong* (2011), a variation on the classic Atari arcade game *Pong* (1972), politicizes social activity by combining weather-mood correlations on Twitter and atmospheric data streams. *O-Tū-Kapua: My Personal Cloud* (2016–2017), by the art collective F4 (Aotearoa New Zealand) and Aotearoa New Zealand's National Institute of Water and Atmospheric Research (NIWA), binds climate science and Māori customary knowledge of weather. Such meteorological artworks act as unruly mediators for humans and our technical instruments with the physical and spiritual worlds.

When Hannah Arendt reflected on space technologies in the 1960s, she found that modern science has shown us vast gaps in our knowledge of nature that escape not only the "coarseness of human sense perception but even the enormously ingenious instruments that have been built for its refinement" (2006, 261). Arendt evokes Max Planck's observation that data sets, for physics researchers, are like "mysterious messengers" from the real world. In weather-forecasting, we only know about future weathers when shifts in light and heat affect our measuring instruments on distant satellites. Transmutations take place between the numerical language of measuring instruments, the swarms of data they generate, and their final translation into pictures by visualization professionals. Perhaps because of the gaps in our knowledge, a tacit acceptance of scientific knowledge and computational mechanisms has emerged, as Vilém Flusser ([1985] 2011) has argued. Yet for Flusser, those who visualize information are not merely working in service of science and industry; they are "envisioners" of our social world who draw out the visual patterns that impact our lives. An artist teases apart accepted data routes and normative software interfaces to diversify the number of stakeholders who envision the atmosphere.

Digital anemometers, barometers, and satellites are essential to scientists as sources of data for computer-based visualizations and climate projections to represent the atmosphere—only to become invisible once maps have been made to communicate the weather. The maps themselves are eventually discarded as yesterday's news. I was given thousands of black-and-white printed photographs of satellite clouds that had once been used by the Bureau of Meteorology (BoM) in Melbourne to make analogue animations for televised weather forecasts—now useless objects to meteorological forecasting, but still captivating documents to me. The humanities have historically "banished" technological and informational objects from the "world of meanings"; as Simondon (1958) argued, they are considered neither human nor natural. On the other hand, aesthetic art objects, such as Turner's *Clouds*, have been given special attention in cultural discourse, as indeed they have in this book. Yet, like many artists, I am intrigued by weather instrumentation, meteorological maps, and satellite images as compelling entities in themselves.

Meteorological Visualization and Mapping

Scientists and visualization experts translate weather phenomena into maps and diagrams using codified color schemas and regulated instruments and software. By employing a homogenous language (longitude and latitude, geometry, time-space axes) the weather map defines the way we understand borders, much as we understand the geographical markers dividing sovereign territories. Such geopolitical borders are clearly imposed despite the lived reality of cultural-linguistic regions, and they are subject to historical movement. Much the same can be said of boundaries constructed in meteorological maps. Latour (1986) coined the term *immutable mobile* to describe how scientific visualizations have the property of mobility to convince dissenters or raise financial resources. Yet they are immutable as they are encoded with particular formal features. A weather map organizes our pursuit of agriculture, leisure events, and travel, so it needs consistency. Repetitive processes keep particular paradigms stable, and, as such, meteorological visualizations are repeatable "gestalts" that we all recognize (Ihde 1998). For general acceptance of a form to take hold, Nigel Thrift argues, their forms must be "reliably repetitive" and "consistently consistent" to be understood and to compel (2004, 177). Artists, on the other hand, will often seek formal deviances, rather than the restrictions of repeatability, or they will invent their own schemas.

In the era of expanding empires, maps of prevailing winds oriented ships along sailing routes. An elite number of citizens could imagine that they "gathered up the world" using visualization of the winds to speed their passage to remote lands. Early maps of the trade winds, for instance, were used to advantage ships in their journeys between Europe and the Americas. According to Latour, visualization is about persuasion. He characterizes the role of a map as follows: "You doubt what I say? I'll show you. And, without moving more than a few inches I unfold in front of your eyes figures, diagrams, plates, texts, silhouettes, and then and there present things that are far away and with which some kind of two way connection has now been established" (Latour 1986, 13). Visualization remains one of the most powerful explanations to muster allies to a cause. Through the opening of visualization processes to a non-scientific audience, artists create new ways to envision, revisit, or resist the power relations of meteorological mapping.

During the Enlightenment, objective reality began to be divided into quantifiable units—from dots and dashes to indicate wind direction to fractions and decimals in mathematical notation to bars and measures in musical notation to perspective in painting, drawing, and cartography. At the same time, graphic marks of weather began to be layered over the contours of the land masses; both cartographic and statistical systems of representation converged on one map. Edmund Halley's early meteorological map of tropical airflow (1686), for instance, layered data about prevailing winds, magnetic variations, and tides from ship's logs to construct a map of tropical surface winds. Halley annotated his isometric projection map with short, swirling dashes to indicate wind direction (Tufte 2001, 20). This process of abstracting nature, Mathew Fuller observes, turns "a live thing, a dynamic, or an object into something that exists as a numerical representation of its properties, or that has such an abstraction of itself embedded within it" (Fuller 2005, 165). The oscillating dynamic between real and abstract systems of phenomena is a lure for many artists.

Ever since Galileo pictured us wandering in a "dark labyrinth" without God's geometrical figures as a guide, measurement has been synonymous with positivist science. Yet painting and architecture have historically played a part in the development of mathematical perspective in maps of the globe. Northern Renaissance painter and printmaker Albrecht Dürer's book on the perspective of the human body, *De Varietate Figurarum* (1537), was circulated widely among cartographers and probably reached Gerhardus Mercator, the Flemish cartographer par excellence. Renaissance perspective in painting gave cartographers the means to reproduce material reality on flat surfaces by using foreshortening, pulling, and stretching to create spatial distortions. The Enlightenment's cartographic accomplishment of a standardized perspectival earth is only one vision of our world, however. To accept this measured, mathematical version of reality was in fact, as Alfred Crosby (1997) has argued, a blind leap of faith into a particular Eurocentric framework.

For Arendt, the problem with mathematical operations that reduce "sensually given data" to "numerical truths" is the removal of the "eyes of the mind, no less than the eyes of the body, from phenomena" through the force of distance. She writes, "Under this new condition of remoteness, every assemblage of things is transformed into mere multitude, and every multitude, no matter how disordered, incoherent, and confused, will fall into certain patterns and configurations possessing the same validity and no more significance than the mathematical curve" (Arendt 1958, 267). Science and mathematics have come to overrule "the testimony of nature as witnessed at close range by the human senses" and reduce it to the uniformities of geometry (ibid.). Artists instead bring the body and social exchange back into mapping processes.

The empirical weather maps of Indigenous navigators persisted successfully as alternative spatial models, without the mathematics of European maps. Take the Marshall Islands' cowrie shell, coconut fiber, and stick maps, for instance, that convey complex information such as ocean swell to guide seafarers around Micronesia. In Australia, stringybark paintings functioned in ceremonies to pay homage to local weathers and plant and animal life. In the bark paintings from Arnhem Land in the Museum of Contemporary Art (Sydney) collection, such as Djimbarrdjimbarrwuy's *Totem Cloud Pattern* (ca. 1970), the graphic marks of wind direction can communicate and without recourse to a numerical system. Spirits lie within these maps that communicate spatiotemporal, social, and atmospheric systems simultaneously (Mundine 2008, 84). Measurement has never been essential to weather mapping; geometry is a culturally inscribed form of representation.

By the turn of the twentieth century, technologies such as radio and the telegraph were used to communicate weather forecasts, largely by observing how fronts traveled from place to place. Ground-based observations in Australia were delivered by telegraph infrastructure to forecast weather between states. If Melbourne experienced rain and a southerly wind, for instance, the same conditions would soon come to Tasmania. The telegraph networks were extended to deliver warnings about the coming weather fronts that drifted across the Tasman Sea to Aotearoa New Zealand. A crucial point in the predictive numericalization of meteorology came in 1904, when Norwegian meteorologist Vilhem Bjerknes claimed weather forecasting to be a problem of physics (Friedman 1989). Ruling equations could be predicted based on recent observations of an initial state of atmosphere. By 1950, early computers enabled the numerical prediction of weather that Bjerknes anticipated: programs could plot weather from one point to another to convey future weathers.

From the first kites equipped with meteorographs in the late 1890s to the panoramic sweep of the weather satellite image, meteorology from above changed forecasting forever. A transfixed television audience viewed large-scale cloud formations from space for the first time via the Television Infrared Observational Satellite (Tiros I) in 1960, at the beginnings of remote meteorology. The cloud patterns were interpreted as "signatures" of the weather systems that would impact the earth far below. Morris Tepper, deputy director of the Space Applications Program at the National Aeronautics and Space Administration (NASA), stated in 1960 that "pictures taken by the Tiros satellites showed that the Earth's cloud cover was highly organized on a global scale. ... The cloud structure as seen by Tiros has been superimposed on the weather map. It is remarkable how closely the cloud systems delineate the weather systems. It is as if Nature were actually drawing her own weather map directly onto the Earth" (NASA 2012). Tepper's enthusiasm for the inscription of nature via technology echoes Henry Fox Talbot's mid-nineteenth-century understanding of solar photography in his book *The Pencil of Nature* as both a natural and a cultural phenomena (Batchen 2002, 10). Both suppress the complex technical operations involved in making images to naturalize an emergent technology. A television "weather lady" would further feminize this technological assemblage as a form of infotainment.

Satellite imaging plays a crucial part in contemporary accounts of the weather system as global and interconnected. After the first Apollo mission, camera-based photographs were no longer taken from space; instead, binary codes were computed from a flow of numerical data to create images. Virilio (1994) describes satellite perception as "sightless"; numbers stand in for physical phenomena that humans must visualize. The vast improvement in the accuracy of mid- and long-range weather forecasts justi-fied the enormous financial and computational power needed for the maintenance of satellites. Transgovernmental meteorological institutions released a limited amount of declassified weather satellite data to the public through popular television or radio and later as continuous real-time uplinks to satellites. However, most weather data is still withheld for scientific, military, or commercial applications. For Foucault, the satellite is a "disciplinary apparatus" from space, a "mechanism that coerces by means of obser-vation" (Foucault 1979, 170). The overlaying of lines demarcating territorial boundar-ies between regions or countries is a convention of satellite weather imaging derived from military operations to render them readable.

When weather is represented from numerical data and false-colored by a visualiza-tion expert, science's hermeneutic practices become opaque. The outline of the isobars become the traced "figure" against the "ground" of a territorial map. By the 1980s, Flusser proposes, the "technical image" had fundamentally transformed our modes of cognition. We moved from an alphanumeric process, in which pictograms were lined up to tell a narrative, to the current chaotic "swarm of particles" and "fields of possibili-ties" of digital code (2007, 19–21). The new role of the visualization expert, or Flusser's "envisioner," is to "press buttons to coax improbable things from the whirring particle universe that the apparatus is calculating" ([1985] 2011, 37). For Flusser, the automatic dissemination of calculated numbers by computer deposes linearity and challenges the human imaginary to new modes of thought.

There are constraints nevertheless on contemporary visualization processes; weather maps are unable to include all phenomena in their sample size, so they reduce infor-mation to the measurable. In weather measurements, phenomena are split into unit variables like temperature, pressure, wind speed, and direction and reassembled by apparatus and maps. The sample size is limited by the fact that we only receive data in zeros and ones, leaving no room for the infinitesimal measurements of our phenom-enological reality. In a presentation at the *Data Landscapes Symposium* hosted by the Arts Catalyst in London, scientist David Walton stresses that nothing is certain in mea-surement: "Data models are based on very large grids with a lot of information missed in-between" (Walton 2011). Each margin of error has potential to accumulate. In addi-tion, supercomputers deal in scales of data processing that are too large for human comprehension; working in patterns simplifies data sets to make them readable again. Not only is information missing, but the original data sources become all but invisible; we know little about the instruments that capture phenomena or the algorithms that underpin the software we rely on. Our own physical actions are quietly tracked by software, and in biophysical terms, we are playing a role in the feedback loop with the sensitive atmospheric system. Artworks render visible such patterns of activity with the physical atmosphere, and set these in relation to instruments of weather monitoring and visualizations of weather.

Artists and Satellite Weathers

Artists, unlike scientists, have traditionally operated in the realm of the unmeasurable; sensations are created perceptually that cannot be described mathematically—for example, qualities of shape such as roundness, smoothness, or the subjective operations of color. In science, atoms, particles, photons, or genes are designations of primary qualities of things, and qualities such as colors, odors, or lights are secondary. While the primary qualities of things suggest universality, the secondary qualities have traditionally divided us according to the specifics of our geography, our languages, our cultures, our cosmologies. Artists often draw together so-called primary scientific systems of measurement and secondary sensory qualities. The tradition of scientific empiricism needs to understand phenomena through standardized routines of demonstration, but artists are concerned with variation. Scientific visualizations strive to communicate clearly, yet many artists eschew an informational function entirely. The communication of useful facts is only one conceivable result of measuring and visualizing the weather.

For much of the twentieth century, restricted access to computerized weather data meant that satellite weather media was out-of-bounds for artists. Yet artists still subverted the political potency of the cartographic map, such as in the Uruguayan modernist Joaquín Torres-García's *América Invertida* (1943), used politically to draw attention to South America's marginalized global position. In Torres-García's map, the sun shines brightly over an upside-down South America; weather is used symbolically to represent the hope of a political revolution. The psycho-geographic maps of the situationists and the nonlinear device of the *dérive* anticipate the meandering flows of information that are a feature of contemporary culture and art. By the closing years of the twentieth century, both scientists and artists could access weather data in digital forms online, albeit with unequal access to classified data.

Although the blind vision of satellites compresses weather phenomena into digits, they offer a mobile vista that supplants anything we ourselves can reach unaided, as Lisa Parks (2007) has argued. Parks describes artists who engage with satellite materials as "satellite translators" who unbind satellites from predetermined military and industrial uses in favor of aesthetic-phenomenological explorations. Rather than positioning satellite weathers solely as a hegemonic form of data production, artists approach satellite visualization as an affective arena that far supersedes their surveilling function. Satellite imaging appeals to artists and scientists alike by opening human perception to scales we cannot sense. We find a scopic pleasure in "seeing the whole," as philosopher Michel De Certeau writes (1984, 92), an aerial lift into voyeurism, now widely available via the Internet weathers sourced from remote satellite. The chief threat of this panoramic perspective is the one-sidedness of the gaze, where the detail disappears into the context, in the "vertigo of distance." Yet the ideological values and dangers of *un regard surplombant* (a look from above) that De Certeau questions, when encountered in art, do not necessarily suppress local and experiential knowledge.

Recent art installations by Billy Apple, Thorbjørn Lausten, and Lise Autogena and Josh Portway perturb the binary distinction between distant meteorological satellites and earthly weathers. Apple's *Severe Tropical Storm 9301 Irma* fuses the satellite view of storm Irma from above and his encounter with the same storm at sea, whereas Lausten's video installation *Magnet* (2008; figure 3.1) elicits a sensory-perceptual, embodied response to color fields produced by live satellite meteorological data. In Autogena and Portway's *Most Blue Skies* (2006–2009), the same data used by scientists for measurement has a qualitatively different purpose: to assess "blueness." These artworks hitchhike on existing meteorological data streams to immerse us in the transient effects of weather. Satellites are perceptual devices that operate with senses (or sensors) that are designed by humans, yet we can still be surprised by the sensory experiences they produce. Although the weathers detected by satellites imitate our own intellectual efforts of perception and memory, they are not bound to the physiology of a human body. Artists bring the body back into account.

Thorbjørn Lausten: Perceptual Maps

The installation *Magnet* (2008) hitches onto live geomagnetic and meteorological data from Scandinavian science institutions. The artwork is an abstract grid of pulsating colored shapes based on the live feeds of physical phenomena. Lausten's visualization was projected in an exhibition space at ZKM Center for Art and Media in Karlsruhe, at the same time as it appeared on a public web page on the Internet, engaging both an online and an onsite audience for the work. In the gallery, each projection divides into four weather zones, with a series of potential color responses to a flux of weather and geomagnetic measurements. The numbers are converted into 256 color values that flicker and change along with the weather, leaving powerful afterimages. Geomagnetic

Figure 3.1
Thorbjørn Lausten. Magnet. 2008. Installation view at ZKM Center for Art and Media, Germany. Software and four video projections. Photograph: ONUK (ZKM Center for Art and Media, Karlsruhe). [See color plate 4]

data was continuously supplied from four measuring stations in northern Norway and processed by the University of Tromsö, Norway. The geostationary satellite Meteosat, positioned above the equator, transmitted infrared weather data visualized as shifting color fields every fifteen minutes. Four areas of meteorological and geomagnetic information from Aalborg, Guldborg, Roskilde, and Karlsruhe were selected by software written specifically for the project. These fifty-kilometer by fifty-kilometer physical zones correspond to the four color zones of the installation, although the shapes produced are abstract, without recognizable local features.

Like Hans Haacke, Lausten describes his artworks as systems, but in this case as visual systems. Lausten told me that he sees the field of data visualization as entirely open because neither artistic nor scientific expertise has clearly defined or claimed this area. The ever-changing meteorological data itself also provides an open field of possibilities. Familiar hexagonal, circular, or rectangular shapes create perceptual gestalts in which weather variables become optical sensations that have no immediate reference to a conventional weather map. As we have seen, scientists use color and figure/ground relations in visualizations hierarchically to draw attention to specific information. Instead, Lausten uses color to create a moving abstraction of an existing data stream. These abstract color-fields make us aware that data is recomposing our senses, as opposed to a scientific visualization that directs vision along culturally learned lines. Color can only be understood through vision, so Lausten harnesses a unique aspect of human sense and ties it to nonvisual scientific data. Although the mathematical (one-to-one) correspondences between color data and weather data may be described as isomorphic or equal, they also share a homologous structural effect, as both color and weather create optical, haptic sensations in the body. Weather shifts and perceptual sensations in the body also share correspondences as they are mutable and temporal.

In scientific visualization, the geometrical orientation of perspectival maps that have been transferred into regimes of colors are the outcomes of the standardized grid of the raster array. The gridded array is also at the core of dominant media forms of spreadsheets, maps, and databases that are the substrata of visualization technologies in social management and science. Yet in the hands of conceptual artists—take Sol LeWitt, for instance—mathematically structured wall drawings undermine the expectations of the regimental function of the grid to defy perceptual logic. LeWitt writes: "Logic may be used to camouflage the real intent of the artist, to lull the viewer into the belief that he understands the work, or to infer a paradoxical situation (such as logic vs. illogic)." (1967, 79). Visualizations working from numerical data can only ever be as open as whole numbers will allow, just as grids cannot take in all the contours of a territory. Lausten works within the confines of gridded data, yet the retinal response to the colors in randomized sequences is generated from unpredictable combinations that emerge from the weather itself. The physical sense of disorientation in the body produced by the afterimage of the geometrical pattern undoes the regimental function of the grid arrangement by confounding logic, in Sol LeWitt's sense.

Instead of occupying a god's-eye view of the weather system from above, Lausten's perceptual schema produces a weather-like bodily experience. *Magnet* activates my senses through the optical play of color afterimages. Retinal effects, such as a red afterimage following a green shape, interferes with the smooth transmission of the weather data in a logical manner. As the afterimage from the video shapes forms, I catch myself in a process of seeing. The perceptual effects forming inside my retina spill into the dynamic space between myself and the data screen and outwards toward the shifting weather. In *Magnet*, a new system of weather visualization emerges, based on pulsation, movement, and temporal responsivity—more closely aligned with winds, clouds, solar winds, and magnetic fields produced by the sun. Conventional whole-earth-mapping

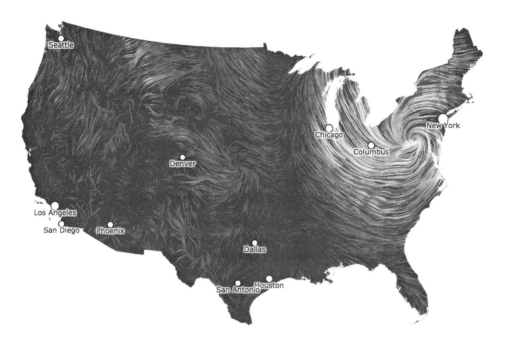

Figure 3.2
Martin Wattenberg and Fernanda Viégas. *Wind Map*. 2012. Screenshot of online artwork. With permission of Martin Wattenberg and Fernanda Viégas.

features such as longitude and latitude, geometry, and time-space axes disappear. The weather map now exists in between the perceiving observer and image. *Magnet* is literally made up of natural phenomena, but the work is not about nature in the Romantic sense. Instead, Lausten (2008) draws our attention to weather as an "inseparable part of our own nature."

In other works, the distinction between an art object and a scientific visualization is much less obvious than in Lausten's bold geometric forms that draw on the legacy of concrete abstraction. Visual communicators Martin Wattenberg and Fernanda Viégas's (United States) project *Wind Map* is an intricate, digital drawing of winds over the United States driven by live data feeds in real time. When the work was first made public online, the creators felt bound to issue the following disclaimer on the same page as the artwork itself: "The wind map is a personal art project, not associated with any company. We've done our best to make this as accurate as possible, but can't make any guarantees about the correctness of the data or our software. Please do not use the map or its data to fly a plane, sail a boat, or fight wildfires" (n.d.). The potential threat of false weather information reaching the public through art projects, and causing alarm with unverified data, is a real concern among scientists. I encountered initial resistance from meteorological scientists to share data with me for the art project *Neighborhood Air* (2013) because they had valid fears about "non-quality-assured" data produced by air quality instruments reaching the public unchecked through the online interface. Machinic irregularities are frequent, and aberrant data in science is cleaned up and eliminated by a human safety check. Artists, on the other hand, will often celebrate the machinic glitch. The responsibility is on us, however, to ensure that an artwork doesn't cause social harm.

Billy Apple: Recomposing a Storm

Wattenberg and Viégas's visualization could be mistaken for a scientific map, however Billy Apple's *Severe Tropical Storm 9301 Irma* (figure 3.3) is formally unlike a conventional weather map, yet retains an internal logic that is consistent with navigational charts. Rather than negotiating with science institutions to harness live data as Lausten does, Apple's departure point is the chance occurrence of a severe storm while he was a passenger on the refrigerated cargo ship *Chiricana*, a vessel laden with high-quality squash for export en route from Napier in Aotearoa New Zealand to Osaka in Japan. On March 15, 1993, as the ship crossed into the Equatorial zone, Tropical Storm 9301 Irma was brewing. Apple describes how the work began as a daily process of gathering weather material on board the *Chiricana*, including printouts of satellite charts of the approaching storm from the radio operator as they came in on the ship's bridge. He collated entries from the ship's log book with assistance of the ship's navigator. Their position in the Pacific Ocean was charted using the marine Beauford scale, used to codify the chaos of real experience into orderly tables of sea states and wind speeds. Later, Apple retrieved satellite weather forecasting data from the Japan Meteorological Agency to track the remote view of the storm from above. In something of an anticlimax, the storm Irma and the ship *Chiricana*'s paths never crossed at the storm's height—a catastrophe averted. Still, the remote view and the nautical data fueled Apple's complex audiovisual and typographical schema in *Severe Tropical Storm 9301 Irma*.

A delight in calculation, measurement, and bureaucratic detail are part of Apple's art practice, along with his formal attraction to orderly disorder in meteorology and navigation. Scientific practices of measuring and diagramming at sea are the compositional spur for *Severe Tropical Storm 9301 Irma*'s five iterations from 1998 to 2015. The site-specific elements of the artwork consist of three parts: an animated navigation map plotting the twin paths of the ship and the storm; two sets of coded typographic scores or sound charts—with thirteen storm charts for the storm and eight charts for the ship;

Figure 3.3
Billy Apple. *Severe Tropical Storm 9301 Irma* (coded schema representing satellite data details the upgrading of the 1993 Pacific Ocean tropical storm to a severe status). 2015. Image courtesy of the Billy Apple® Archive. [See color plate 5]

and a large-scale wall painting in pale blue and shades of black, like a tonal bar graph, to visualize the wind and wave conditions during the storm. At the Window gallery in Auckland in 2005, at midday each day (the same time as log entries were made on the *Chiricana*), a sound composition plays in a duet: one stereo channel indicates the ship's passage and the other the rising storm. Like Lausten's *Magnet*, *Severe Tropical Storm 9301 Irma* establishes a language of transactional exchange between art and computational logic.

In the Window gallery, the *Navigation Chart* animation (2002) is bordered by a panel of red lights on the left and green lights to the right—the nautical symbols for port and starboard. The green and red orienting devices bring to mind Ihde's description of the repeatable perceptual "gestalts" used in mapping. Red and green are also recurring colors in Apple's self-branding language. The colors first emerged in his iconic apple Pop artworks, such as *Apples, 2 for 25¢* (1962–1964), as a mnemonic for his new identity as artist. Art historian Wystan Curnow writes that the "commercial ordinariness" of the *Chiricana*, in the business of commodity trading of squash, is "an Apple kind of ship" (Apple et al. 2015, 2). Apple clears away the mess of human emotions in a storm that would characterize such a subject in Romantic art. Yet the artwork is not completely devoid of expressive elements; there is still a sense of compositional drama as the sound intensifies, as the storm and the ship's paths draw close.

The three-step electronic sound score and programming system of *Severe Tropical Storm 9301 Irma* was devised by Apple with composer Jonathan Besser's assistance. A code was developed in letters and numbers to lend sound to the normally silent cartography of the weather map. This alphabetical, numbering, and musical notation system, entitled *Sound System* (2002), is based on the course of the ship from the log book and the remote satellite information tracing the storm's path. Apple pointed out to me that he used red for the numbers and blue for the notes and corresponding numbers and letters in the sound schema, as a reference to the color of the pencils used in the *Chiricana*'s log. Rather than a mere translation of the movement of weather phenomena into sound, curator Andrew Clifford notes that Apple's approach obfuscates information, as an encryption, rather than a sonification process that would disseminate data in "more tangible, more cognitively ergonomic ways" (Apple et al. 2015, 9–11).

In 2015, Apple published an artist's book to further unfold the typographic correspondences between numbers, letters, and musical notes that the storm Irma had become. The book graphically lays out the alphanumerical schema for the severe storm and the ship's route based on the log entries from March 12 to March 18 and digits from the Beauford scale, each matched with a musical note. At its center, a foldout navigation map, condensed into blocks of blue (waves) and black (wind), with proportions derived from the golden ratio, recalls the wall painting of earlier iterations. Where Lausten starts from scratch for his visual system, Apple recomposes his own experience into an eccentric temporal and spatial weather scheme.

In a similar vein, the numerical automation of the weather system is investigated by British artists Thompson and Craighead. The online work *Weather Gauge* (2005) is a digital record of global weather data from 150 countries, constantly updated in real time. We see masses of names of cities on the globe, quickly replaced by the local time, and then the temperature (in Celsius and Fahrenheit) in rhythmical swaths of digits. Thompson and Craighead foreground the statistical analyses and algorithms that drive current understandings of natural phenomena, in a work that overwhelms with the sheer speed and complexity of numerical computation. The particular event of Irma in Apple's weather schema fixes the weather in time, whereas the weather relentlessly rolls across places and time zones in *Weather Gauge* in a constant process of renewal.

Lise Autogena and Josh Portway: Machinic Blue

The algorithms in Lise Autogena and Josh Portway's *Most Blue Skies* (2006–2009) trawl the skies to determine where in the world at any given time is the "most blue." The artwork, first shown in Kwangju in Korea, takes the form of an installation with a simple blue square projection and a global map illuminated with the location of the "most blue" sky. The deceptively simple question of "Where is most blue in the world?" becomes a complex navigation through scores of remote-sensed meteorological data sets to produce a single location in the world with the bluest sky. The research into both human perception and the science required to answer this question was as intensive as any scientific whole-earth data-gathering project for the artists. Fed by live global atmospheric data, the installation continuously calculates sky colors of millions of places on earth at once. An algorithm compares these calculations so that the software can identify the intensity and location of the "most blue sky" in our world.

The color is calculated by simulating no less than the passage of sunlight through the atmosphere, based on the spectrum of radiation reaching the ground, based on the altitude of the ground, time of day, latitude and longitude, air pressure, aerosol density, and water vapor density, among other parameters. A suite of computers is required to perform this big data operation, which points to the genuine possibility of a numerical calculation to answer a subjective question. The artists describe the realization of *Most Blue Skies* as "grueling" in terms of technology development and cross-institutional negotiation (Autogena and Portway 2011). The labor of programming was undertaken by Portway and Tom Riley, and the atmospheric radiative transfer model was based on an algorithm developed by Chris Gueymard to calculate the "most blue." They obtained atmospheric aerosol data from the MODIS (Moderate Resolution Imaging Spectroradiometer) instruments on NASA's Terra and Aqua research satellites and the cloud and water vapor data from GOES (Geostationary Operational Environmental Satellites) and Meteosat satellites. Institutional partners included the Space and Atmospheric Physics Lab at Imperial College, the UK Meteorological Office, the UCL (University College London) Color and Vision Research Laboratory, NASA, and the Physical National Renewable Energy Laboratory (United States). *Most Blue Skies* was dependent on these high-level scientific institutions to access data streams, implicating the artwork in infrastructures of control.

Environmental sensors and the software algorithms that produce visualizations rely on their energy supply, wireless networks, and the rules and protocols of an ever-increasing number of regulatory interfaces. In the era of the predictive power and behavioral monitoring of large companies like Google, as cultural theorist Scott Lash (2010) points out, nonlinearity and self-generating systems are also mechanisms through which capitalist power moves in contemporary information society. Nonlinear dynamics, in computing in particular, has taken on a different meaning now than in twentieth-century discourse; generative artworks do not automatically have transformative potential over the sameness of the commodity market when they are embedded in multinational conglomerates. The dynamic circulation of the meteorological artwork online is thoroughly supported by the information society as a zone of activity within capitalism's intensive cultural networks. New-media art or "digital" art easily can be recuperated into capitalist technoindustrial formations.

Although *Most Blue Skies* is equivalent in complexity to a scientific visualization and relies on much of the same regulatory infrastructure as science and industry, the artists' question remains socially orientated. Autogena and Portway (2011) suggest that an overwhelming beauty is present in visualization "that is very specific to data," yet a political point also emerges. At the outset, *Most Blue Skies* was not intended as a direct comment on the climate crisis, although the artists later stated: "It addresses our changing relationship to the sky as the subject for scientific and symbolic representation: how the hopeful image of the pure blue sky has become problematized and confused: an imaginary and increasingly vulnerable shelter against the uncertain effects of climate change" (Autogena and Portway 2011). There is pathos in the attempt to seek a meditative experience of color in light of the deep environmental ill health of our age.

Autogena and Portway also are concerned with socializing their data sets in several ways. "The most blue" is a culturally specific identification. They found that scientists, who appeared to know the most about color, could not necessarily help them determine their measurements. Eventually, they selected a human color perception model to try and measure blue as it passes through the atmospheric spectrum to the ground. They would often try to contact someone in the place where the "most blue" had been selected, whether it was in the outback of Australia or the heartland of China, to further qualify or augment the data set with everyday perceptions. The artists once spoke to the owner of Al's Trailer Park in the Australian outback for twenty minutes, by telephone, about the blueness of the skies there that day (Autogena and Portway 2011). One participant in the Data Landscapes Symposium (2011) commented that *Most Blue Skies* generates a democratic "citizen blue," as opposed to the individualism of artist Yves Klein's branding of blue. *Most Blue Skies* surely offers a "machinic blue," produced by a computer algorithm, via which the audience becomes part of a global polity of sky watchers who can compare or contradict the software's decision processes.

Art invites us to think about the origins of the technical image. As visualizations become an increasingly natural part of our environment, we need to attend to their conditions of production. The daily selection of the most blue is an application that in the near future we may happily leave to machines on our behalf, just as choosing favorite clouds is computerized in New Zealander Douglas Bagnall's *Cloud Shape Classifier* artwork (2007; figure 3.4). In this software-based artwork, participants select a series of clouds by pushing one of four buttons on a projected grid connected to a computer. The *Cloud Shape Classifier* eventually will offer a profile of your favorite cloud type depending on your selection from an initially random set of cloud shapes. The endless stream of satellite and other atmospheric data offers only one choice of blue in *Most Blue Skies*, yet it is part of an ever-changing sequence of events. Our choice of cloud, or blueness, allows these machines to learn about human nature.

French-Chinese artist Maurice Benayoun's interactive work *Emotion Winds* (2014) sources "emotional" data from 3,200 cities to form a pattern of the winds laid over a global map. I notice that Aoteaora New Zealand disappears under a swarm of lines representing our heady emotional traffic sourced from online posts. The linear tracks of wind recall Halley's Enlightenment isometric projection map with its rhythm of swirling dashes, and the softer contours of Chinese ink drawings. Visitors can "play the emotion strings like a musical instrument" (Benayoun 2014); the piece also produces the sound of the crowd as we move closer to a particular city. *Most Blue Skies, Emotion Winds*, and *Cloud Shape Classifier* make apparent the ubiquitous presence of calculative processes in daily life online, and the availability of our data to capture and manipulation. Social media platforms such as Tumblr, Instagram, Snapchat, or Flickr enable the constant upload, retrieval, and archiving of an unlimited number of digital images, and Twitter and Facebook tap into our words. These artworks remind us of data-mining

Figure 3.4
Douglas Bagnall. *Cloud Shape Classifier*. 2006. Installation view at MIC Toi Rerehiko, Auckland.
Software, projection, electronic buttons. Image courtesy of the artist. [See color plate 6]

operations that are now performed by algorithms that were once considered to be the
preserve of the human, from face-recognition software to accounting for emotions.
Artist Zune Lee also introduces social encounters into the weather map, by wedding
emotional and air quality data in the form of a game.

Weather Pong: A Game of Eco-mediation

Korean artist Zune Lee acts as a data hitchhiker and a social agent in his software-
based art practice. Lee's game *Weather Pong* (2011) draws together air-quality data
sourced from environmental sensors and social feelings about the weather as expressed
on Twitter through live feeds. I played *Weather Pong* when it was installed at Auckland's Audio Foundation in 2011. By sliding a paddle along the base of the Ming-blue

Figure 3.5
Zune Lee. *Weather Pong*, v. 1.0. 2011. Audio Foundation, Auckland. Computer game program, joystick, LCD monitor.

projection screen with a gaming console controller, a colored ball ricochets around a screen full of spheres. The ball explodes bubbles of weather that represent ratios of pollutants and atmospheric conditions of sun, rain, and smog from commercial and citizen weather data streams. Floating bubble emoticons represent emotional states produced by weather that are data-mined from Twitter. Common idioms such as "I'm feeling under the weather" or "it's a happy, sunny day" are translated into six emotion bubbles. Lee transforms established application programming interfaces (APIs) from Synth-catch, a program for turning sentences into icons, for the analysis of human emotions. Positive emotions and healthy air quality encourage a tree to grow through the center of the screen. Negative emotions combined with NOx and CO_2 cause the tree to darken and wither.

As an act of hitchhiking, *Weather Pong* generates rhythms of data from sounds, shapes, and colors that connect our senses to weather. The screen is divided in half to compare two streams of weather and air quality data, including carbon dioxide and nitrogen dioxide levels from Auckland and from Seoul in version 1.0 of the work, which I played at the Audio Foundation. Color plays a fundamental role to create patterns in scientific visualization and in art: the 256 RGB colors in *Magnet*, the blue in *Most Blue Skies*, the red and green in *Irma* direct our attention, while the whimsical pastel tones of *Weather Pong* designed by Lee are decidedly unscientific. Still, retinal color effects in the brain generate a heightened reflexivity of our own perception, a vital dynamic that couples an "affect with an effect" (Massumi 2007, 14). The electronic xylophone-like sound designed by Changgyun Jung creates a gentle mood, punctuated with disturbing rattling sounds or base subsonic rumbles when negative properties or emotions are encountered, further associating the data sets with sound. The bubbles sometimes collide and form a new bubble state with an accompanying sound; for example, Fear and Fog combine to produce a Smog bubble, and Sad and Cloud fuse into a Fog bubble.

Weather Pong was later included in the group exhibition *The Weather Tunnel* in Beijing (2011), using the data sets from Auckland and Seoul. Seasonal "yellow storms" drift from China to the Korean peninsula, causing poor air quality and amplifying the politics of Lee's work when installed in Beijing. Fears about poor air quality and toxic rain for South Koreans came to the fore after the nuclear power plant breakdown in Japan caused by the 2011 earthquake and tsunami. Closer to home in Seoul, Lee is concerned about the air pollution caused by the excessive use of air conditioning units and the carbon emissions of the transport networks. Anxieties about Korea's air quality and related health issues are frequently expressed via online social communities such as Twitter. Lee's game operates as a social tool to bridge the gap between both human-qualitative modes of sensing weather phenomena and instrumental-quantitative data sets.

The Auckland live weather data for *Weather Pong* was sourced from Weather Underground, a website via which citizens can upload weather information from home weather stations. Weather Underground has operated since 1993 as a challenge to "the conventions around how weather is shared to the public" in order to bring weather forecasting to parts of the world that are underserviced by mainstream weather providers (Weather Underground, n.d.). At the other end of the spectrum, statisticians employed by large conglomerates, such as Google or Hollywood production houses, data-mine social media for commercial purposes. Nonprofessional users need the right training in computer science and statistics to obtain meaningful results from data-mining. Lee puts data-mining algorithms to ecopolitical use in *Weather Pong* in collaboration with software designers Inho Wohn and Chihyoung Shim, who were sponsored by Art Center Nabi in Seoul. Creative uses of data-mining techniques, such as *Weather Pong*, resist ubiquitous corporate surveillance, democratizing an elite medium to make it serve the community. Nothing is difficult about reading the weather or air quality in *Weather Pong*'s interface, so long as we concentrate on the ball, play, and listen. While playing the game, I felt a sense of agency over my weather world that defied immediate

Figure 3.6
F4 Collective (Susan Jowsey, Marcus Williams, and Jesse and Mercy Williams). *O-Tū-Kapua: My Personal Cloud.* 2016–2017. With New Zealand's National Institute of Water and Atmospheric Research (NIWA); Maree Sheehan, Claudio Aguayo, and his assistant, James Smith, from AUT; and Roy Davies, the CTO of Imersia.

logic. Game playing like this diffuses psychic fears around a real ecological threat by creating a dialogic space of encounter.

O-Tū-Kapua (*What Clouds See*)

Like *Weather Pong*, *O-Tū-Kapua* (2016–2017) is a participatory art project that connects science and the social world. Indigenous cosmologies and meteorology are drawn together to visualize local weather and air quality in Auckland. The project was developed for TEMP, a program of art/science and community assemblages in which artists and climate scientists brokered new artwork. *O-Tū-Kapua* was initially developed by the art collective F4 (Sue Jowsey, Marcus Williams, and their children, Jesse and Mercy Williams), who collaborated with a team of researchers from NIWA. Their goal was to investigate how weather data and air pollution information could be made meaningful for children. *My Personal Cloud*, an early phase of the project, included the composition of a waiata (Māori song) by Mercy Williams, a bilingual song writer. Mercy cocreated this "climate change waiata" with children from Prospect School and Te Kura Kaupapa

Māori o Hoanu Waititi. The *kura* (school) is an immersive Māori language school in Glen Eden in West Auckland. Māori sound composer and academic Maree Sheehan contributed the aural dimension to the mixed reality experience in a later part of the project. The haunting stories of Hauāuru (the West Wind), were composed using contemporary instruments and *taonga pūoro* (traditional Māori instruments), fused with the songs of the birds and insects that fill the air in the Waitakere Ranges.

The team was concerned with the relation between our internal senses and exterior weather as a culturally specific experience. They write: "The voluminous size and scale of clouds and their ethereal qualities were reconfigured through *My Personal Cloud*: cloud became something that fitted into the personal space of the child." (TEMP, n.d.). Dr. Josie Keelan, of the Ngāti Porou iwi, gifted the name *O-Tū-Kapua* for the project, which, loosely translated, means *what clouds see*. *My Personal Cloud* asks "how we inhabit the atmosphere, and conversely how it inhabits us" (TEMP, n.d.). A perspectival shift asks us to imagine the world from the above, wrapping us in living ancestor-clouds. For many Māori, *te mea*—"the things" or stuff of our cosmos—connects human and nonhuman elements in a bond of care. Systems of religion, power, and capital associated with colonization have systematically excluded Māori spiritual knowledge. *O-Tū-Kapua* expresses a counterflow to normative representations of weather within scientific parameters by infusing data with cultural forms of knowledge.

The project unfolded over several years in three stages: the first stage was to engage children with the invisible movements of weather by using different senses such as smell, taste, and touch. The atmosphere was linked to the children's own life experiences and cosmological understandings, rather than by imposing a Eurocentric version of the physical universe. Formal portraits of the *tamariki* (children) holding their clouds were videoed for one second to form an animated sequence. The waiata became an accompaniment to this film and an aerial cloudscape of children's personal clouds suspended in Te Uru gallery. The clouds, made from organic wool, were personalized and made tangible. The second stage, the *AirScience Pilot*, elicited the students' cultural perceptions of air and sky and then linked their insights to processes of observation in atmospheric and climate change science. Collections of data from particulate matter sensors were introduced to show how qualities of air are measured in science as one form of generating environmental knowledge.

The third stage of the project was the development of a mixed-reality project in which F4 and the NIWA scientists were joined by mobile education researcher Dr. Claudio Aguayo and his assistant, James Smith, from Auckland University of Technology (AUT), and Dr. Roy Davies of Imersia. *O-Tū-Kapua* (*What Clouds See*) eventually took the form of a physical and aural mixed-reality installation, designed for imaginative play using a marker-based interface. The physical installation takes the form of a forest; two-dimensional props, including stage-set-like trees, are gradually populated with flora and fauna produced by children. With a mobile phone held up to a marker, the augmented-reality interface comes alive, producing data in a fourth dimension linking city pollutants and weather data to the growth of the forest. When I visited the exhibition, the children around me painted and collaged their own pictures of colorful birds and insects to add to the installation. When they held up their mobile devices to particular markers, they discovered how wind speed, humidity and pollution levels effected the virtual tree in front of them. Air quality and climate science are folded into an experiential atmosphere rich with bush sounds and the strains of *taonga pūoro* in a sonic connection to the ancestors of sky and forest.

The interdisciplinary team of researchers chose to focus on children—the generation that will inherit environmental and social issues associated with a changing climate. F4 wrote: "Scientific discussions around the mechanisms, impacts, and options for adaptation predominantly exclude the input of children. Climate science is perceived to be beyond the scope of children, often categorized as dry in both subject and methods. We believe participatory projects such as this can introduce atmospheric science to children in a meaningful way, using imagery, language, music and other creative activities that enable them to creatively converse, question and understand climate science and our interdependence on the environment around us" (TEMP, n.d.). Sustained attention to the voice of children prizes open accepted routes of visualization in art and science. The bridging of knowledge between Indigenous values and mathematical data sets is crucial territory for visualization. The hackneyed separation of "prescientific" understandings of nature and scientific knowledge is very far from the truth, as Arendt observed (2006, 263). She challenges the prevalent idea in modern science that "we have come to live in a world that only scientists 'understand'" (ibid.). The generative collaboration of F4, NIWA, technology designers, and school children erodes the annexing of science from cultural life.

Critical questions about the relation between art and science are raised in data hitchhiking practices that ride on institutional meteorological data sets. Despite forming links with science organizations to use a wide range of data, the process of scientific collaboration often disappears from view in an art installation. When the complex negotiations with science organizations are made invisible, we are offered sensations yet left without a deeper understanding of how an artwork came into being. Art that obscures its scientific mechanisms can be likened to Ihde's insight about scientific visualization; for scientific depictions to convince, the instrumentation must withdraw so that the patterns can stand out more clearly (1998, 472). But why should the relationships with science organizations be foregrounded for art to perform affective-political operations? Artists are not bound by the demand in conventional weather mapping for an envisioner to make data readable within a defined field of signification. When artists forage for satellite signals and weather information from multinational companies or governments, they engage in a particular ethos of reuse of capital investment. An aesthetic politics emerges through the release of weather data into unforeseen assemblages.

Meteorological art redistributes knowledge and privileges a roving, embodied interaction with data. Mobile applications for accessing air quality and weather information in science and commerce also are increasingly personalized and adaptive. Yet the very lack of fixity of the weather when it appears in art implies the constant questioning of perception, human or machinic. The flickering color changes of Lausten's *Magnet* allow us to optically sense weather shifts rather than to defer to scientific interpretation of data. *Severe Tropical Storm 9301 Irma* unsettles the institutional framework for interpreting the weather map; *Most Blue Skies* mathematically works through a simple question of blueness; *Weather Pong* provides an outlet for social anxieties; and *O-Tū-Kapua* (*What Clouds See*) reveals that Indigenous, scientific, and children's weathers are never mutually exclusive. Far from Latour's description of a scientific visualization as an "immutable mobile" in which dissenters are forced to concede their positions, or Ihde's repeatable "gestalts," artists visualizations travel and change. Scientific visualizations tend to standardize representations of the atmospheric system, yet artworks imply that scientific mappings can only ever be understood as situational, rather than universal.

4 Meteorological Art Instruments

The flux of weather has a long history as a driver for wind-based instruments—from the Aeolian harp to today's chance-based electronic scores fashioned by home weather stations. Audio artworks trigger new opportunities for exchanges among instruments, weather phenomena, and listeners through the extraordinary sensations they produce. Sound as a compositional element distinguishes the artworks in this chapter from the silence of scientific meteorological representation. Rather than trying to naturalize an instrument's role in data production, modifications of weather instruments by artists expose their inner mechanisms. Artists will vary manufactured weather instruments to their own ends—or devise new meteorological art instruments entirely. At one end of the spectrum, New Zealander Philip Dadson uses a radio tower as a found-sound producing object; at the other, Australian artists Joyce Hinterding and David Haines' *Earthstar* (2008) produces solar sounds from custom-made radio antennae. Anaïs Tondeur's *The Eophone's Whistle* (2015) is a fictional instrument that powerfully connects us to the climate science of the changing thermohaline circulation in our oceans.

The second part of the chapter foregrounds Andrea Polli's (United States) practice of intensive collaboration with science institutions in *Sonic Antarctica* (2008), and in *Energy Flow* (2016–2017), in which an entire bridge is turned into an instrument. Slovenian artist Marko Peljhan's mobile *Makrolab*, meanwhile, is an instrument for sociopolitical leverage outside the gamut of any institution. These artworks question our tacit acceptance of weather apparatuses, and the data they transmit, as transparent windows into natural phenomena. The idiosyncrasies of place and weather become the material for sonic experiment. Artworks will be positioned as open entities or *quasi-objects*, borrowing a term from Michel Serres (1982b), and adopted in Latour's oeuvre. In the 1960s, systems theorist von Bertalanffy also described the open system as a "(quasi-) steady state … in which material continually enters from, and leaves into, the outside environment" (1968, 121). Quasi-art, quasi-instrument assemblages foreground the instabilities between subject and object, human and ahuman, technologies and environments.

The quasi nature of meteorological instruments, invented by artists or in commercial use, generate contingent alliances among audiences, weather phenomena, and science. Instruments harnessed by artists for their qualities will be treated less as black box technologies that are separated from our senses or cultural discourse than as changeable entities that belong equally to politics, nature(s), and technologies. In scientific practice, once proven, instruments must be treated as if they transmit data that can have only one possible meaning; the relation between meteorological referent and instrument is based on efficient information exchange. Artworks are polysemic; they have multiple levels of interpretable meaning for the audience.

Weather art instruments can perturb the "business as usual" of the communication of weather data by meteorological agencies. Take British artist Richard Garrett's real-time installation, the *Weather Songs Project* (2007), a musical composition made from the fluctuating patterns of the wind, rain, and atmospheric pressure. A small, home-user weather station with sensors to record air pressure, humidity, wind direction and speed, and rainfall is connected to music software. Each time Garrett's software requires a new note, the computer checks recent numerical inputs from the weather station and selects a pitch, intensity, and duration based on the numerical values of the live weather. Depending on the weather, different sounds will emerge; humidity and temperature usually produce bass drones, wind produces a lead vocal, and rain is a random percussive event (Garrett 2007, 32). The weather analogically now has its own "voice"—at least, we feel like we hear the weather's voice in Garrett's work. Artworks such as this raise the question of how the weather is constituted as information: in its collection, in its transmission as sound, or in us, the audience?

We make meaning from the quasi-art instrument in a relational encounter between the body and weather phenomena. In Karen Barad's account of the evidencing of matter in scientific apparatus, "phenomena are the ontological inseparability/entanglement of intra-acting agencies" (2007, 139). Phenomena (in physics) are produced from differential patterns of *mattering*, or becoming evident to our instruments and our senses as observers. In meteorological sensing, we are no less entangled in the weather, but sometimes we sense it first and ask questions later. As animals, we can feel a storm coming on, we might get drenched by rain, and then later we watch the weather forecast on the news to understand how long it might last or whether it will intensify. The artworks described here as "quasi" have a meteorological referent, but they expose and refer to both the signals of the instrument and an interpreting receiver—ourselves, where some of the meaning of the work is constructed in our internal response. The performance of "worldly mattering" generates intense intra-actions between apparatuses, phenomena, and audience in meteorological art.

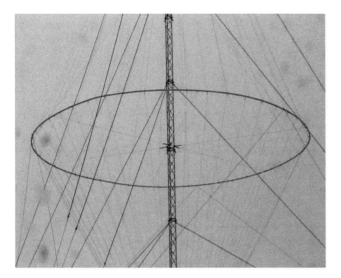

Figure 4.1
Philip Dadson. *Aerial Farm*. 2004. Still from *Polar Projects* (2003–2005). HD video.

Phil Dadson: Found Sounds of Weather

Phil Dadson's *Polar Projects* series transforms "found" weather sounds from scientific instruments that he encountered at McMurdo Base in Antarctica during an artist fellowship in 2003. The *Flutter* (2004) and *Aerial Farm* (2004) videos document the unintended sonic by-product of a lonely flag and a radio aerial mast through sound and video. *Flutter* is a single eighteen-minute-long shot of the relentless flap of a marker flag against the wind, reigniting Dadson's interest in working with the vagaries of wind in *Hoop Flags* (1970; see introduction). The wind blows the flags to produce an abstract composition from the "flap," with a different rhythmic character according to the strength of the wind. The red flag is attached to a bamboo pole, the strongest material the scientists could find to withstand a hostile weatherscape. In his diary, Dadson describes his experience of the Antarctic as strangely silent, apart from his own footsteps, until he discovered the sounds of the human-installed structures.

While *Flutter* is a study in audible rhythms, *Aerial Farm* is a study of sonic tones. *Aerial Farm* is composed of wind-generated aeolian tones from a circular radio aerial mast and the multiple wires that tie it to the ground. Dadson placed a microphone at the base of the largest aerial mast in the wind farm to collect the sounds generated by a wide-frequency band of wire tones in fifty-kilometer winds. High-pitched, fluted sounds are the by-product of the relentless rush of Antarctic winds, muted a little by the intermittent effects of snow drift. The sounds of the wires recall the Aeolian harp, named after Aeolus, the Greek god of the wind. The harp takes the form of a wooden box, with strings stretched lengthwise across two bridges and usually placed next to an open window. Aeolian vibrations produce an alternating vortex in the wires that produce sounds. Despite the fact that the scientific data produced by the aerial mast was invisible to him, Dadson made the melancholic hum of the instrument's physical matter and the presence of the wind perceivable.

Rather than inventing new instruments altogether, as Len Lye did with the *Wind Wand*, Dadson uncovers the poetic-sensory qualities of existing instruments in this series of weather-based work. The instruments deployed in *Flutter* and *Aerial Farm* express much more than mere utility or scientific function. The meteorological flag or radio mast are quasi-objects that have different meanings for Dadson the artist, the scientific researchers who installed them, and another for the winds themselves. The variable use of technologies by artists "indetermines" media, as Douglas Kahn (2011) has argued, in moments of escape from technologically determined regimes. By gifting an affective reprieve from conventional flows of information in the polar mechanosphere, Dadson engages in a politics of close listening at a time of rapid anthropogenic-induced change in Antarctica.

The winds are also made visible in unexpected forms in Australian artist Cameron Robbins' *Wind Section Instrumental* (2013–2014). This art instrument is an outdoor wind turbine and weather vane on an eight-meter-high tower that captures the wind's "drawings" on large sheets of paper. Gusts of wind are connected to an indoor drawing machine to create dense, circular records of wind over time. When this work was installed at the Museum of Old and New Art (MONA) in Tasmania, it caught the strong southeasterly weather systems from the Southern Ocean that batter the Derwent Estuary. The drawing mechanism inside the gallery uses this powerful wind to drive an ink pen, the wind's direction to swivel a drawing board, and time and electricity to move the paper slowly along at 250 centimeters per week.

The drawing assemblage was installed next to a large window from which the turbine tower could be seen in operation; this allowed the movement of the exterior winds and the interior experience of shelter from the weather to be sensed simultaneously. Robbins (2014) speculates that the difference between his own interest in the dynamics of wind and a scientist's is that he does not try to predict the outcome of his experiment in advance; he leaves the drawings to the fluctuations of wind. *Wind Section Instrumental* opens up its workings to public view, unlike the self-contained "black boxes" of remote instruments. The meteorological art instruments of Dadson

Figure 4.2
Cameron Robbins. *Wind Section Instrumental*. 2013–2014. Installation view from *The Red Queen*, Museum of Old and New Art, Hobart, Tasmania. Mixed media, wind powered mechanical parts, electric paper feed, pigment ink on watercolor. Photograph: Rémi Chauvin. © Cameron Robbins. Image courtesy Museum of Old and New Art (Mona), Hobart.

and Robbins become quasi "us" when we experience the making of the drawings the winds produce. In the seeing, hearing, and feeling of the power of the winds that hammer these weather apparatuses, we encounter the elements anew.

Hinterding and Haines: Inventing Weather Instruments

Australian artist Joyce Hinterding's invented instruments openly reveal their inner workings. Since the early 1990s, Hinterding's gallery-based and site-specific installations have used instrument devices of her own invention to attune to energies beyond the human senses. Her custom-built instruments respond to synoptic-scale meteorological events to translate invisible frequencies into forms that we can perceive. Hinterding's radio-antennae instruments generate live audio compositions from the musical potential of electrical storms, lightning, and other Hertzian frequencies. I first experienced the intensity of Hinterding's sound works in *Aeriology* in 1995 at Artspace in Auckland, although she had been working with atmospheric energies since *Electrical Storms*, featured in the Ninth Sydney Biennale (1992). At Artspace, a 15–20 km length of copper wire was wrapped around the columns of the entire exhibition space, causing it to crackle and hum continuously. De Maria's *The Lightning Field* waits passively for the event of lightning, instead *Aeriology* constantly draws energy from the immediate electrical ambience of the urban weather environment.

In the *Transmission from the Sun* performance (2017), the sounds of the crackling and popping of the electromagnetic energy of the Milky Way were rendered audible with a custom-made VLF instrument made from coils of copper wire over a frame, as well as the energy of the gallery building itself. Under the open-domed ceiling of Te Uru gallery at sunset, Hinterding wielded a large, square, custom-built antennae with copper coils that attuned to the sound of the solar interaction with the ionosphere within magnetic field lines. The background noise of the Milky Way and the local electromagnetic environment of the gallery produced crackling and popping sounds. Hinterding's antennae capture low-frequency electromagnetic impulses, such as whistlers, the circular looping sounds of sferics (short for atmospherics), and descenders that viscerally resonate through the body as low rumbles, or "notes" generated in the electrically charged atmosphere. Hinterding's practice inhabits contemporary science with invented instruments, to model transferences of energy akin to the atmosphere itself.

As well as her independent practice, Hinterding has a long-term collaborative relationship with David Haines, and Haines also has his own art practice. Their often-large-scale collaborative work incorporates Hinterding's (2010) "energy scavenging" sound practice, while Haines attends to the visual and, for the last decade, to the olfactory sense. Like environmental scientists, Hinterding and Haines often spend long periods of fieldwork outside the gallery to generate video and audio recordings. In July 2002, Hinterding and Haines led a new media artists' camp, together with local Indigenous artist Thompson Nganjmirra, in Oenpelli, Arnhem Land. Technologies were used as processual mediators between the traditional owners, new media artists, and the terrain and atmosphere. The traditional owners led the artists at the camp to significant cultural sites. Before installing their instruments at Oenpelli, the artists were invited to reach an understanding of Indigenous protocols relating to the imaging and sound recording of place, a process that has been neglected traditionally in scientific monitoring.

Hinterding and Haines had to reframe their activity in an Indigenous setting under cultural lore at Oenpelli. The group of artists built their own hydrophones (electronic receivers that pick up sound traveling through water), lashed video cameras to helium balloons for aerial footage, and worked with a diverse range of equipment, from astrophotography cameras and infrared sensors to VLF antennas. The use of scientific instruments in a remote landscape might estrange the human from the environment if care is not taken, as writer Linda Carroli reflects (2005, 47). Hinterding recalls that the Indigenous community was very responsive to the signals of the VLF antennae, suggesting that the instruments become quasi-cultural objects in this context. The artists were readily granted permission for balloon launches; in an Aboriginal worldview, "the skies are for everybody" (Haines and Hinterding 2017). Later, Hinterding and Haines extended their rudimentary tests to affix instruments to helium balloons at Oenpelli for the stratospheric launch of *Soundship* (*descender 1*) in 2016 (see chapter 8). Haines found that the camp presented two intensive experiences for the artist-participants, however: first, interacting with the community; second, an intensive period of technological experiment within the environment. The artists' camp was a generative yet sensitive process, allowing for cultural paradigms of place to inflect the instrumental outcomes.

Earthstar and Instrumental Mediation

Although weather is often understood to mean storms, clouds, or rain, the sun is the predominant driver of the terrestrial weather system. Haines and Hinterding's installation *Earthstar* (2008 to present; figure 4.3) is an instrumental mediation of solar radiation through the ionosphere. As a study in energies, the work is an ecopolitical lever, as well as a contemporary homage to the life-giving and life-threatening star. *Earthstar* brings us closer to the sun with the help of three elements: a pair of customized VLF antennae tuned to the radio bursts emitted by the sun and fed through an amplifier to provide real-time sounds of the sun; a single projected image of the solar chromosphere captured using a hydrogen-alpha telescope; and aroma molecules that approximate the aromatic scents of the sun.

The radio antennae are laid out as tight coils of copper wire around a long pipe, supported by two long, wooden tables, suggestive of laboratory workbenches. The amplifiers beneath the table produce a continuous soundscape of hisses, pops, and scratches that ebb and flow in intensity as they pick up the sun's frequencies. In the first version

Figure 4.3
Joyce Hinterding and David Haines. *Earthstar*. 2011. Installation view from *Star Voyager*, Australian Centre for the Moving Image (ACMI). HD video projection, live sound, two custom VLF antennae, graphite and polythene-coated copper wire, mixing desk, stereo speakers and geodesic dome-shaped scent dispenser. Image courtesy of the artists. [See color plate 7]

of *Earthstar* at the Gallery of Modern Art in Queensland (2008), a fridge full of phials contained perfume propositions of the smell of the sun. These were stored like samples at "smell stations," at which the participant could try a limited-edition ozonic perfume called *Solaire Amour*. Art theorist Lizzie Muller (2009) notes that the "smell-displaced" of a perfume strip she took home from *Earthstar* had the power to evoke the experience of the artwork more intensely than any image. In a later version in the *Star Voyager* group exhibition at the Australian Centre for the Moving Image (ACMI) in 2011, the "Ionisation Aroma" was housed in a geodesic dome-shaped dispenser made from black, acid-free, Stonehenge paper, rather than the perfume strips used in Queensland. A third means of delivering aromas in glasses was tested in subsequent iterations of the work. Although scent-based artworks, including the multisensory Flux kits, have existed since the 1960s, smell remains an unfamiliar encounter in the predominantly ocular-centric sphere of the gallery.

The flickering edges of the projected video image in *Earthstar* correspond to the movement of electrons around the hydrogen atoms in light frequencies. Haines became interested in a hydrogen-alpha telescopic lens for his camera in the early 2000s. This lens enabled solar activity to be observed by revealing hydrogen, the major gas in the sun's make-up. The hydrogen-alpha telescope contains a filter gel that only allows light from the sun centered at 6,563 angstroms—also known as the *hydrogen-alpha line*—to reach the human eye. Looking through the telescope produces a red solar disk by shifting the ultraviolet light to the red part of the visual spectrum. The electromagnetic frequencies from the sun that create sound are produced by the same type of radiation as the ultraviolet light revealed by the hydrogen-alpha telescope, although with differences in wavelength and frequency. When hydrogen levels fall, we see an emission of energy on the spectrum; when they rise, they absorb energy. The amount of energy absorbed or released affects the wavelength produced in the ultraviolet region of the light spectrum. The artists hypothesized that they might see sunspots with the hydrogen-alpha telescope, which in turn might produce more intense levels of electromagnetic activity in the ionosphere with a corresponding level of sound frequencies detected by the antennae. Haines captured many solar flares during his year of recording, but no sunspots appeared.

The animated hydrogen-alpha sequence in the *Earthstar* projection is made from thousands of composite images animated at twenty-five frames per second to form a four-minute long sequence. Haines made intuitive decisions about the exposure lengths and frame rate of the animations. The animation sequence begins with a bright white orb, almost too bright to look at, against a red background. The next phase is a black orb with a circular red frame, which is the hydrogen stretching out—flaring wildly. The final sequence shows a yellow orb flecked with red solar activity. The color phases depend on the length of exposure of each image, with the longest exposures at two minutes. Each image leaves an afterimage on the retina—a perceptual effect that suggests the intensity of looking at the sun with the naked eye. These are raw frames with little postproduction, although they are false-color images, shot in monochrome. The dynamic range of the image is a composite of many exposures. For Haines and Hinterding (2017), the human eye meets machinic perception in *Earthstar*: the telescope gives us a renewed capacity for seeing.

The experimental pursuit of sensory experience for the audience is most apparent in the use of smell to represent the sun. In *Earthstar* at ACMI (2011), a list entitled "keywords" on the wall text reads, "Fresh sea breeze, ocean waves, air and dust, lightning strike, transparent, clean, chemical, summer rain, burning molecules, power lines, aurora amber, orange peel." Haines has developed synthetic aromas with a molecule

broker in America and in doing so has become attracted to scientific taxonomies such
as ozanil, helional, ocean carboxaldehyde, maritime, and hedione. Haines is a *nose*, a
person skilled in smelling, remembering, and putting names to smells. A small number
of multinationals produce most of the aroma materials worldwide, and they are pur-
chased on an industrial scale. Captive molecules are not released into the wider market,
but Haines has access to over 1,500 molecules in his "perfume organ" (collection of
aromas), collected over a decade of practice. Haines experiments with a range of simple
or complex "notes" or solar aromas, in a parallel practice to the sonic tones produced
by Hinterding's VLF antennae. Traditional methods of aroma construction are based
on *accords* (ratios of molecules that give an olfactory experience). Some accords are
patented; for instance, Johnson's baby powder uses the carnation accord. Rather than
selling commercially patented aromas, Haines' atmospheric aromas, such as ionization,
are offered freely to the public where the work is exhibited.

Hinterding and Haines treat accepted facts about natural phenomena experimentally. When we first met in 2010, Haines was intrigued by an emergent theory in quan-
tum biology that it is not the shape of aroma molecules that affect what we smell, but
their molecule-stretch frequencies: how the atoms are bound together and how they
vibrate. The sense of smell activates the temporary ecologies of memory in the nervous
system in response to coming weather changes, which might simultaneously trigger
our enculturated knowledge about the sun. Often, science professionals have found
it revelatory to experience Hinterding and Haines's reconfigurations of atmospheric
materials in artworks, and are able to offer further explanations of the phenomena
sensed in scientific terms (Haines and Hinterding 2017). A discursive relationship is
generated between art and science, with the artwork as catalyst. To position *Earthstar*
as a means of escape or resistance to universalizing tendencies in science would be to
limit the meanings of the work.

Earthstar opens out our senses via telescopes and antennae, expanding perception
to scales we could not otherwise reach. For some time, Hinterding has used the physics descriptor *sympathetic resonance* as a "word for artistic investigations into materials and properties, where …, 'almost by accident' information occurs/evidences itself"
(van Kranenburg 2006). Sympathetic resonance attends to human perception in relation with the phenomena sensed, rather than through the production of a singular
intense sensation. This gradually achieved feeling of connectedness is far from the
hyperesthesia, or the overplayed sensuality of late capitalism, exemplified in shock
advertising strategies. The notion of sympathetic resonance invites comparison
with Len Lye's empathy discussed in chapter 1, in which the mediation of instruments chimes with both our accumulated memories and immediate perceptions.

Hinterding and Haines's art oeuvre makes us conscious of the way instruments organize the senses.

Earthstar's subject, the sun, has political resonance within the context of the increasingly volatile weather of the Australian continent. In the interstices among the technical instrumentation of telescopes and antennae, the sun's radiance, and our senses in *Earthstar*, we encounter our solar dependencies and limits. A politics of sympathetic resonance recalls Massumi's emphasis on the importance of artworks, which express "what the human shares with everything it is not: a bringing out of its inclusion in matter, its belonging in the same self-referential material world in which every being unfolds" (2002, 128). An ecopolitics of affect occurs through the art instrument that plays the sun's frequencies on the body as we reflect on how we use energetic forces. The next set of artworks discussed refer to climate politics more pointedly.

Anaïs Tondeur, Marco Peljhan, and Andrea Polli: Politicized Instruments

How can we respond to the signals of climate change amid the noise of the world? Using instruments, advanced computers and numerical climate prediction models, scientists now detect the patterns that conclusively prove the climate is changing. Artists transform pieces of complex aggregate data through strategies of data sonification, signal hacking, and narrative. French artist Anaïs Tondeur's *The Eophone's Whistle*, Solvenian Marko Peljhan's *Makrolab*, and Andrea Polli's oeuvre broach the science of climate change as represented through data. Both Peljhan and Polli's artworks present assemblages of instruments that attune to the biosphere while modeling sustainable art practices. The peripatetic *Makrolab* living unit and Polli's large-scale projected visualizations are meteorological art instruments designed for political leverage. Tondeur conjures an instrument from her imagination to equally potent political effect. These artworks reimagine climate and weather representations through alternate articulations of meteorological data.

Anaïs Tondeur: A Fictional Instrument

Anaïs Tondeur's *The Eophone's Whistle* (*Le Crie De L'Eophone*) (2015) is an installation centered on a quasi-fictional data-gathering instrument. Real and imagined data about the oceanographic thermohaline circulation and its influence on climate balance are drawn into a narrative-based installation. The Eophone is presented as a series of graphite drawings, glass-plate cartographies, and a nine-minute-long film, shot in high-definition (HD) video. Tondeur developed the project as part of a residency with

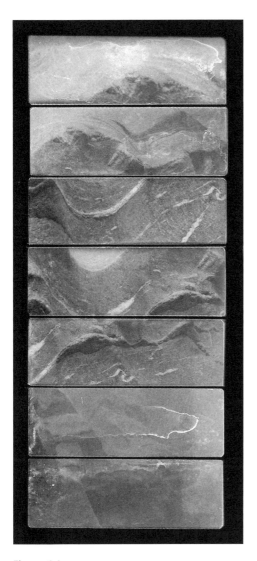

Figure 4.4
Anaïs Tondeur. *Eophone* (detail). 2015. Glass plate with thermic variations imprints, C print,
7.5 × 16 cm.

paleo-climatologists and oceanographers from the National Natural History Museum and Pierre and Marie Curie University as part of Demain, le Climat, for exhibition at ARTCOP21. A male narrator (Pierre Grandry) opens the film: "The Eophone (from the Greek, *eol*: wind, and *phone*: voice) is an enigmatic oceanographic tool. So the story goes, the physicist and inventor Benjamin Thompson, set one adrift in the currents of the Atlantic in 1799." However, we soon discover that "the Eophone only rises to the surface once every 72 years. No one caught it in 1871 nor in 1943. Victor Turpin tried his luck in 2015." The Eophone is the elusive quasi-object of the film.

The narrative continues with Turpin in pursuit of the lost Eophone, setting sail on a small sail boat on the Atlantic toward the Canary Islands, hoping to retrieve a rich data archive of ocean and the climate information from across the centuries. We learn that the Eophone is a long, narrow cylinder capped by a horn. When the Eophone reaches the surface of the sea, "wind dives into the cone and creates a whistling noise that attracts passing sailors." At one point, Turpin catches the heart-rending cries in the wind, somewhere between a bird and a human cry. The narrator describes the cries as containing "the amplitude of the breath of an organ blown by the wind." These sounds seem to reveal centuries of the ocean's pain. Turpin gropes around in the darkness trying to retrieve the instrument (perhaps an allegory for the scientific search to understand the role of oceans in climate change), but it sinks out of sight once more. We have missed our chance: "In another 72 years perhaps the Eophone will rise again." Tondeur's exhibition text states that she collaborated with oceanographer and navigator Victor Turpin to produce the artwork; however, the film reveals him to be an invented character.

The black-and-white film is largely set at sea, where the soft-focus, long shots, and the classical music of Max Richter offer an elegiac mood. The Eophone instrument, suspended by canvas balloons, is also represented in a series of soft graphite images in the installation. As a further dimension of the work's narrative, Tondeur produced glass plates with "thermal variation imprints" to suggest the kind of data set that the Eophone would produce. Each element of *The Eophone's Whistle* alludes to the factual scientific research that underscores her quasi-scientific narrative. Such departures from the real gently remind us that a compelling narrative also plays a part in scientific accounts of instrumental findings. This creative strategy developed from Tondeur's earlier project *Lost in Fathoms* (2014), in which she explores the disappearance of the fictional Nuuk island in shadowgrams after intensive research during a residency with the LadHyX Hydrodynamics Laboratory in France. A reference to debates about the "truth" of climate change also underscore these artworks. For Tondeur, the lab is a research environment in which to brew imaginative stories that reflect back on the changing climate, allowing us to process, and seek to learn more about what is happening in our own world.

Russian media artist Aleksey Grachev's *Weather Station 1, Atmospheric-Acoustic Transducer* (2012) is a sound quasi-object that is also based on an imagined instrument of Russian scientist Lev Termen, or Léon Theremin, as he was known in the United States. Termen is well known for his invention of the electro-music instrument the theremin (patented in 1928). *Weather Station 1, Atmospheric-Acoustic Transducer* is an artist's imagining of how a portable-acoustic transducer, designed by this inventive electro-engineer might look and sound. Grachev evokes the period during Termen's eight-year imprisonment at the design bureau TKB-29 NKVD in the Soviet Union when he developed the concept of transmitting information by tonal-rhythmic musical drawings (CYLAND 2018, 23). A dark Soviet-style grey metal box attached to portable speakers produces crackles and hisses by transforming atmospheric data from sensors into a rumbling composition. Marko Peljhan's *Makrolab*, considered next, opens the box further to generate a weather-sensing instrument in which to live.

Makrolab: An Instrument Institution

In Hinterding and Haines's work, the gallery becomes laboratory-like; Tondeur immerses herself in lab residencies to research her imagined scenarios; but in Marco Peljhan's *Makrolab* (1997–2012), a countermodel altogether of an art/science institution emerged. Peljhan's socially motivated approach became an exemplar of a mobile, sustainable ecological research center, as envisioned by a media artist. *Makrolab* was open to artists, scientists, hackers, and cultural workers for the collection and transformation of local and space-based environmental data. The solar-powered pod was fitted with a host of radio-transmission and radio-reception technologies and a large array of sensors. Remote sites and fragile ecologies from the poles to the deserts became home to *Makrolab*'s crew within the shelter of an experimental craft. The autonomous living pod could sustain its crew for up to 120 days. First installed in an urban location at Documenta X in Kassel, Peljhan's *Makrolab* became a roaming, countercultural interloper into the signal traffic of our atmosphere.

Makrolab Mark II was stationed at Wadjemup (Rottnest Island) in the Western Australian desert as of February 5, 2000, facilitated by the Art Gallery of Western Australia. The orange-and-white hexagonal pod, covered in insulation material, was made from easily reassembled parts designed by architects Matevz Francic and Aljaz Lavric. For the installation in Australia, *Makrolab* invited "artists, activists, writers, scientists and strategic and tactical information analysts" to interact with global systems of "telecommunications, weather and migration" (Peljhan n.d). The lab was equipped to hack into signals from wireless digital signal-processing (DSP) networks and weather satellites. In the Rottnest Island phase, a self-named *IWD-PHII* function aimed to integrate all available open-source atmospheric space and weather data for this specific geographical zone. The temporary occupation of Wadjemup spurred the development of water collection, purification systems, and ventilation for the living systems of the lab. The lab also tapped into data about whale migration patterns and bird migrations near the island.

Remote sites are often the object of intensive scientific research, but they also fuel our collective anxieties about climate warming. The isolated location in the desert recalls De Maria's remote site of environmental communion in *The Lightning Field*. However, the ability to stay networked via satellite and radio meant that *Makrolab's* collaborative art activities were continuously available on the Internet in real time. A critique nevertheless has been leveled at tactical media interventions based on a lack of deep connection with Indigenous and local communities that might need this data the most. Hinterding and Haines's Oenpelli camp, in comparison, carefully adhered to the cultural meanings of place of the Aboriginal traditional occupants for their instrumental activity. As *Makrolab's* activities developed in later years, however, community participation increased. Bird-monitoring activity with a Doppler radar instrument, for instance, was shared with the Slovenian bird-watching society when *Makrolab* was installed in Slovakia in 2006.

The larger question addressed by waging signal interceptions is one of freedom of usage of airspace for nongovernmental or non-corporate-affiliated groups. Peljhan argues that the radio amateur is "a civil exception in the world ruled by governments, international treaties and last but not least, capital" (Peljhan 2001). The cultural process of electronic media monitoring by artists taps into the highly regulated economies of telecommunication. In general, it is only through complex negotiations with state and commercial interests that artists can receive this data. The airspace itself is often treated as "territory" that is object-like or bounded. New "architectures of air," Adrian Mackenzie proposes, are replacing ground centers of calculation in intensive contemporary computing (2009, 1295–1297). The conceit of the quasi-object, quasi lab instrument is the widening of atmospheric knowledge for the layperson in resistance to the accumulation of capital value from environmental data.

For Peljhan (n.d), "If the methods and systems of art give us freedom, methods and systems of science give us the ability for progression and reflection." The dream of radio communicators was once for universal contact, for everywhere to be accessible to everywhere else. *Makrolab* extends the ideal of openly accessible channels to the Internet but shifts away from the twentieth-century dream of total communication.

Figure 4.5
Andrea Polli. *Sonic Antarctica*. 2008. Installation view at MIC Toi Rerehiko, Auckland. Three-channel HD video projection and sound on headphones.

Its activity represents a democratization of the "spectrum commons," in which radio atmospheric spectrum is positioned as a site of tactical resistance to control, beyond the contingent moment of access (Joyce 2008, 6). Peljhan's radical gesture lies in modeling both the sustainable intra-actions for the occupants of a future living unit in a remote location and the opening of antennae to technological and atmospheric signals beyond the limits of regimes of capital.

Andrea Polli: Collaborative Instruments

Peljhan's *Makrolab* operates outside formal institutional structures, whereas Andrea Polli's collaboration with scientists aligns with the climate activism at the heart of her art practice. Polli works with scientific instruments and digital data sets, matterings and atmospheres, the "actual" and the sonified signs of climate change. The early project *Atmospherics/Weatherworks* (2002) started as a sound and video performance in which Polli played intensifying notes of severe storms through a sound-mixing desk. The sounds were generated directly from sonified meteorological data produced by a simulation of a cyclonic storm generated by scientists. Polli wrote a program for a data logger to interface with live weather inputs to make randomized sound compositions. In the *90 Degrees South* project (2007–2008), she worked with scientists in the Antarctic environment to source sonifications of long-term climate monitoring and to make live recordings. By 2017, rather than negotiating the use of digital data streams, Polli created a collaborative, wind-turbine powered visualization with light for the Rachel Carson bridge.

The *90 Degrees South* project evolved from a seven-week National Science Foundation (NSF) art residency in 2007 to 2008. Polli found that when we talk about "saving the poles," what most people really are concerned about is saving "us," humanity, from sea-level rise, desertification, and flood. Her activist strategy is to use the intra-actions of data to speak about the irreversible changes occurring to all inhabitants of

Antarctica. As part of the public, online dimension of the project, Polli interviewed Antarctic scientists who were willing speak to her publicly about their research. In the political climate of a "war on science," many scientists were afraid to engage in open defense of the clear evidence of global warming. The Antarctic scientists spoke to Polli of the frustration that their messages were consistently ignored by governments still engaged in resource exploitation. A decade after Polli's project began, the situation for climate-research scientists enlisted by the American government in particular is still highly precarious.

Sonic Antarctica (2008) is a ninety-minute-long album of compositions from human, biological, and technical sources—a "collective listening" to the Antarctic atmosphere. The abstract clicks and pulses are the sounds of geosonifications of ice-acceleration data, weather, and climate data. The Geiger counter is a common application of sonification of otherwise imperceptible radiation data. Artists' sonification requires a relatively simple shift from a numerical output to another kind of medium that makes it perceivable to our senses; Max/MSP is one software Polli advocates to make this translation. One of Polli's sonified representations is the sound of Iceberg B15A breaking up, collected by a seismometer in numerical form. To make the long period of break-up of the iceberg audible, the data was accelerated by a factor of a thousand by scientist Dr. Douglas MacAyeal, then transformed using audio software to produce a corresponding, or isomorphic, representation in sound.

While in the Antarctic, Polli also recorded ambient sound samples of the mechanics of monitoring the weather, including helicopters, radio waves, and footsteps crunching over a glacier. A collage of live field recordings of water flows beneath Taylor Glacier is layered over the electronic sonified data. Voice recordings of scientists describe their interactions with pressure sensors, anemometers, and tropospheric ozone detectors. The sound recordings are immersed in the homomorphic tradition of the observational scientist who makes direct recordings in fieldwork, as well as an homage to the "site-listening" tradition in sound art and the radio documentary format. When the sonified data is intermingled with real-time microphone recordings, different forms of ecological evidence of climate change irreverently coalesce.

The fusion of representational systems in sound is mirrored in the video sequences that accompany *Sonic Antarctica*. In one sequence of a three-screen video projection, shown at MIC Toi Rerehiko (Moving Image Centre), in an exhibition I curated in Auckland, a wireless camera transmits video while attached to a weather balloon. As viewers, we inhabit the position of a remote observer, hanging precariously over the snow while the wireless video connection flickers uncertainly. From the perspective of the balloon, we experience a jerky ascent from the ice, and we hear the anxious preparations of the artist as a countdown to launch is shouted out by a team of Antarctic meteorologists. Another screen shows the ground-based view of the balloon, and another the whirring of an anemometer. In the accompanying audio composition, sonified, tropospheric weather data collected by the balloon is combined with the ground-based experience of the adrenaline rush of the instrument's launch. While the image falters, the audio data streams warble, chime, pulsate, and eventually overpower the scientists' voices; the atmospheric whirr eludes science's best efforts at interpretation.

In Polli's "sound walkabout" workshops (2009a) at Scott Base, she created a social collaborative event to record environmental sounds. The walkabouts hosted a cross-section of Antarctic workers, from physicists and engineers to boiler-room technicians and carpenters, some with DIY recording devices. *Ground truthing* in science triangulates the findings of remote instruments with surface-based experience, which in artists' hands was adapted to the sound walkabouts. To collect sounds while walking or drifting elicits a temporal auditory experience of the "thicks and thins" of the actual world (De Certeau 1984, 93). The invitation to present the resulting sound compositions in the Scott Base coffee house generated so much interest that the performance became "standing room only" (Polli 2009b). The coffee house performances created social and environmental networks that transcended the regulated environment of the Antarctic base.

Polli echoes Latour's (2005) exhortation to return to a democratic republic of things or "res publica" through activating instruments in aesthetic/political formations. Polli speculatively asks: "What of the voice of the Poles themselves? Can the soundscape of the poles and the translation of polar environmental data into sound contribute to public understandings of climate change?" (Polli 2009b, n.p). Instruments of measurement augment our sense perceptions, yet scientists often struggle to make their complex data meaningful in lay contexts. Polli proposes that the intimacy of sound connects the human to the nonhuman in a collective experience of hearing. Data in the form of audio is democratic in the sense that it does not need technical expertise to generate an affect.

In the last decade, Polli's attention has turned toward air quality and real-time visualizations as an extension of her sonification practice, using instruments such as mobile phones, LED light arrays, and wind turbines. Polli and Chuck Varga's *Particle Falls* (2010–2015) is a large-scale real-time visualization of particulate pollution, first projected onto the AT&T building in San Jose, California, using laser projection and a mobile phone interface. The animated particles in their first phase are a blue vertical stream, but the schema changes to a cloud of fiery orange or red when particulate pollution is nearby. The animation is responsive to large vehicles such as trucks that produce volatile organic compounds. At the Museum of Contemporary Art in Zagreb, *Particle Falls* was visible though the museum windows, illuminating the entire side of the building.

On a similar scale, French collective HeHe's *Nuage verte* (2008) used spectacular methods of disseminating information about air quality to a local community with large-scale public projections. Green laser projections of cloud forms illuminate the night sky, revealed by real clouds of industrially produced factory smoke. *Champs d'Ozone* (2007) was a computer-generated cloud that illuminated the city: the over-saturated colors were a response to the concentrations of nitrogen dioxide, sulfur dioxide, ozone, and particle dust suspended in the air. Meanwhile, the Preemptive Media collective's *Area's Immediate Reading* or *AIR* (2006) miniaturized wearable air-sensor instruments to self-monitor levels of pollutant gases. In an Australian Network for Art and Technology (ANAT) workshop in Melbourne (2008), led by the late Beatriz da Costa, "carriers" (myself included) were invited to make and wear sensor instruments to collect the air pollutant shifts over a day. The *AIR* project renders explicit "otherwise unrepresented entities (i.e. particles) as stake-holders in a common situation," as workshop participant Michael Dieter argues (2009, 57).

At a local scale, my online color field *Neighborhood Air* (Randerson 2012–2014) shows fluctuating urban air pollutants recorded by air quality instruments in a disused traffic control booth in Auckland. The instruments were installed in collaboration with urban meteorologist Jennifer Salmond. Although we live on a South Pacific island, New Zealanders are only beginning to realize that we cannot rely on the wind to blow away chemically produced toxins from our ubiquitous cars; there is no "away" from our global atmospheric container. The national mythology of the "100 Percent Pure New Zealand" tourism campaign has created an atmosphere of denial that does not reflect the actual experience of many city dwellers. Auckland's air has been found to be poorer than several larger cities in Australia (WHO 2011). When even the air in small island states is industrially altered, the global implications of the "age of atmospheric toxins," to borrow Peter Sloterdijk's phrase (2009), becomes devastatingly apparent.

Neighborhood Air was driven by instruments to measure volatile organic compounds, nitrogen dioxide, and carbon monoxide, as well as weather parameters. Levels of toxicity are represented by photographic stripes of the sky to form a pale color field, with an accompanying sound to correlate to an instrument. I recorded video images of Auckland's photochemical smog events from the top of a central volcanic cone in a homomorphic registration of air pollution, as distinct from scientific "count" mechanisms. I also gathered written observations and sensations from breathers of city air. Jeff Nusz wrote the software for a sound and abstract visual interface. When *Neighborhood Air* was installed at Screen Space in Melbourne (2012), a randomly occurring button in the software interface fades in with the option to print a postcard, inscribed with a sentence-long "air quality story" from a citizen of Auckland. Postcards of twenty different "air samples" (viewed as colored strips) could be printed from a postcard-sized Canon printer. The stories inscribed on the postcards were full of hope and contradictory understandings of the health of our air. At ISEA (2013), *Neighborhood Air* was exhibited inside a car converted to a garden by Ian Clothier.

When the secondary qualities of matter such as color and sound describe our intra-actions with instrumental counters, we unsettle the acceptance of mathematics as the only way to describe physical data sets. Sensor instruments such as those used in Polli's *Particle Falls*, da Costa's *AIR*, and *Neighborhood Air* provide orders of sensation that flow beyond the body. The urban infrastructure of instruments can be understood as "an automatic, collective sensorium," as Jennifer Gabrys (2007) has suggested. By managing urban environments, sensors effectively generate a new version of the urban environment itself, albeit in digital form. When information about humidity and temperature or tiny particulate matter that is too minute for human detection is transmitted via machines, rather than directly to human skin or our respiratory systems, we become reliant on machinic interfaces as mediators.

Polli's *Energy Flow* (2016–2017) is a real-time visualization of the "energy potential" of wind power on the Rachel Carson bridge in Pittsburg, in homage to its namesake, the pioneering environmentalist. Polli worked with a team of lighting experts and with Pittsburgh-based wind turbine manufacturer WindStax to power arrays of over 27,000 multicolored LED lights positioned along the bridge's vertical cables. The strong winds that flow down the Pittsburg Valley activate sixteen wind turbines attached to the catenary arches of the bridge. The colors of the lights change with the oscillations of wind speed and direction captured by a weather station. Engineered bridges, for Polli, are large-scale, obsolete monuments to the fossil-fueled industrial age that must now be relinquished. She demonstrates the viability of wind power as a permanent energy solution by repurposing the remnants of the modernist, industrial environment. The first version of this concept was developed in the *Queensbridge Windpower* project (2008) in New York. In both projects, the bridges become part of a giant bridge-turbine instrument; in *Energy Flow*, the highly visible light show emanates across the river in a spectacle of sustainable energy.

Meteorological art gives sensory correlatives for live weather that center on difference, rather than uniformity, evading the tendency in modern science to "augment and to order" (Arendt 2006, 261). Artists' custom-made instruments, such as Hinterding and Haines's *Earthstar*, produce ecologies that resonate perceptually rather than

Figure 4.6
Andrea Polli and Rod Gdovic. *Energy Flow*. 2016–2017. Rachel Carson Bridge, Pittsburgh. Photograph: Larry Rippel. Image courtesy of the artist. [See color plate 8]

merely transmit messages. Live weather phenomena detected by instruments may be consistent with anterior versions of reality based on scientific accounts, yet artworks generate a feeling for data that defies rationality. Peljhan's *Makrolab* hacks into digitized weather frequencies to throw instrumentalist reason into a state of emergency. The limits of scientific and governmental inscription mechanisms, their hold over information, and their associated claims to truth become culturally unstable. Tondeur's fictionalized *Eophone* instrument provokes our poetic imagination in light of a seemingly hopeless situation. Polli's attention to ground observation, together with the aerial view, activates relations between ourselves and nonhuman others. For artists, meaning occurs in the ongoing performance of the world as "a differential dance of intelligibility and unintelligibity" (Barad 2007, 149), in which we sense energetic forces through sensations and our social settings.

The reorientation of instruments in art "makes concrete sense of the abstract and absurd universe into which we are falling" in ubiquitous digital culture, as Flusser argues ([1985] 2011, 37). When artists invent or repurpose meteorological instruments, we treat them as agents capable of political interference. Art practice extends political participation to the weather through quasi instruments, challenging us to reconceive our atmosphere as a shared place. Many scientists, sustainable commercial entities, and mobile platforms also are working toward a radical overhaul of our fossil-fuel-reliant economy. Artists foster such emergent art-science and technological alliances carefully. Tending to collaborators quashes the differences among art, science, and lay knowledge in place of situated exchange, as I will investigate further in the next chapter. Art brokers unlikely coalitions between people and weather to forge new ways to see, hear, and feel. If we take a step further to think of shared art-science instruments as "quasi us," we disturb the normative boundaries of where the apparatus ends and the human begins.

5   Social Meteorology and Participatory Art

Meteorological art projects are always embedded in cultural life, but the artworks in this chapter attend to the weather-knowing held in particular communities. Social weather practices and the natural sciences historically originate from shared observations, but in the twentieth century the terms *ethno-meteorology* and *amateur weather observation* surfaced to separate the weather intuitions of the layperson from the professional. These terms are inadequate, I make the case, to express the complexity of Indigenous weather knowledge and the intricate social exchanges that artists create within the spectrum of weather politics. Assemblages of art, meteorological science, activism, and Indigenous knowledge exist now that were scarcely conceivable in science during the last century. The phrase *social meteorology*, coined by cultural theorist Andrew Ross, locates weather knowledge as part of quotidian experience, to bring to light the expertise beyond the realm of professional science.

Social meteorology, according to Ross, is "meteorology on the ground and of the ground, as well as from the air, the traditional vantage point for forecasting. A meteorology that builds fronts from below in addition to one that sees fronts coming in advance. And, above all, a meteorology that can explain some of the desired connections between social life, natural life and economic life" (1991, 13). The common appearance of rain at a Māori *tangi* (funeral) or at the opening of a new Māori *marae* (communal meeting house) is a social meteorological phenomenon in Aotearoa New Zealand. The rain is understood as a *tohu* (sign) of grief from the spirits in response to human loss. In early European culture, belief systems also were bound to weather phenomena—from Roman weather auspices to the eighteenth-century British "meteorological apparition narratives," in which military affairs were linked to severe weather. In the intense visions of the disenfranchised laboring class likely to be sent to war, clouds were reported to form into fierce sky battles (Jankovic 2000, 66). Weather beliefs often are grounded in a restorative faith in the signs the weather offers.

With the discovery that our consumption of fossil fuels releases the gases that are changing the usual course of our weather patterns, cultural analogies between human action and atmosphere are physically borne out. Now more than ever, we see that human social behavior is inextricably linked to the atmosphere. Social accounts of weather therefore are becoming increasingly valuable to science. Scientific institutions such as the Bureau of Meteorology (BoM) in Australia and the National Institute of Water and Atmospheric Research (NIWA) in Aotearoa New Zealand now are taking note of Indigenous accounts of the changing seasonal cycles of flora and fauna. Writer Henry Thoreau's nature observations in his journal at Walden Pond are becoming valuable evidence for science of climate shifts (Howden-Chapman 2016), and urban meteorologists in Britain are analyzing John Constable's cloud paintings as historical evidence of London's air quality (Thornes 1999). Yet social meteorology extends beyond the building of cultural bridges between community or art-based ways of knowing and scientific knowledge to include the nonhuman.

In this chapter, a range of art strategies are conceptually divided by the terms *polity*, *politics*, and *the political*, following political philosopher Chantal Mouffe's (2005) distinction. *Polity* refers to the interphylum dialogue of the atmosphere's constituents; by *interphylum*, I mean the relations between both human ethnicities and the nonhuman. *Politics* refers to the ontic register, or the practical doing or playing out of debate between parties, often in online forums in the cases herein. *The political* refers to artworks that address ontological questions about our relations to atmosphere and to each other. The Australian collective theweathergroup_U can be understood to operate in the realm of the political. The group creates an online space for Indigenous, art-based, activist, and sustainable technical activity around the weather. Social unrest and climatic turbulence are conjoined from geographically dispersed regions of the Australian continent. The collective theweathergroup_U was formed to bring together stories by Indigenous and nonindigenous participants, on subjects from ecological lore to neo-colonial politics. Scientific climatology may be recognized as the primary authority in defining the exact physical nature of the global crisis, but there are important questions raised by artists as a form of "cultural climatology" (Thornes 2008) that have ramifications for policy making and social justice.

Māori concepts such as *mauri* (life force) and *kaitiakitanga* (guardianship) offer a rich, alternative account of ecological relationships to environmental science. A sense of ecological reciprocity is also shared by many Pākehā (European New Zealanders) to acknowledge that we are only one element of the given world. In 1991, the New Zealand Government's Resource Management Act recognized the Māori concept of kaitiakitanga as a concept for the joint custodianship of physical resources between iwi and local authorities. The swiftly changing weather of Aotearoa-New Zealand is enmeshed with ancestral weather narratives for many Māori artists. Lens-based media artist Natalie Robertson (Ngāti Porou, Ngāti Puai, Clann Dhònnchaidh) generates weather narratives that have a community-binding purpose, and Rachel Shearer (Te Aitanga ā Māhaki, Rongowhakaata, Ngāti Kahungunu) uses sound to signal ancestral presence in the atmosphere. Robertson's work represents a specific Māori polity (Ngāti Puai) of the East Cape of New Zealand, yet Indigenous cosmologies also offer a worldview that exceeds the regional issues that define the most commonly recognized polity of nation.

In a very different milieu, British artists Corby and Baily made *Cyclone.Soc* (2006–2008) from the heated opinions and unmoderated outrage of online newsfeeds. This socially oriented artwork addresses the parallel development of the severe storms that are indicators of global warming for most scientists and the vociferous online reactions to the 2008 financial crisis. The advance and recession of online attention to the global financial crisis and the ebb and flow of discussion on "global warming" converge in *Cycone.Soc*. A nonrepresentational form of politics is also enacted in *Talking about the Weather* (2006), created by the Australian collective Out-of-Sync. The artists collect personal contributions to a carbon "breath collection" that is archived in a blog. The act of human respiration is linked to climate politics through the written descriptions and sound recordings of participants' breath that Out-of-Sync collects. This connective forum convenes our hopes and fears about the changing weather in a temporary coalition. *Incompatible Elements* (2010–2011) and *And the Earth Sighed* (2016) by Australian artists Josephine Starrs and Leon Cmielewski politicize the issue of forced environmental migration with topographical images of extremes of drought and deluge in Australasia. By looking closely at their manipulated satellite or drone images, we join a polity that bears witness to climate change–affected regions.

Well before Mouffe, Arendt argued that ethical questions concerning ecology, science, and technology should be open to a wide polity. Art can facilitate social discussions of atmosphere—not to provide answers, but rather to reflect on "our newest experiences and our most recent fears" (Arendt 1958, 5). This chapter investigates how meteorological art questions the human will to master nature with alternate paradigms of ecological reciprocity. The well-known work *The Weather Project* serves here as a preface to highlight social systems of value concerning weather.

Socializing the Institution

73% OF LONDON CAB DRIVERS DISCUSS THE WEATHER WITH THEIR PASSENGERS
(Eliasson 2003, 132)

Figure 5.1
Olafur Eliasson. *The Weather Project*. 2003. Installation view at Tate Modern, London. Monofrequency lights, projection foil, haze machines, mirror foil, aluminium, scaffolding, $26.7 \times 22.3 \times 155.44$ m. Photograph: Andrew Dunkley and Marcus Leith. Courtesy of the artist; neugerriemschneider, Berlin; and Tanya Bonakdar Gallery, New York. © Olafur Eliasson. [See color plate 9]

This statement was posted in a London taxi on a yellow poster as part of the marketing poster campaign that preceded Danish-Icelandic artist Olafur Eliasson's *The Weather Project*. Excerpts of opinion polls about the weather were published in magazines, on taxis, on the exhibition invitations, and on billboards around London. The half sun, mirrored ceiling, and water vapor mist created dramatic perceptual effects in the Turbine Hall of Tate Modern (2003–2004). Yet Eliasson is an artist who felt bound to open his perceptual explorations further to create public dialogue around the escalating climate crisis. In April 2003, prior to the opening of *The Weather Project* installation, Eliasson conducted the "Tate Weather Monitoring Group Survey" among gallery staff at the Tate. He posed a series of questions such as "On an average day, how often would you discuss the weather?"; "If you discuss the weather, is your encounter likely to turn into a friendship or are you more likely never to talk to them again?," and "Do you think the idea of weather in our society is based on Nature or Culture?" (2003, 59–64). Eliasson used the survey playfully to suggest that our supposedly universal experiences of weather are also specific to us as private individuals and as members of a particular culture. These questions function in the ontic register to reduce the specter of climate change to specific facts by uncovering the staff's opinions. The questionnaire, as a precursor to Eliasson's visually compelling installation, underscores his concept that experiences of weather, like nature, cannot be regarded as common to all.

As I lay beneath the false sun made of industrial parts in the Tate's turbine hall, I found that it gave no warmth. In the context of out-of-control human effects on the climate, *The Weather Project* made me think about our estranged relations with nature. For geographer John E. Thornes, *The Weather Project* has instrumental value as a work of "cultural climatology" to visually represent the new dialectic between society and atmosphere (2008, 570). Eliasson's practice also has intrinsic value as a mediation on the perceptual effects of light and the interconnected nature of the weather and ourselves. The artwork's politics might be understood as working internally through the body. But there is a parallel need to stop thinking about nature as an exterior entity to ourselves, and to reunite scientific facts with the social values that surround weather and climate. Eliasson's later work *Ice Watch* (2015), made for COP21 and discussed in more detail in chapter 7, continues his political intervention in the public sphere.

A widespread blindness persists toward recognizing ourselves as part of the natural system that we care for. Our connected ecological systems and nonhuman things need tending as "matters of care," as María Puig de la Bellacasa has argued (2017), rather than exploitation as a resource. A feminist materialist approach of "care" overlaps with Indigenous paradigms of environmental care in several ways. I draw on the Māori concept of mauri, or the life vitality possessed by all living things—from the Indigenous cosmological paradigm that I am closest to—as a form of social meteorology in this chapter. Kaitiakitanga, another core Māori concept, links environmental care to well-being. Politician and academic Pita Sharples defines kaitiakitanga, the role of caretaker or guardian, from the perspective of his tribe, Ngāti Kahungunu: "Kaitiakitanga seeks balance in sustaining our natural resources as the basis for our well-being—rather than limitless commodities to use at our will" (Selby, Moore, and Mulholland 2010, vii). I offer a connection between postanthropocentric thought and the ecological values inherent in mauri and kaitiakitanga.

Indigenous Weather Knowledge

Kaitiakitanga (custodianship) and mauri (life force) are central to Māori environmental lore and increasingly recognized in mainstream culture in Aotearoa New Zealand. Mauri is vital within Māori systems of resource conservation as part of a cyclic process, where to damage one part might have far-reaching consequences to the whole. As a "process-oriented concept," mauri underlies the conservational effect on the traditional prohibitions on human action, such as *tapu* (restrictions on sacred sites) and *rahui* (temporary prohibition), which are inserted in the chain of being to prevent harm to nature and to people (Park 2006, 25–26). Harm to land, air, and water compromises mauri through colonial and neocolonial exploitation of resources that ultimately effects our people adversely. Artist and writer Huhana Smith observes, "If pollution, contamination, or desecration affected the mauri, or life vitality, of revered places within the natural environment, then this influenced the communities who relied on the land, often manifesting in disquiet, disunity, or fragmentation within those communities" (2012, 16).

Māori are progeny of the earth and atmosphere ancestor-beings; such an ontology of connection calls for a continually enacted ethic of care. For many Māori, kaitiakitanga is the inherent obligation to their *tīpuna* (ancestors) and to their *mokopuna* (grandchildren). The capitalist thirst for progress that holds the domination of nature as self-evident is incompatible with Māori cosmological systems. There is also a temporal incompatibility in which the short-term horizon of capitalism is out of step with the Māori conception of obligation to the future. Indigenous polities, weather phenomena, ecology, and climate change are treated as interconnected in the practices of art collective theweathergroup_U, Rachel Shearer, and Natalie Robertson.

theweathergroup_U: Seeing, Listening, and Documenting

The collective theweathergroup_U was founded to create a communal archive of voices that have been systematically excluded from public life in Australia. The group was

Figure 5.2a, b
theweathergroup_U. *theweathergroup_U*. 2008. Installation view at Cockatoo Island, Sydney Biennale. Photograph: Craig Bender. Courtesy of theweathergroup_U.

formed with an agenda to act on the anthropogenic alteration of climate from disparate social standpoints, cultural beliefs, and opinions. Through a public blog, at its most active in 2008, and a grassroots documentary video archive, theweathergroup_U collated geographically diverse voices from the Northern Territory to Wiradjuri activists in New South Wales. The group members included high-profile artist Susan Norrie, David Mackenzie, video/audio artist Sumugan Sivanesan, cultural theorist Dr. Jeremy Walker, media communications expert Bryce Anbinis-King, and Darwin-based videographers Will Tinapple and Danielle Green.

Their activity culminated in a temporary configuration for the 2008 Sydney Biennale at Cockatoo Island that drew on their professional areas of specialism and respective community access. The biennale artwork was a video storytelling forum that presented Indigenous and nonindigenous weather knowledge and experience. Their stated aim was to explore "ways of seeing, listening and documenting the interactions with natural systems that punctuate our daily existence" (theweathergroup_U 2008). The installation was an antispectacular, distributed composition including small television monitors, small projections, and headphones, placed on simple desks with chairs in an otherwise empty shed. Each monitor played a separate documentary loop using the vernacular mode of recorded video of elders' voices.

The installation, however, presented a critical challenge to the biennale norms by powering the installation with a sustainable energy supply. The multiple television monitors were powered by wind and solar energy, using the weather to alternately power their art installation over the long period of public exhibition. Bryce Anbinis-King, of theweathergroup_U , designed the simple "e-gipsi" supply unit, in collaboration with Charles Darwin University. The solar-powered generator provided Internet access to a local area network anywhere in Australia. To operate the e-gipsi on Cockatoo Island for three months in winter during the exhibition, a wind turbine was introduced to supplement the power production of the solar panels. This connection was used to provide live, online content for the exhibition to link remote parts of Australia. The adoption of the e-gipsi and wind turbine resists the dominance of state or private power supplies, based on fossil fuels, in light of increasing scrutiny of exhibition practices. This quiet modeling of an energy-efficient exhibition practice is one of the first instances I can recall in a biennale setting. The artists implicitly drew attention to the energetic cost of powering digital media installations day and night.

The blog forum of theweathergroup_U assembled new and preexisting videos that record both social and climatic disturbance. The videos include documentation of protests against radioactive waste dumping, Sumugan Sivanesan's documentation of the Redfern riots in *Fire of the Island*, weather video stories of local observations of climate change, and the activity of the Firestick Theater in Arnhem Land. *Fire of the Island* documents Aboriginal activist Isabel Coe and Robert Corowa as they establish the Sacred Fire and move the mobile protest unit known as the Aboriginal Tent Embassy to Cockatoo Island after the Sydney Olympics (2000). Other videos record the revival of the practice of cultural burning in remote Arnhem Land in the Northern Territory of Australia. Controlled burning of sections of land reduces the intensity and spread of the dry season bushfires and reduces the amount of CO_2 released into the atmosphere. The volatility of the weather recorded in the video documents has a social parallel in the urgent actions of cultural self-determination in other video vignettes.

The recurring motifs of storms and burning fires contain the apocalyptic resonance found in theweathergroup_U member Susan Norrie's art practice. Norrie's video works such as *Undertow* (2002) and *Havoc* (2007) combine a geographical spread of natural and manmade disasters, using smoke, steam, and fire as allegories for her vision of a planet in turmoil. There is a long history of narratives of environmental apocalypse in film, which links to biblical day-of-reckoning scenarios. The climate crisis often is situated as a near-future apocalypse in fantastic cinematic representations, such as director Roland Emmerich's *The Day after Tomorrow* (2004) or Dean Devlin's *Geostorm* (2017). The danger is that such spectacularly extreme weather events as entertainment may dissociate us from the cumulative effect of everyday decisions that contribute to the present warming atmosphere. The documentary context of the purposely lit fires in the Northern Territory in theweathergroup_U video pieces, however, is a grounded attempt to restore social and ecological balance. Video narratives are shared from Indigenous leaders in Ramingining in the Northern Territory that pass on urgent cultural knowledge rather than as visual spectacle. Through stories that disseminate the voices of a particular polity, the elders avoid a feeling of helplessness in the face of colonial and environmental forces.

In a similar vein, a toxic meteorology is evoked in the glass cloud installation *Thunder Raining Poison* (2015) at the National Gallery of Australia by Yhonnie Scarce (Kokatha/Nukunu peoples). By suspending over two thousand blown-glass yams as if they were cloud particles in a five-meter-high installation, the artist recalls the clouds produced by British nuclear bomb tests in Maralinga, about 800 kilometres northwest of Adelaide in the late 1950s and early 1960s. The nuclear bombsite turned the surrounding dirt into glass, the artist's grandfather recollected (Baum 2017). The HD video trilogy *Trace Evidence* (2016) by London-based artist Susan Schuppli, also excavates the recent history of Chernobyl's airborne contaminates delivered by a rain cloud in Sweden in April 1986. Along with the creative focus on the issue of climate change, these works evidence the anthropogenic alterations of the weather for specific communities.

Knowledge about the weather and human land use as part of a continuous cycle, even in their destructive effects, gives a sense of place within Aboriginal lore. Author, songwriter, documentary maker, and Gunditjmara man Richard Frankland (2016) describes this knowledge as "a feeling of safety that comes about by seeing, feeling, experiencing the positives of your people and culture which has woven everything together in over 60,000 years of history." Such narratives offer a venue to listen intently to aboriginal voices within a public art setting. Frankland offers the principle of *dadirri* or "deep listening" as a way to attend to the often-excluded voices or suppressed histories in this polity. *Dadirri* also signals an inner awareness (Atkinson 2002).

A *polity* was once defined by Aristotle as the condition of being constituted as a state or organized community in a very different cultural framework. The *body politic* historically has signified the body of the ruler, but in contemporary discourse it describes the demographic composition of a geographical or social area. In Mouffe's terms (2005), we make a polity through the "we/they" distinction that allows us to frame collective identities. Making a distinction between outside and inside forms a polity; yet the we/they distinction that defines the nation-state often can leave Indigenous voices outside. theweathergroup_U demonstrated how the issue of climate change is inseparable from other challenges of inaction at a governmental level on climate strategy in Australia. The group also set up a challenge to mainstream representations of climate by connecting the issue to other potent political struggles. Their pluralistic strategy was less a short-term guerrilla intervention but a validation of a longer, deeper connection to the land and atmospheric system. Rachel Shearer and Natalie Robertson, in Aotearoa New Zealand, offer media artworks for the Indigenous polity in resistance to neocolonial interests, the "conservative" in conservation, and an often-unresponsive mainstream culture.

Kaitiaki for the Polity: Rachel Shearer and Natalie Robertson

In Māori cosmology, weather empathizes with human circumstances. The foundational conflict in the creation story for Māori is the struggle between Tāwhirimātea (spirit of wind) and Rūamoko (spirit of earthquakes and volcanoes), who break apart the heaven from the earth. The wind is Tāwhirimātea's fighting spirit, while cloud and rain are healing entities. Māori cosmology sees the world and nature as formed from conflict. This massive separation conceptually parallels the painful experience of colonialism and the long struggle over sovereignty rights between Crown and Māori, the duty of custodianship for the land and atmosphere and the need for economic survival. Sound artist Rachel Shearer composes from solar energies to signal the vibrant life force of the weather. In solar-responsive sound works such as *Imperceptible Degrees* (2010–2015) and *Wiriwiri* (2017), she uses renewable solar energy. In a version of *Wiriwiri* (2017) at Te Uru Gallery in Auckland, speakers powered by a solar panel are situated on the canopy over the street entrance to the gallery. Speakers also were located in trees in earlier iterations. The speakers play an audio composition continuously from sunrise to sunset.

The position of the artwork at the threshold of the public gallery allows visitors to be greeted with the sounds of the sun. Shearer allegorically finds a sonic equivalent for a hand gesture called a *wiri* in Māori performance. She writes: "The trembling hand iconic in Māori performance is called a 'wiri'—'the tremble of life.' The wiri is an acknowledgement of Tanerore—the shimmering heated air that rises from the ground on a hot summer day, personified as 'te haka a Tanerore' (the dance of Tanerore). Wiri-wiri is to tremble, shiver, quake. This gesture resonates in an idea of vibration at the core of the material world that is performed in this work as a field of trembling sound" (Shearer 2017). In Ngāti Kahungunu cosmology, Tanerore is the son of Tamanuiterā, the sun, and the summer maiden named Hineraumati. The emitted sound has the textural vibration of an insect's wings and modulates in pitch in response to the sun's temperature. The sounds fuse with the chorus of the bush cicadas that also grows louder with the heat of the sun. Shearer's sense that the natural world is "trembling" resonates with Povinelli's (2016) argument that former modes of human governance of nonlife are becoming unstuck, or are "trembling," as exploitation of resources can no longer be sustained. Shearer's composition is suffused by the sun's heat, which literally drives the sonic intensity, in an operation that is outside human instrumental control.

Artist Natalie Robertson uses lens-based media to attend to social and ecological issues in Aotearoa New Zealand. Her iwi, Ngāti Porou, is a polity on the eastern coast of New Zealand's North Island. Robertson's work often expresses relationships between people, ancestral mountains, and rivers and Tāwhirimātea (spirit of wind). In an early video work, *Weatherscape: Mataatua* (2000), weather phenomena reflect the dynamics of a group of artists on a journey on foot through the Urewera ranges. In *The Whispering of the Karaka Trees* (2000; figure 5.3a, b), weather at the mouth of the Waiapu River is read as a tohu of the spiritual journey of Robertson's grandfather after his passing. Recent installations *Waiapu Kōkā Huhua: Waiapu of Many Mothers* (2016) and *He Wai Mou! He Wai Mau!* (2017) use sound, video, and photographs return to Robertson's ancestral river, Waiapu. Locally grounded concepts for care of the ecosystem of land and atmosphere, such as mauri and kaitiakitanga, are brought to bear in these projects. Although many Pākehā New Zealanders embrace kaitiakitanga as a bicultural concept,

Figure 5.3a, b
Natalie Robertson. *The Whispering of the Karaka Trees*. 2000. Video stills. Images courtesy of the artist. [See color plate 10]

many of us question the motives of successive governments that assign relatively small tracts of land to be governed as national parks. Still worse, neocolonial ventures, particularly in the agricultural and mining industries, continue to exploit Aotearoa New Zealand's remaining environmental resources. At a point in our history at which the cataclysmic effect of European colonization and the systematic exploitation of the coastal ecology and Indigenous culture is only just beginning to be recognized, the promotion and revival of kaitiakitanga is urgent.

In interview, Robertson describes her artworks as relational. They are about "relationships between people, the land and the atmosphere, not simply about human politics or ecological issues" (Robertson 2011). The first of Robertson's video weatherscapes, *Weatherscape: Mataatua* (2000), was a commissioned work made on a *hikoi* (politicized walk) in Te Urewera country, one of the last bush-clad strongholds of the Tuhoe iwi. The six-day hikoi was the initiative of Terry Firkin to bring together Pacific artists on a journey that covered seventy kilometers from Mataatua, near Ruatāhuna, across to Ruatoki, not far from Whakātane, through the heartland of the Urewera ranges. The work was first shown in the *Te Totara Paa Te Urewera Hikoi* exhibition at Archill Gallery, Auckland (2000), and later shown in *Experiencing Turbulence* (2003) at Te Papa Tongarewa, the national museum in Wellington.

For the exhibition, Robertson selected one of many fixed-camera-position video recordings she had made on the hikoi, at Mataatua Marae. In the fifteen-minute sequence, a near whiteout of the mist-covered *maunga* (mountain) dissipates as the sun heats up the earth. The gathering and dispersal of cloud contain the surfaceless bodies of spirits. We sense the mauri of the Te Urewera forest, where the cloud shifts endlessly beyond the frame. In Tuhoe cosmology, the iwi did not arrive in a *waka* (canoe) from the Pacific; instead, Tuhoe choreographer Maaka Pepene states, "We were born from the Urewera elements ... we're part of the air, the soil, the wind" (Kamm 2011). Embedded in the heart of a remote range in the North Island's center, the Tuhoe never signed the Treaty of Waitangi; in colonial history, they have made many independent sovereignty submissions to the Crown. As in Robertson's later work, mist is a transitive element indicating movement, change, and resilience.

Cloud for Robertson is also a formal technique to counter the stillness of the photograph, yet still retain the control of a locked-off camera position. Clouds have a strategic function in the pictorial order as "an integrator and a disintegrator, now as a sign, now as a non-sign" (Damisch 2002, 184). The video was originally to be viewed while sitting on a *paepae*—a wooden seat made from concrete rounds and a plank of rimu wood, such as those that could be found at marae such as Mataatua—to emulate the observational position of the camera. A place to rest provides comfort for the meditative experience of watching the incremental shifts of weather. The intensified observation that is required of a fixed camera position pays homage to the endurance and resistance of the Tuhoe embodied in their ancient Te Urewera mountain ranges.

The formal techniques developed in *Weatherscape: Mataatua* (2000) are revisited by Robertson in *The Whispering of the Karaka Trees* (2000), a work that also charts the passage of mist, revealing a prominent geological feature of land (also an ancestor) at the Waiapu River mouth. *The Whispering of the Karaka Trees* is a personal work made shortly after the death of Robertson's grandfather. This work was exhibited in *Te Ata: Māori Art from the East Coast* with an accompanying catalog by novelist Witi Ihimaera and curator Ngarino Ellis. Robertson placed the video camera where the Waiapu River *ngutu awa* (mouth or beak) meets the sea soon after her grandfather's tangi. As she stood there filming, a dark rain cloud moved across the headland and out to the sea. The sign of rain at a tangi is held to be a portent or a tohu that signifies the passing of a spirit. Rain after a significant passing is understood in Māori cosmology as the tears of Ranginui, the sky father. The river mouth was the place where Robertson's grandfather related the story of the significance of the "scratchy whisper" of the karaka trees to her. His mother had told him that this whispering was the sound of the Ngāti Porou spirits leaving the Waiapu River on their way to Cape Reinga, the northernmost tip of Aotearoa, where Māori spirits return to Hawaiiki (the spiritual homeland for Polynesian people in Māori oral histories). Robertson and her grandfather agreed to meet at this sacred place after his passing.

The tohu of the rain cloud signified Robertson's emerging responsibilities as *kaitiaki* (guardian) over the Waiapu River, now in a state of silted degradation from farming and forestry. The karaka trees have long since disappeared, along with much *wāhi tapu* (sacred ground) of ancient burial grounds on its banks due to erosion. In Māori terms, this is a decline in mauri, the life force of the river. This work also raises larger questions surrounding the future of coastal regions of Te Moana nui a Kiwa (the Pacific diaspora). The proximity to the shore of many Pacific communities in marae (meeting house and surrounds) makes Māori coastal communities particularly vulnerable to sea-level rise. Māori ecologist Lisa Kanawa predicts that Te Tai Rāwhiti, the eastern coast of the North Island, near Robertson's tribal land, is predicted to become 20 percent drier but interspersed with very heavy rainfall and flooding by 2070 (2010, 113). The fixed camera position steadfastly records the changing atmospheric conditions of these sites, suggesting that they are watched, and protected, under the patient gaze of a kaitiaki.

Robertson's 2016 body of work, *Waiapu Kōkā Huhua: Waiapu of Many Mothers* at Papakura Art Gallery and ST PAUL St Gallery, includes four vertical black-and-white photographic prints of a tangled mass of driftwood at the Waiapu River mouth. The images, made from negatives taken twenty years earlier, record the environmental impacts of the forestry industry that caused river erosion and the aftereffects of Cyclone Bola (1996). Two giant rocks, the still bodies of *turehu* (fairy people) in Ngāti Porou lore, disappeared from the river in the force of Cyclone Bola, perhaps escaping back to the Urewera forest. The four floor-to-ceiling images are named *Pohautea* after Robertson's ancestral mountain that guards the "bones" of driftwood in the foreground. In one of the long photographs, a shadow of Robertson's body and her camera tripod falls onto the sand and driftwood on the beach. Her body is positioned as a *gnomon*, the shadow of the sundial that indicates the position of the sunlight, implicating the photographer in the surrounding ecology (Robertson 2011). Flood and the increasing incidence of cyclonic weather events are one of most visible consequences of climate change in Aotearoa New Zealand. By reprinting a black-and-white negative of the aftermath of Bola in a new format, Robertson makes a continuous link from the damage of past cyclones to future speculation on the turbulent weather to come. The exhibition is accompanied by a Ngāti Porou *mōteatea* (lament) sung by Rhonda Tibble for an ancestor-chief named Pahoe (Te Whanau-a-Hinetapora), who was drowned in a flood in the Waipau River.

In 2017, Robertson returned once again to the Waiapu with cameraman and drone operator Pat Makiri to trace the deforestation and flood damage of the ancestor river. The title of this series, *He Wai Mou! He Wai Mau!*, comes from a composition written for the signing of a joint management agreement for the Waiapu River between Te Runanganui o Ngāti Porou and the Gisborne District Council in 2015. *He wai mou* signals the water that is for Papatūānuku, the earth mother, for the sustenance of her being. *He wai mau* is the water for us, the living; the water of life that sustains our everyday lives. This is the ecological reciprocity with the nonhuman that the European settler culture is now beginning to recognize as a foundational principle to restore the mauri of the river. The haunting sounds of the mōteatea for young Pahoe's drowned body cast ashore at the mouth of the Waiapu River, fill the airspace of the gallery. The lament expresses grief for an uncertain future, as well as for Pahoe, a revered ancestor.

A drone glides ten meters above the river, from a bird's-eye perspective, as if searching for the body of Pahoe. The airborne perspective of the drone evokes the ethereal realm of spirits from which ancestors depart for Hawaiiki. The camera sails over the remaining pillar of a bridge, destroyed by flood before it even opened in the 1900s. The journey ends at the river, now split into two mouths by Cylone Cook (2017), at the same point at which Robertson watched her grandfather's spirit depart almost seventeen years earlier, recorded in *The Whispering of the Karaka Trees*. The camera tilts upward out to sea and fades to white. The drone imagery is accompanied by a second large-scale projection filmed with a handheld camera on a motorized gimbal, in which Robertson closely combs the river banks on foot in the aftermath of Cyclone Cook. The sea foam has made its way up the river and swirls in foaming eddies. The actions of cyclonic events, predicted to intensify by the IPCC, as well as colonial deforestation, have played a part in the degradation of the Waiapu River, which is now heavy with sediment.

I attended the crowded opening of *He Wai Mou! He Wai Mau!* at Māngere Arts Centre, which included a *pōwhiri* opening, a customary ritual opening in which *kaumātua* (elders) drew attention to the history and value of the Waipu River in Ngāti Porou ecosophy. The care of ecological reciprocity extended even to water ecology at the site of Robertson's Auckland-based exhibition. Close to the Māngere gallery, at the degraded urban Tararata Creek, Robertson facilitated riparian planting of over two thousand sedges and flaxes to support the threatened *inanga* (eel) spawning. Robertson's work is stitched into global ecological debates, including the sensitive use of rivers and coastal ecologies in the changing climatic conditions. Her practice is not only a situated act of resistance to environmental exploitation for her tribal polity; it also resonates widely, as her frequent international showings attest. Robertson has a genealogical and spiritual connection to a specific polity, whereas British artists Corby and Baily's *Cyclone. Soc* exists in a community of voices that are connected, even if only briefly, through the Internet.

Cyclone.Soc: Information Politics

In *Cyclone.Soc* British artists Corby and Baily draw together the political energies surrounding the global financial crisis of 2008 and the issue of global warming in anxious synthesis. This commentary refers to the second version of *Cyclone.Soc* shown at MIC Toi Rerehiko in Auckland. On October 11, 2008, a week before the Auckland show opened, the head of the International Monetary Fund (IMF) warned that the world financial system was teetering on the brink of systemic meltdown. As an immediate response to this crisis, *Cyclone.Soc* collated the opinions of geographically dispersed sets of Internet users in political news feeds about the financial crisis. They visualized the intensifying flurry of words as moving, cyclonic weather patterns. The live text-feeds reflected the rising stress levels and conflicting responses to the growing financial crisis among web users. Online participants heatedly debated topics from defaults on subprime housing loans and the collapse of banks to the breakdown of Iceland's financial system.

Plate 1

William Hodges. *A View of Cape Stephens with Water Spouts*. 1776. Oil on canvas, 135.9 × 193 cm. Image © Ministry of Defence, Crown Copyright 2018.

Plate 2

John Constable. *Clouds*. 1822. Oil on paper on cardboard, 30 × 38 cm. National Gallery of Victoria, Melbourne. Felton Bequest, 1938.

Plate 3
Alan Sonfist. *Crystal Enclosure*. 1965. Photograph courtesy of the artist.

Plate 4

Thorbjørn Lausten. *Magnet*. 2008. Installation view at ZKM Center for Art and Media, Germany. Software and four video projections. Photograph: ONUK (ZKM Center for Art and Media, Karlsruhe).

1 5   M A R C H   1 8 0 0 h

| 1 | 5 | | 13 | 1 | 18 | 3 | 8 | | 1 | 8 | 0 | 0 | 8 |
| A | Cᵉ | | AB | A | AE | B | E | | A | E | – | – | E |

S E V E R E   T R O P I C A L   S T O R M

| 19 | 5 | 2 | 5 | 18 | 5 | | 20 | 18 | 15 | 16 | 9 | 3 | 1 | 12 | | 19 | 20 | 15 | 18 | 13 |
| AF | Cᵉ | AᵉAᵉ | Cᵉ | AE | Cᵉ | | Aᵉ– | AE | ACᵉ | AD | F | B | A | Gᵉ | | AF | Aᵉ– | ACᵉ | AE | AB |

9 3 0 1   I R M A

| 9 | 3 | 0 | 1 | | 9 | 18 | 13 | 1 |
| F | B | – | A | | F | AE | AB | A |

9 8 5 h P a

| 9 | 8 | 5 | 8 | 16 | 1 |
| F | E | Cᵉ | E | AD | A |

L A T I T U D E   1 5 . 3 ° N

| 12 | 1 | 20 | 9 | 20 | 21 | 4 | 5 | | 1 | 5 | 0 | 3 | 0 | 14 |
| Gᵉ | A | Aᵉ– | F | Aᵉ– | AᵉA | C | Cᵉ | | A | Cᵉ | | B | – | AC |

L O N G I T U D E   1 4 9 . 8 ° E

| 12 | 15 | 14 | 7 | 9 | 20 | 21 | 4 | 5 | | 1 | 4 | 9 | 0 | 8 | 0 | 5 |
| Gᵉ | ACᵉ | AC | Dᵉ | F | Aᵉ– | AᵉA | C | Cᵉ | | A | C | F | – | E | – | Cᵉ |

P O S I T I O N   F A I R

| 16 | 15 | 19 | 9 | 20 | 9 | 15 | 14 | | 6 | 1 | 9 | 18 |
| AD | ACᵉ | AF | F | Aᵉ– | F | ACᵉ | AC | | D | A | F | AE |

M O V I N G   N O R T H

| 13 | 15 | 22 | 9 | 14 | 7 | | 14 | 15 | 18 | 20 | 8 |
| AB | ACᵉ | AᵉAᵉ | F | AC | Dᵉ | | AC | ACᵉ | AE | Aᵉ– | E |

1 0   K N O T S

| 1 | 0 | | 11 | 14 | 15 | 20 | 19 |
| A | – | | G | AC | ACᵉ | Aᵉ– | AF |

M A X I M U M   W I N D S

| 13 | 1 | 24 | 9 | 13 | 21 | 13 | | 23 | 9 | 14 | 4 | 19 |
| AB | A | AᵉC | F | AB | AᵉA | AB | | AᵉB | F | AC | C | AF |

5 0   K N O T S   N E A R   C E N T E R

| 5 | 0 | | 11 | 14 | 15 | 20 | 19 | | 14 | 5 | 1 | 18 | | 3 | 5 | 14 | 20 | 5 | 18 |
| Cᵉ | – | | G | AC | ACᵉ | Aᵉ– | AF | | AC | Cᵉ | A | AE | | B | Cᵉ | AC | Aᵉ– | Cᵉ | AE |

O V E R   3 0   K N O T   W I N D S   W I T H I N

| 15 | 22 | 5 | 18 | | 3 | 0 | | 11 | 14 | 15 | 20 | | 23 | 9 | 14 | 4 | 19 | | 23 | 9 | 20 | 8 | 9 | 14 |
| ACᵉ | AᵉAᵉ | Cᵉ | AE | | B | – | | G | AC | ACᵉ | Aᵉ– | | AᵉB | F | AC | C | AF | | AᵉB | F | Aᵉ– | E | F | AC |

1 2 0   N A U T I C A L   M I L E   R A D I U S

| 1 | 2 | 0 | | 14 | 1 | 21 | 20 | 9 | 3 | 1 | 12 | | 13 | 9 | 12 | 5 | | 18 | 1 | 4 | 9 | 21 | 19 |
| A | Aᵉ | – | | AC | A | AᵉA | Aᵉ– | F | B | A | Gᵉ | | AB | F | Gᵉ | Cᵉ | | AE | A | C | F | AᵉA | AF |

Plate 5

Billy Apple. *Severe Tropical Storm 9301 Irma*. 2015. Coded schema representing satellite data details the upgrading of the 1993 Pacific Ocean tropical storm to a severe status. Image courtesy of the Billy Apple® Archive.

Plate 6
Douglas Bagnall. *Cloud Shape Classifier*. 2006. Installation view at MIC Toi Rerehiko, Auckland. Software, projection, electronic buttons. Image courtesy of the artist.

Plate 7

Joyce Hinterding and David Haines. *Earthstar*. 2011. Installation view from *Star Voyager*, Australian Centre for the Moving Image (ACMI). HD video projection, live sound, two custom VLF antennae, graphite- and polythene-coated copper wire, mixing desk, stereo speakers, and geodesic dome-shaped scent dispenser. Image courtesy of the artists.

Plate 8
Andrea Polli and Rod Gdovic. *Energy Flow*. 2016–2017. Rachel Carson Bridge, Pittsburgh. Photograph: Larry Rippel. Image courtesy of the artist.

Plate 9

Olafur Eliasson. *The Weather Project*. 2003. Installation view at Tate Modern, London. Monofrequency lights, projection foil, haze machines, mirror foil, aluminium, scaffolding, 26.7 × 22.3 × 155.44 m. Photograph: Andrew Dunkley and Marcus Leith. Courtesy of the artist; neugerriemschneider, Berlin; and Tanya Bonakdar Gallery, New York. © Olafur Eliasson.

Plate 10
Natalie Robertson. *The Whispering of the Karaka Trees*. 2000.
Video stills. Images courtesy of the artist.

Plate 11
Francis Alÿs (in collaboration with Julien Devaux). *Tornado*. 2000–2010. Single-channel video projection, 39 minutes, color, 5.1 surround sound. © Francis Alÿs. Image courtesy of David Zwirner, New York/London.

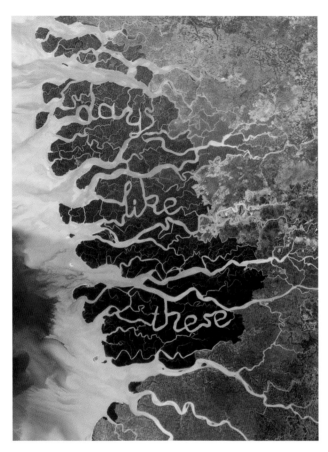

Plate 12
Josephine Starrs and Leon Cmielewski. *Incompatible Elements*. 2010.
Still from media arts installation. Image courtesy of the artists.

Plate 13
Amy Howden-Chapman. *Uncertainty Italicized*. 2013–2014. Performance image at 2201 Gallery, Los Angeles, 2013. Image courtesy of the artist.

Plate 14
Layne Waerea. *Bruce Pulman Park, Papakura, 2014*. 2014. Part of *Chasing Fog Club* (est. 2014). Image courtesy of the artist.

Plate 15
Ursula Biemann. *Subatlantic*. 2015. Video still. Image courtesy of the artist.

Plate 16

Karolina Sobecka. *Cloud Machine*. 2013. Commissioned as part of the *Amateur Human and Nephologies* exhibit at the V2 Institute for Unstable Media, Rotterdam. Image courtesy of the artist.

Plate 17
Tomás Saraceno. *Aerocene*. 2015. Pilot launch at the White Sands Desert. Courtesy of the artist; Pinksummer Contemporary Art, Genoa; Tanya Bonakdar, New York; Andersen's Contemporary, Copenhagen; Esther Schipper, Berlin. © Photograph: Tomás Saraceno. Image courtesy of the artist.

Figure 5.4
Corby and Bailey. *Cyclone.Soc.* 2006–2008. Installation view at Ambika P3, 2015. Photograph: Richard Stonehouse.

The live text on a projection screen curled into the shape of the tight isobars that signal the low-pressure system of cyclones, allowing the gallery audience to follow the growing public conversation on multiple news feeds. The isobar forms were distilled by the artists from publicly available satellite forecasts for the East Coast of the United States in autumn 2005. The storm patterns linked the climate issue to the financial system, both once assumed to be relatively stable, or at least slow to change. Now they were thrown into increasingly violent patterns in which one element threatens to destabilize the next. By streaming online news feeds, *Cyclone.Soc* became a lively barometer of the public mood, or a "landscape of feeling," as Tom Corby described this work to me in a 2008 interview. The graphic text acts "as metonyms for different types of cultural and ideological tension." The audience in the gallery could interact with a mouse to zoom in on parts of the streaming text and scroll around the black-and-white graphic atmospheric patterns.

As noted in chapter 3, information visualization is a political, regulatory tool in online networks for managing complex streams of data through design and digital cartography. The pairing of topical, emotive data sets and isobar lines forges a link between the physical world and the financial systems that has cycles of growth and recession, like the intensification of weather fronts. The 2006 version of *Cyclone.Soc* combined intense debates between extremist religious and political groups in the United States with the isobar lines of the cyclones at the height of the war on terror. The visualization makes tangible growing fears about the personal impacts of the crisis, together with the patterns of a severe storm that shape the superstructure of the immediate human catastrophe.

Cyclone.Soc makes the connectedness of the global financial and ecological systems apparent. The work signals that we should pay attention to the energy spend of the earth's resources and the functioning of banks and the stock market system simultaneously. We have become proficient at describing human behavior (in relation to fossil fuel consumption) in terms of carbon credits, debits, and losses. Ross notes that the language of financial markets became increasingly translated into environmental discourse in the early 1990s. He tracks an emergent "eco-mercantilism" in the new logic of planetary management that applies to climate and capital alike (Ross 1991, 207). If global warming is positioned as a potential threat to our economic livelihood, then self-interest may prevail among business leaders and governments. Corby and Baily's concern with the current politics of the financial crisis and the war on terror operates at an ontic register. A social atmosphere is created in which audiences can discern patterns in the ebbs and flows of global opinion. Mouffe argues that the concerns of the majority often fail to be captured through conventional political means, *Cyclone.Soc* however, offers a place for the expression of political passions freely.

On the capacity for *Cyclone.Soc* to produce connections, Corby states, "By translating data into pictures, with IV (information visualization) we aim to capitalize on humans' natural ability to spot patterns and relationships in visual fields" (Corby 2008, 461). In advanced computing, such as the computing used to model climate, millions of generative calculations form the background to a prediction. A new phase of "qualculation" that involves using data to make qualitative human judgments is emerging. According to Nigel Thrift, "It is no longer possible to think of calculation as necessarily being precise" (2008, 90). A shift is afoot from quantitative calculation methods, such as listing, numbering, and counting, to the excessive possibilities of the calculative, via which we must make qualitative judgments about information and work with ambiguity. Corby and Baily exploit and extract this ambiguity within information visualization in *Cyclone.Soc*. In the *Data Landscapes* series (2011–2015), in collaboration with the British Antarctic Survey, Corby and Baily further developed data representations and animations of Arctic sea ice loss. These works continue to create an affective

Figure 5.5
Francis Alÿs (in collaboration with Julien Devaux). *Tornado*. 2000–2010. Single-channel video pro-jection, 39 minutes, color, 5.1 surround sound. © Francis Alÿs. Image courtesy of David Zwirner, New York/London. [See color plate 11]

atmosphere with data patterns, bearing out Edwards's (2010) observations in the sci-entific sphere that without models, there is in fact no available data; it has become impossible to see the whole.

From the societal flux of the financial crisis in *Cyclone.Soc*, I turn briefly to the social upheaval reflected in the Belgian artist (and resident of Mexico) Francis Alÿs's prac-tice of storm chasing. The video *Tornado* (2000–2010) documents the artist's personal recordings over a decade during which he would read the signs of storm over Mexican plateaus such as Milpa Alta, patiently waiting for the onset of the storm, then plunge into it on foot carrying his camera. The work, first exhibited in 2010, is composed of fragments of dust-storm chases over a long duration and is presented as a large-scale video (fifty-five minutes long). *Tornado* is an immersive experience in which the audi-ence inhabits the perspective of the artist deep in the heart of the storm. Like storm-chasers ourselves, we whirl with the vortex of golden dust. Alÿs's sensorial action in *Tornado* is described by Adrian Searle (2010) as follows: "The artist pants across the dry earth with his handheld camera and steps right into the thunderous sizzle and roar, the no-visibility brown-out. Inside the vortex there is a sudden momentary stillness, as he stands in a column of dead air, before being pelted once again by the infernal dust."

The periods of calm within the storm have been likened to periods of social stability in Mexico, and the barrages of the yellow dust storm (see color plate 11) are analogues for surges of political turbulence. The video expresses the sublime terror of an unfurling tempest, yet Alÿs had to carefully attune to the meteorological conditions that were favorable to the development of tornado phenomena to prepare for the filmmaking. He attempts to make aesthetic sense of the randomness that generates the higher order in a tornado in meteorological terms. Alÿs himself describes the structure of the experience he was trying to capture in the video installation: "It took me years to figure out what I was looking for … At the end I realized I was looking for order within disorder. Paradoxically, it takes a lot of order to create a tornado" (Loos 2011). Alÿs's elliptical politics emerge somewhere in the chaos and paradoxical stillness of the storm. *Tornado* and *Cyclone.Soc* visually represent the turbulence of weather as an allegory for the social patterns of the bios politikos. *Talking about the Weather* intervenes in political life by collecting opinions on the street.

Talking about the Weather: The Politics of Breath

Australian artists Maria Miranda and Norie Neumark of Out-of-Sync translate media rhetoric and public paranoia surrounding climate change into art material. The motivation for *Talking about the Weather* (2006) was "sheer terror" at the threat of global warming. On the Out-of-Sync blog, participants can donate to the "world's largest breath collection." The artists' aim was to poetically demonstrate the "widespread effect we unwittingly have everyday [sic] on the planet, by collecting breath, both metaphorically via a written blog and by personal encounters with people on the streets" (Out-of-Sync 2007). The 2007 installation at Govett-Brewster Art Gallery in Taranaki included chemist's phials of captured breath, boxes of breath, and installed wall speakers that played the sound of breath from their New Plymouth street recordings with local inhabitants. The artists offer the humorous reassurance that the stored breath will be used eventually to "blow back" global warming, a proposition only a little more farfetched than many current geoengineering strategies to combat climate change technologically, such as giant mirrors or cloud layers (see chapter 8).

Talking about the Weather was motivated by a lack of policy initiative to reduce carbon emission levels despite the pledge of the New Zealand and Australian governments to the Kyoto protocol. The artists turned to the grassroots tactic of asking passersby to participate in their social project. Using a microphone, they collected the sound of participants' exhalations to get them talking. These audio recordings and the wide range of written opinions posted on the *Talking about the Weather* blog expose a polity that is a diverse and incommensurable grouping. In recent art, the modernist tradition of the avant-garde artist as radical outsider has been partially supplanted by the community-binding role of artists as social mediators or facilitators. However, political philosophers such as Mouffe (2005) and Rancière (2010) criticize the postpolitical, cosmopolitan worldview that automatically assumes that consensus democracy and, by extension, political art might be able to forge agreement on global issues. Mouffe opposes the cult of action that is legitimized through a hoped-for consensus, like Adorno's critique of "blind praxis" before her. This social participatory art project acknowledges the conflicts and agonisms that exist within local communities and allows them to be voiced safely.

The political community convened by Out-Of-Sync on the group's blog is full of fractures and hopes, "where political being-together is a being between: between identities, between worlds" (Rancière 1999, 137). But the social participation in the blog forum orchestrated by Out-of-Sync provides only one level of engagement with *Talking about the Weather*. The poetic illogic of a sound recording of a carbon emission posted on a website invites us to consider how we can represent the invisible. The project bemuses with its nonrational appropriation of scientific authority that would claim the climate change space. As Out-of-Sync demonstrates, the very act of exhaling is part of a dense system of interactions that are only partially human, and we cannot control their recursive effects. *Talking about the Weather* suggests that by voicing our concerns about anthropogenic impact on the atmosphere, we can come to grips with our part in the bios.

Adorno's *Negative Dialectics* ([1973] 2004) suggests a method of political encounter with the nonidentical other of breath, or the impacts of carbon dioxide. Climate change is nonidentical, but the climate itself is undergoing a process of being objectified into a coherent sociotechnical problem awaiting a solution. There is an ethical task in grasping for the nonidentical other that displaces the Cartesian subject as sovereign, along with the desire to master nature. The absurdity of capturing carbon emissions by microphone or describing breath on a blog reveals a shift toward "an identification *with* the thing itself—as opposed to an identification *of* the thing itself" (Adorno 2008, 92). The sense of incapacity or ridiculousness in Out-of-Sync's proposition produces generative confusion. We are asked to consider our contribution to the sphere of the uncontrolled and unknown that operates though the wider ecological polity, beyond our individual bodies.

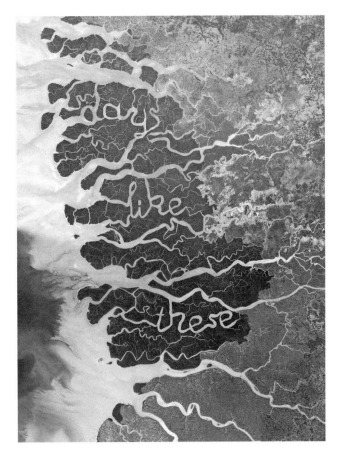

Figure 5.6
Josephine Starrs and Leon Cmielewski. *Incompatible Elements*. 2010. Still from media arts installation. Image courtesy of the artists. [See color plate 12]

Facing Incompatibility

Australian media artists Josephine Starrs and Leon Cmielewski's project *Incompatible Elements* (2010–2011) draws together Māori knowledge of weather, Australian aboriginal proverbs, and the science of remote satellite mapping. The artwork highlights the human displacements caused by violent weather patterns of drought and flood. People in the Southern Hemisphere, particularly in Te Moana nui a Kiwa, are threatened by rising sea levels and intensifying storms, as I will examine more closely in chapter 7. Ecological reasons are frequently cited for migrations, although the term *climate refugee* has been contested. Starrs and Cmielewski direct attention to current and future human climate change migrations through the vistas of the satellite and drone. Both Indigenous citizens and migrants might be considered nonidentical humans—with the Indigenous the people of the land and therefore almost excessively citizen, whereas migrants are not citizen enough. Both occupy a border zone at which the definition of the citizen is becoming less clearly demarcated.

Incompatible Elements was first exhibited at Performance Space in Sydney in 2010. The work consists of slow-moving pans of composited satellite images as floor projections or light boxes of some of the regions that are most affected by climate change—for instance, in the Ganges Delta in Bangladesh, where floods are displacing millions of people. The sandy banks of the Coorong River in South Australia after a period of prolonged drought and the deforested Mount Taranaki in the central North Island of Aotearoa New Zealand are also documented. As the videos unfold, the satellite imagery is incrementally altered by the formation of lines of text from features of the landscape itself. The sources of the animated words derive from various sources. The line "And the River was Dust" that emerges from the Murray-Darling basin is from a poem by Australian environmentalist poet Judith Wright. John Lennon's song lyric "days like these" (from the song "Nobody Told Me") unfurls from the waterways of the Ganges. A phrase from the Ngarrindjeri culture, "a living body," rises out of the dusty banks of the Coorong.

The Māori words "Puwai Rangi Papa" in one projection (2011) translate as "waters of the radiant sun and earth mother," as explained by kaumātua (elder) Te Huirangi Waikerepuru. Te Huirangi introduced this phrase to Starrs and Cmielewski on a hui (public forum) in the Owae marae on the West Coast of New Zealand, where local iwi suggested they make a work about the erosion of Taranaki maunga (mountain). In Māori terms, the mauri of the mountain's iconic physical form is being eroded by the impact of increasingly severe storms that signify the changing climate (IPCC 2014). The soundtrack of the artwork includes the tumbling of stones from the mountain that keeps residents on the edge of Taranaki maunga awake at night.

And the Earth Sighed (2016) is a large-scale floor projection, first exhibited at the Arts House in Melbourne. Footage of fragile Australian desert landscapes is recorded by drone technology, and single words made from rivers or rocks rise from the earth's surface. The crafted digital postproduction again integrates the words into the very material of the mediated earth. We climb steep stairs to a high platform and look down on the land and waterscapes from an Archimedean perspective, yet the words emerging from the land and water locate us firmly as part of this media-nature-cultural encounter. The artists build their politics into the spectacular visuality of the weather's devastating

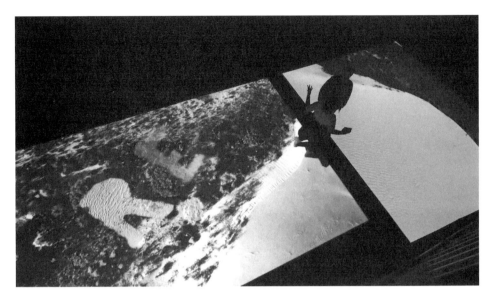

Figure 5.7
Josephine Starrs and Leon Cmielewski. *And the Earth Sighed*. 2016. Installation view at Arts House Melbourne. Image courtesy of the artists.

effects, to which we might otherwise become inured. To work across cultures signals a necessary shift from viewing a landscape or weatherscape as inert matter and toward the "living bodies" encompassed in Ngarrindjeri or Māori cultures. Social meteorological encounters are forged by providing philosophical openings to Indigenous systems of value and possible reconciliation. Artworks mark a moment in time as we move toward a reconfigured political ecology—a sometimes-contradictory ecology in which the seemingly incompatible systems of environmentalism and Indigenous knowing must equally shoulder responsibility for care of the earth and atmosphere.

Socially orientated meteorological art provides momentum for both reflection and political action by convening different publics. There is often a clash of values between the weather knowledge that exists in social news groups or in Indigenous cosmologies and the designation of climate change as a particular kind of technoscientific, economic object. The prevailing climate discourse enshrines instrumental, rationalist values in the service of capitalist production as arbiters of how we should best live. For Adorno, the profit motive that divides society and "potentially tears it apart" is also the factor by which society reproduces its own existence (2008, 9). This is the immanent contradiction from which many antagonisms emerge within society. The artworks considered here reflect such quandaries and produce different narratives, or real survival strategies in the case of the solar-powered generator of theweathergroup_U. Cumulatively, the works in this chapter present an alter position to recognized authorities, often using online networks to conjoin disparate communities. Rather than acting as politicians, the artists considered here facilitate alternative forums for political expression. Art can probe the paradoxes without which there would be no change, in us or in the wider political world.

To return to *The Weather Project* with a hermeneutic approach, the artwork has an overwhelming sensuous effect, but at the same time aesthetic beauty can also impinge on how we make meaning. In the process of watching, hearing, moving, or lying still, we can experience a sense of the nonidentical other that is never fully revealed. Robertson creates sublime weatherscapes, yet hovering over or through them is an unseen layer of environmental degradation that undermines the mauri of the ancestor-river Waiapu. Indigenous relations to weather coexist with normative mainstream culture, but not without conflicts. Productive interphylum and intercultural exchange appears possible in Starrs and Cmielewski's fusions of remote satellite imaging and poetry, even if the work's title, *Incompatible Elements*, suggests this will be difficult work. Those who are left out of democracy are the nonhuman and the faceless uncounted, the noncitizens, the unquantifiable people, the refugees. The task of distributing political value more generously requires attention to the disenfranchised humans and the nonhuman.

Such art projects are necessary critiques of postindustrial systems of value, using aesthetic means to highlight ecological tensions. In comparison to the social weather knowledge argued for here, scientific knowledge often is held up as unmarked and universal, but on closer analysis many so-called global visions are the product of regional circumstances. Through the detection of Adorno's ungraspable, nonidentical other in art, we might find that our representational schemas are not all-determining and coherent. The climate issue generates different patterns of emotions, sympathies, and disagreements, as Latour has argued: "There might be no continuity, no coherence in our opinions, but there is a hidden continuity and a hidden coherence in what we are attached to" (2004a, 15). Meteorological artworks reveal our implicit and explicit attachments to "things" such as cyclones, financial markets, CO_2, airborne dioxins, ancestor maunga, biospheres, and satellites or drones, and, to follow Puig de la Bellacasa (2017), these are things to care for.

The task of democratic politics is not to overcome difference or we/they conflicts through consensus, as Mouffe (2005) argues, but to reconstruct and energize the public forums in which debate can occur. The artworks considered in this chapter work around conventional politics or operate outside state political institutions. Corby and Baily data-mine real political opinions from newsfeeds so that we intuitively feel their ebbs and flows. The Out-of-Sync collective polls opinions and records them on a blog site—the kind of survey of social temperature that seldom concerns governments. These artworks create a vibrant public sphere of contestation, or equally a shared commitment, among online participants, gallery audiences, or the willing who plant sedges to purify the water for *inanga* along riverbanks, in the case of Robertson's *He Wai Mou! He Wai Mau!* (2017). In the next chapter, the public discourse of climate change as mediated through scientific language—in particular, that of the IPCC—is examined as art inquiry.

6   Climate Dialogues: Acts into Nature

To act into nature, to carry human unpredictability into a realm where we are confronted with elemental forces which we shall perhaps never be able to control reliably, is dangerous enough. Even more dangerous would it be to ignore that for the first time in our history the human capacity for action has begun to dominate all others—the capacity for wonder and thought in contemplation no less than the capacities of *homo faber* and the human *animal labo-rans*. (Arendt 2006, 62)

Arendt wrote the preceding lines in the context of Cold War nuclear proliferation. Now, with the rise of new weather, there is a renewed call to examine our "acts into nature." The paramount danger of the actions of *homo faber*, the tool maker, is the unpredictability that is built into the human condition. For *homo faber*, "the end justifies the violence done to nature to win the material, as the wood justifies killing the tree and the table justifies destroying the wood" (Arendt 1958, 153). Our more aggressive dealings with the environment start "man-made natural processes" of our own, which Arendt pinpoints at the splitting of the atom. Such acts "increase our power over nature to destructive effect" (Arendt 2006, 60). Chapters 6, 7, and 8 deal with meteorological art in a warming climate, an ongoing natural process that we have accelerated, rather than the instantly destructive effect of the nuclear bomb seen in Arendt's time. Contemporary artists who act on the climate issue probe our internal political conflicts, but they also return us to the ethical question of care examined in the previous chapter. To maintain climate change on the political agenda calls for creative strategies that inspire a capacity for wonder, thought, and action to stave off despair.

This chapter concerns artworks that produce dialogue through material artifacts and concepts in light of the obstinate fact of climate warming—the developed world's collective creation. Against climate deniers, dithering politicians, and multinational industries backpeddling on mitigation strategies, artists work to generate change in social and political systems, often together with scientists. Amy Howden-Chapman, Amy Balkin, Layne Waerea, the *Dear Climate* collective, and Mark Harvey, part of the

Maldives Exodus project, negotiate both a *committed* mode of art (Adorno's term) and a poetic or playful engagement with politics, particularly the language of climate discourse. To make artwork about climate change today, artists must find ways through climate-fact fatigue, to imaginatively redirect obvious ways of consciousness raising.

For *homo faber*, or Haraway's (2015) "fossil-fuel-burning humanity," the imperative for growth continues to exacerbate the climate crisis while the wheels of industry furiously turn. Physical testimony about the exhaustion of resources, extinction events, air pollution, and the devastation of extractivism lives not only in Indigenous knowledge systems but also within two hundred years of European environmentalism. Yet a failure of political memory still allows the living to neglect the fate of the human and nonhuman inheritors of this planet. In collaborative art actions, there is hope: history tells us that because of the *initium* of people as "acting beings," the more "heavily the scales are weighted in favor of disaster," the more vigorous creative actions will be in response (Arendt 2006, 169). Artists, I believe, are in a position to unravel paradoxes, hopes and fears, and speculative possibilities for the future, often by focusing on situated details.

Amy Howden-Chapman's performance work *Uncertainty Italicized* (2013–2014) and Amy Balkin's *Reading the IPCC Fourth Assessment Report on Climate Change* (2009) dwell on the collaborative findings of the Intergovernmental Panel on Climate Change (IPCC). Both art projects experiment with events that navigate the weight of information in the IPCC documents for the layperson. For artists, in direct or mediated collaboration with scientists or scientific information, the artwork is more than a public-relations exercise to promote or illustrate climate science. Balkin and Howden-Chapman produce and reveal the creative-social patterns that exist within scientific activities and language. Scientific enquiries often are framed by complex quantitative language, whereas meteorological art can suggest patterns, or feel through difficult issues. In his writing on the information dynamics of climate, Paul N. Edwards (2010) argues, "In a knowledge-production process that involves continuous contestation, you are never going to get a single universal data image, or a single uniformly agreed-upon projection. Instead you will get shimmering data, shimmering futures, and convergence rather than certainty" (Edwards 2010, 398). The projects in this chapter operate at this shimmering edge of the mirage of data, often by taking specific actions or creating affective situations.

Artist Søren Dahlgaard's peripatetic caravan, the *Maldives Exodus* project, confronts political apathy, condemnation, and inertia toward those made economically and politically vulnerable by climate change. Aotearoa New Zealand artist Mark Harvey's *Political Climate Wrestle* is a performance-based contribution to the *Maldives Exodus* art platform on which I will focus. Like Balkin and Howden-Chapman, Harvey creates an opportunity for debate about climate change through a playful invitation to wrestle with the artist himself in public space. Harvey probes the human problem that Adorno describes as "manic fixity"—or, in this case, a solidifying of social-ecological injustices into "laws of nature" (2002, 71). Through a one-on-one, head-on, yet humorous confrontation in the form of a wrestle, positive change becomes thinkable. *Dear Climate*, a collective including Marina Zurkow, Una Chaudhuri, Oliver Kellhammer, Fritz Ertl, and Sarah Rothberg, invites the gentler act of writing a letter to the climate, taking cues from the tradition of activist campaign. These artists challenge seemingly immutable societal laws of consumption and the destructive effects of the "law of progress" at the expense of our shared ecology.

Scientists measure and track climate trends, but mitigating actions are needed from all of us, in coalitions of activists, professionals, the media, the arts community, citizens, and noncitizen and Indigenous groups: whoever we can muster. Howden-Chapman and curator Abby Cunnane's *The Distance Plan* journal is a collective platform to both work constructively within creative communities and to reach out to invested communities beyond the art world. A language of crisis and catastrophe, with accompanying tactics of shock and melancholy, are affects that are produced often in "climate art." Timothy Morton's well-circulated description of climate change as a "hyperobject" (2013) captures this constructed, inflated dimension. The focus here instead is on participatory art strategies to stimulate critical thought, aesthetic sensitivity, and humor in light of the complex assemblage that is climate change.

Committed Art: Adorno and Arendt

I turn to critical philosophers Adorno and Arendt in this chapter to position *homo faber* not only as the prime carrier of the debt for destructive "acts into nature" but also as the species capable of correcting this imbalance. Both Arendt and Adorno observe humanity's dangerous exploitation of the natural world through the lens of history. Arendt's recognition that in the modern world we "make nature" as we used to "make history" (2006, 58) never seemed more prescient than today. On the one hand, neoliberal economies toy with *intended* decarbonization to mitigate climate change without relinquishing the freedom to profit from the earth's resources. On the other, drought and storms rage in the "tropic of chaos," converging with poverty and struggles over scarce resources, often resulting in human conflict (Parenti 2011). During COP21, Bangladesh, alongside other countries that undercontribute to global warming, called for deep emission reductions from developed nations to address an out-of-balance historical climate debt and high per capita emissions. The call went largely ignored.

The Paris agreement made during COP21 was a quasi decision that only goes part-way toward addressing the mammoth task we face in reducing emissions (Latour 2016). The aspiration to keep temperatures below two degrees was thwarted by the current emissions targets submitted by participating countries, which are predicted to cause a dangerous rise of at least three degrees. This points to the disturbing fact that the dominant political regimes have not yet learned from past environmental injustice; in Arendt's words, remembrance is one of the most important "modes of thought", yet there is "no mind to inherit and to question, to think about and to remember" (2006, 6–7). Although all entities human and nonhuman have equal agency insofar as they act on other entities, we humans are the preeminent species to have accelerated global warming. The irrefutable fact of climate change due to anthropogenic forcing remains our legacy for future generations.

Artists faced with the climate issue confront Adorno's perennial question—"What is to be done?"—in times of political crisis. The answer, Adorno says, should not be an automatic reflex before the political thought is fully comprehended, nor should it emerge from a "blind praxis" (2005, 276). We feel our way through the current situation of political inertia. Despite what we know from the IPCC reports and media coverage, and the real experience of severe weathers that are the effects of the changing climate, many politicians, industrialists, and citizens engaged in their immediate daily life would rather forget about climate change for the short term. Stengers addresses "all of us who are living in suspense" by acknowledging that there is a "quasi-stupefying contrast—between what we know and what mobilizes us" (2015, 22–23). We know we ought to do something, and only a small push might be necessary to join the growing tide of people who are prepared to work out what that something is. The scientific community's attempt to spur government action by rendering data transparent through reports, policy guidelines, and visualization processes is not producing the necessary changes in politicians. Therefore, the artist's task is not so much consciousness raising as it is signaling to "others out there" that they are part of a community of concern and willing to keep the climate issue in the foreground. Art, I will argue in this chapter, finds ways to do this through inventive material, language-based, and performance practices.

In the essay "Commitment" ([1977] 2007), Adorno cites the long-running controversy between "committed art" and "autonomous art," which he believes are at odds with each other, mustering Sartre and Brecht's plays to his argument. Socially committed art can run the risk of functionalizing art as a mouthpiece of science or institutional politics; on the other hand, artists who avoid political content altogether abdicate their responsibilities as political citizens. He writes, "A work of art that is committed strips the magic from a work of art that is content to be a fetish, an idle pastime for those who would like to sleep through the deluge that threatens them, in an apoliticism that is in fact deeply political" (Adorno [1977] 2007, 177). Autonomous works of art, or "art for art's sake," is a "spiritual catastrophe" in Adorno's eyes. He is equally cautious about conspicuously political artworks, on the other hand, in which "for the sake of political commitment, political reality is trivialized." The danger is a reduction of the political effect ([1977] 2007, 184–185). Taking these pitfalls on board, artworks that attend to the issue of climate change directly run the risk of becoming didactic or unsubtle expositions. Yet, for the climate activist, conceptual art strategies may seem inadequate for the urgent task of social change.

I argue, nonetheless, that when artists use creative strategies such as playfulness, inference, or evocations of the atmospheric conditions that envelop us, art is working politically. As I work through the perennial question of the political value of art, Arendt's view that *we cannot act in isolation* is vital. Adorno observes how the "bourgeois coldness" of social and ecological inequity has become accepted as a "law of nature" (2005, 274). Yet, against all odds, Adorno and Arendt go on searching for a better political future after the trauma of the holocaust. Many artists today also foster attentiveness to others, both human and nonhuman, beyond our immediate, individual demands by offering alter experiences to media or scientific reporting of climate affairs.

Practicing Collaborative Language

Art publications and events are critical platforms to resist the neoliberal drive for progress—less as reactive dealings with the ecological "crisis" than through the forging of sustainable relations over a longer period. For Amy Howden-Chapman (Aotearoa New Zealand; United States), performance events, installations, videos, and printed publications are means to engage with the language of climate politics. The Distance Plan Press (which produces a journal, among other publications) is curator Abby Cunnane (New Zealand) and Howden-Chapman's publication platform. *The Distance Plan* journal was launched in Wellington, New Zealand, in 2010, as a connective forum for people engaged with climate politics from infrequently crossed discipline boundaries. Essays, page works, and interviews are invited from a diverse range of contributors, including urban planners, environmental researchers, pedagogues, migration lawyers, indigenous activists, and artists, all to try to "figure out what art can do" to counter the numbing effects of the climate crisis. By connecting artists to other fields of knowledge, *The Distance Plan* tests "what specific ways art, as a field of practice, can contribute to addressing the problem of climate change, and what can be achieved through 'companionship' with those in other disciplinary fields" (Cunnane 2016). Communities of care are sustained in the journal by returning to a core group of artists as their work evolves over time.

Cunnane describes the journal as "a working model of a way of worrying at a problem together" by practicing the often-complex languages of science and other areas of discipline expertise in an art context. *The Distance Plan* orients itself away from the academic elitism of much climate discourse and toward the everyday. Often, Cunnane suggests, climate change art obscures the intersections between environmental well-being and social justice for vulnerable communities. Instead, Cunnane and Howden-Chapman ask what climate change means for everyday life and socialize these ideas through exhibitions and the online readership of *The Distance Plan*. For Cunnane, the publicness of the platform invites a collective processing of what is possible and what can be voiced on the climate issue in a socially accountable form.

To use art's capacity to speak "immediately of the immediate" (Adorno 2002, 15), Cunnane and Howden-Chapman have developed a lexicon that connects climate warming to governance, the refugee crisis, materialist feminisms, the impact of technologies, and financialization of life-worlds; this lexicon is intended to operate alongside the specific language of environmental scientists. *Art & Climate Change: A Lexicon* brings together a broad range of invited writers to generate new or recognize existing terms and to provide descriptions as a focusing device to understand the climate crisis. Terminology in the lexicon ranges from brute force infrastructure, citizen science, deniholism, climate debt, climate hostage, and precautionary principle to social tipping points, among others. In the editorial for the 2016 issue of *The Distance Plan*, containing *Art & Climate Change: A Lexicon*, Cunnane and Howden-Chapman write: "Through proposing neologisms and promoting less well-known terms, we wish to propel interdisciplinary discussion, and by extension accelerate the pace of action. Through this lexicon we propose that the science around climate change is developing so rapidly that we need new language to articulate its processes and effects. The lexicon is also based on the recognition that evolving science produces evolving policy, and politics must be commensurate with this" (Cunnane and Howden-Chapman 2016). Artwork is a means to punctuate indifference and silence by galvanizing the imagination, in service of the political statement that "climate change is now" (Howden-Chapman 2016). Joint publication is a key mechanism to put collaborative language into action.

Howden-Chapman suggests that the onus on artists is not to solve the problems of climate change alone, but to imagine things differently by bringing social narratives to bear on ecological problem-solving. *All the News I Read about Climate Change in 2014* (2015) is a printed publication published by Distance Plan Press that encapsulates Howden-Chapman's research-based art practice. In a thick, black ring binder, a

Figure 6.1
Amy Howden-Chapman. *All the News I Read about Climate Change in 2014*. 2015. Artist book. Image courtesy of the artist.

vast number of newspaper clippings are cut from the papers and arranged in pointed juxtaposition. The IPCC committee summarizes all published scientific literature on climatology and related issues in biology, hydrology, and oceanography based on peer-reviewed research, Howden-Chapman, on the other hand, collects climate-related clippings on a smaller, domestic scale, from a vast array of journalistic news sources. This potted newspaper collection, however, reveals some societal trends: for instance, an increase in lifestyle articles that report on the economic impacts of climate change, such as ski areas closing or the problems retailers have selling winter clothes. The absurdist task of keeping abreast of the overwhelming number of reports evidences one citizen's full-time attempt to process the realness of climate change, producing a sense of futility that many of us will recognize. Howden-Chapman operates through an (almost) obsessive level of research into the projects she launches, a relentless search for patterns in the language of the public debate around climate change.

In the performance *Uncertainty Italicized* (2013–2014), Howden-Chapman responds to the cautious use of a scale of "likelihood" in the predictions made and conclusions

Figure 6.2
Amy Howden-Chapman. *Uncertainty Italicized.* 2013–2014. Performance image at 2201 Gallery, Los Angeles, 2013. Image courtesy of the artist. [See color plate 13]

drawn by the IPCC reports' scientific contributors. *Uncertainty Italicized* was first performed at 2201 Gallery, Los Angeles, and then again in 2014 at YNKB Artspace, Copenhagen, Denmark. The piece is based on the Intergovernmental Panel on Climate Change's guidance note (released in 2013) asking scientific contributors to the fifth assessment report to maintain consistency by adhering to a "likelihood scale." The performers in this event are Howden-Chapman's friends, performance artists and actresses, and people roped in—in a mobilization of her immediate community around a shared matter of concern. In the prologue to the piece, Howden-Chapman is in the spotlight, dancing to fast Spanish music. At first, she dances in a state of apparent abandon, perhaps in a last dance of freedom in the carbon-fueled economy. Then, as the intense orb-like spotlight grows larger, she begins running on the spot more anxiously, even desperately, running as if there is an internal conflict that she can't escape from. She tries to run both backward and forward simultaneously, trapped; the movements are an attempt to "embody" the unknown atmospheric future. She comes to rest and reads aloud from a piece of paper, at which point the tone of the performance changes, becoming more sober. "Uncertainty exists so that it is possible to see certainty, that is, alternatives" is the last line Howden-Chapman reads.

Following the prologue, seven performers enter, dressed in pastel shades, and stand in two rows, one on each side of the room. The spotlight glints off glass panes they each hold up and momentarily blinds the audience. A male voice reads out a measure of certainty, taken from the likelihood scale of the IPCC guidance notes. Each time the narrator reads a scientific fact, using a qualified term to indicate the level of scientific agreement, one of the seven performers steps forward, holding a pane of colored glass aloft that is etched with the same word or phrase. The precarious nature of ornamental glass, etched with melted metals, lets light through yet may shatter; the soft pinks and blues of the glass suggest the fragile results of a litmus test. The narrator announces each performer by name. The following is an excerpt from the script:

It is Mireya: *Very likely* that there has been an overall decrease in the number of cold days and nights and an overall increase in the number of warm days and nights.

It is Scott: *Likely* that anthropogenic influences have led to warming of extreme daily minimum and maximum temperatures at the global scale.

It is Scott: *Likely* that there has been an increase in coastal high water related to increases in mean sea level.

It is Scott: *Likely* that anthropogenic influences on increasing coastal high water due to an increase in mean sea level.

It is Sarah: *Virtually certain* increases in the frequency of warm daily temperature extremes and decreases in cold extremes will occur in the twenty first century at the global scale.

It is Tyler: *Exceptionally unlikely* that the global pattern of warming can be explained without external forcing. That is human action.

It is Gracie: *Unlikely* that emission growth rates will be significantly moderated during the coming decades.

The pragmatic descriptiveness of the qualified scientific language somehow intensifies into an affective cry as the layers of text mount up. To conclude the performance, each performer lines up silently in turn, holding the glass sheets high once more. In silence, the performers take one step forward, then take one step backward, and then file out of the room. Victoria Wynne-Jones likens the performers' collective movement to "a colourful human wave, an ebb and flow of certitude" (Wynne-Jones 2013, 3), whereas I feel as if I have witnessed a sensory, ritualized form of protest.

In the likelihood scale of the IPCC, the italics leap out as recurrent notes of caution in the scientific findings. Howden-Chapman explores the complex attempt to quantify greatly differing opinions by using qualifiers. The Fifth IPCC Summary for Policymakers states that a level of confidence is expressed using qualifiers: very low, low, medium, high, and very high, and it notes that "assessed likelihood should be typeset in italics, e.g., *very likely*." Howden-Chapman's script mirrors this language for assessing the likelihood of an outcome on a scale extending from "virtually certain 99–100% probability" all the way down to "exceptionally unlikely 0–1%" (IPCC 2014). The Fifth IPCC Summary also acknowledges a human lack of motivation, in many cases derived from a lack of agency, which means we are slow to act: "Inertia in many aspects of the socio-economic system constrains adaptation and mitigation options (*medium evidence, high agreement*). Innovation and investments in environmentally sound infrastructure and technologies can reduce GHG emissions and enhance resilience to climate change (*very high confidence*). {4.1}" (ibid.). These observations reveal the social dimensions of climate change that the IPCC contributors are beginning to consider. Such statements, we might note, also have high agreement outside of the scientific community, where art performs the distribution of complex information through the senses.

Howden-Chapman describes *Uncertainty Italicized* as an attempt to "embody uncertainty" through patterns of color, language, and movement. The work is part of an ongoing investigation of human decision-making—specifically, how a series of smaller choices leads to larger, collective decisions (Howden-Chapman 2016). Howden-Chapman has a keen sense for the ways in which language becomes more or less flexible in different cultural spheres and how such flexibility is signaled and controlled. A secondary processing of language takes place in scientific writing that is obtuse to those outside the world of science and policymaking. The omniscience of the hundreds of scientific voices and the now-hidden processes of evaluation of underlying evidence and agreement behind the IPCC report are countered by the naming of specific participants in *Uncertainty Italicized*. To make complex information easier to understand, each statement read is associated with a real person and with visual clues of color (Wynne-Jones 2013). Each performer's character or a color (of the glass, the costumes) can help us hold information about a likelihood that we may not be able to mentally process in the details of the IPCC document.

Voices, gestures, and signs are special forms of praxis in the *bios politikos* that sustain the political function of the polis (Arendt 1958, 13); such events draw a community together to collectively absorb the implications of scientific findings. *Uncertainty Italicized* also acts like an artist's bulletin, interpreting the IPCC reports from a tangent to work through these foundational documents of our time. Howden-Chapman's willingness to "linger with the particular"—in this case, the humble italic—has an affinity with Adorno's strategy to combat brutality, whether in language or the ecosystem with particular detail. His last hope for thought is a gaze that is "averted from the beaten track," from which fresh concepts might surface, "not yet encompassed by the general pattern" (Adorno [1951] 2002, 67–68). In art as well, this indirect gaze might find a means to communicate otherwise.

Nonhuman Rights

The art practices in this chapter can be located along a spectrum of tactics from direct and unmodified communication of science fact to a more abstract or conceptual engagement. At one end, we might place the theater piece *2071*, directed by Katie Mitchell; at the other, Layne Waerea's *Free Social Injunctions*, which speculates on cultural understandings of fog and air. *2071*, a theater performance at the Royal Court in London, consisted of a monologue from climate scientist Chris Rapley, cowritten with dramaturg Duncan Macmillan, that focuses on the link between fossil fuels and climate change. The climate scientist's own words, subtly crafted by the screenplay writer, carry the weight of the performance. The *Guardian* gave *2071* a five-star review and rated it as a "compelling" vehicle calling for urgent collective action through the calm and factual delivery of a scientist seated centrally on the stage (Billington 2014).

The mere presence of a scientist, firmly ensconced within the cultural sphere, had a sobering and even a politicizing effect among the theatergoers. For performance theorist Peta Tait (2016), this work raised the following problem: When there are so many means for the arts to communicate about climate change beyond merely giving information, what else can performance do? On the other hand, the simple displacement of a scientist into a theater appears to connect a new audience to climate politics. The voice of a scientist, responsible for the "real" analysis of our physical world yet placed in a cultural forum, invites different stakeholders to invest in climate-mitigating action. Adorno's politics encourages reflection from within practical action: "Thinking has a double character: it is immanently determined and rigorous, and yet an inalienably real mode of behavior in the midst of reality" (Adorno [1969] 2005, 261). We are brought head on into an encounter with climate science from which we cannot easily walk out or switch off in the theater context.

American artist Amy Balkin's video *Reading the IPCC Synthesis Report: Summary for Policymakers* (2008) is also a direct conduit for scientific findings reframed within a nonscientific art context. The video work was shot in one continuous take; with a clear pedagogical intent, the artist carefully enunciates each sentence with appropriate gravity to the IPCC document. Like political philosopher Noam Chomsky in artist Cornelia Parker's video *Chomskian Abstract* (2007), Balkin is spotlighted against a studio-black background. The looped video (38 minutes, 53 seconds) is a direct appeal to both the public and government policymakers. In a second, participatory version of this work, *Reading the IPCC Fourth Assessment Report on Climate Change* (2009), over fifty volunteer readers took part in a three-day attempt to read the entire eight hundred pages of the third volume of the Fourth IPCC Assessment Report in Manchester, during the Futuresonic festival in 2009. The facticity of scientific language and the sheer volume of climate change evidence are encountered in a durational public event. Balkin writes that this performance attempts to "make these documents more public through a participatory public reading" (Demos 2013b, 11). Balkin's belief in the value of publicness resonates with Arendt's observation that "the presence of others who see what we see and hear what we hear assures us of the reality of the world" (1958, 57)—in this case, of the reality of the IPCC document that is collectively spoken.

In Balkin's earlier project, *Public Smog* (2004–present), the artist provocatively proposes to make the atmosphere a protected UNESCO World Heritage Site. In her contribution to *dOCUMENTA (13)*, Balkin assembled approximately fifty thousand signed postcards and sent them to Germany's minister of the environment, Peter Altmaier, requesting that Germany lead a coalition to lobby for the earth's atmosphere to be included in the UNESCO list. Although the German ministry declined to take this proposition forward, the project has gained recognition as art in the form of real-world policy-making. Balkin invited countries all over the world to lead this coalition to lobby UNESCO. In general, governments have not responded to Balkin's serious proposition. However, Dr. Ana Maui Taufe'ulungaki, the minister for education and women's affairs and culture from the Kingdom of Tonga, responded positively to Balkin's move to protect the atmosphere. In 2009, Taufe'ulungaki presented her research on the "Safe-Guarding of Intangible Cultural Heritage" to her government. Unfortunately, however, she was prevented by budget restraints from leading the campaign on behalf of her small island (Demos 2013b, 13). The attribution of value to the atmosphere is easily dismissed in a Euro-American context but is part a foundational tenet of many Indigenous cosmologies, as I explore further in Layne Waerea's work ahead.

In light of general governmental reluctance to address climate change, T. J. Demos argues that disruptive artworks like Balkin's can offer quasi-legal alternatives, or what he calls "experimental jurisprudence," to spur "new, if as yet unrealised, possibilities for intervening positively in the way human governance systems define, use, and protect the environment" (Demos 2013b, 11). Such artworks make our common atmosphere tangible as an entity. To paraphrase Arendt, we enter the earth's atmosphere when we are born and leave it behind when we die (1958, 55). The atmosphere transcends our individual lifespans, yet the conceptual shift toward its preservation is very hard for

Figure 6.3
Layne Waerea. *Bruce Pulman Park, Papakura, 2014*. 2014. Part of *Chasing Fog Club* (est. 2014). Image courtesy of the artist. [See color plate 14]

Euro-American governments to make. A sense of the long temporality of environmental custodianship, central to Indigenous systems such as Māori kaitiakitanga, is barely conceivable in dominant modern cultures' *now-focused* mode of operation.

Artist Layne Waerea's *Chasing Fog Club* (2013–present) is a parallel case of "experimental jurisprudence" in action, in Aotearoa New Zealand. Waerea's *Chasing Fog Club* is an online platform via which participants are invited to post videos of their fog-chasing activities across property boundaries. Participants chase elusive fog vapors across farms, parks, or the lands of their neighbors, flouting trespass laws. In return for video documentation of their transgressions of social and legal mores in the act of chasing fog, participants receive a free t-shirt and can join the club. Waerea herself engages in a fog chase across a field near her home in the video *Bruce Pulman Park, Papakura, 2014* (2014). In Mātauranga Māori cosmology, fog has *wairua* (spirit), as a manifestation of ancestors' tears.

Trained as a lawyer, Waerea locates her performance practice in public squares or online forums. Through the tactical deployment of brief humorous performance moments, she interrupts social and legal norms of public behavior. In her *Free Instructional Video: How to Catch Air* (2014), as part of her *Free Social Injunctions* series (2012–present), Waerea offers participants the chance to catch free air via an untethered large-scale plastic bag in a public plaza in central Auckland. Air freely enters into and escapes out of the open-ended shape. The art interventions, positioned here in the context of atmospheric politics, comically contravene the state policing of boundaries over air and water. Waerea playfully references Māori rights to determine how natural resources are shared, and implicitly challenges the individual, rather than communal property rights over common resources created in (neo)colonial legal systems. Our founding document, the *Treaty of Waitangi*, signed by many Māori iwi and the British Crown in 1840, was subsequently contravened by Pākehā mass settlement and sovereignty wars in the 1860s, leading to Māori land confiscation by the Crown. Her work points to specific legal claims, such as the Wai 262 claim (2011) brought before Aotearoa's Waitangi Tribunal, which targeted amendments to New Zealand laws by proposing Māori sovereignty rights over language, resource management (including air space and water), wildlife, conservation, cultural artifacts and art forms, environmental protection, patents, and plant varieties. Prior to this claim, the Waitangi tribunal largely had dealt with claims concerning the return of or compensation for illegally confiscated Māori land.

In an unprecedented development in 2017, a major river in the North Island, the Whanganui, has been deemed a legal entity in itself, owned neither by the government nor by Māori, in accordance with the wishes of the Whanganui iwi (Davison 2017). In other words, a nonhuman entity has been recognized as having the legal rights of a person in this important legal decision. The specific politics in Aotearoa New Zealand made it conceivable for a nonhuman entity to gain this legal status, yet perhaps this decision brings Balkin's proposal for the entire atmosphere one step closer. The collision of worldviews from the legal to the spiritual in Waerea's artwork returns us to Arendt's reflection that, despite our vast differences in perspective, we can gather around a common object such as atmosphere. The end of the common world comes, according to Arendt, "when it is seen only under one aspect and is permitted to present itself in only one perspective" (1958, 58).

Befriending Climate Change

Dear Climate is an online platform for design activism, formed by a group of artists and environmentalists including Marina Zurkow, Una Chaudhuri, Oliver Kellhammer, Fritz Ertl, and Sarah Rothberg in New York. Their expertise spans permaculture, research theater, ecocritical writing, land art, and design. Rothberg is coeditor of the digital zine called *Smog*. The group advocates for active yet intimate dialogue about climate change through letters, as well as spoken word–based podcasts and posters that visitors are encouraged to download and distribute. *Dear Climate* is described online as "a collection of agitprop posters and meditative audio experiences that help you meet, befriend, and become climate change" (Dear Climate, n.d.). The artists' collective statements assert that climate change needs to be spoken about otherwise: "Now that the weather's changed, is it also time to change the way we talk about it?" (ibid.). They take their starting point from activist formats for launching a campaign, the letter or poster, but the invitation to recognize a nonhuman entity by writing to the climate reorients the usual activist tactics.

Dear Climate invites letters to the climate from us, the public, and the artists also model letters themselves. Their collectively signed letter has the tone of a Dear John confessional: "We know: we blew it. We got distracted, as usual. ... In fact, we never really thought about you. We thought about (and we loved to complain about) The Weather. ... We want to find a way to shift relations—with the spheres, with you, and also with our own uncertain and unruly inner climates." (Dear Climate, n.d.). The intimate language invites us to share the problem of being human: we make mistakes. To make the necessary changes to our patterns of consumption, we do not have to suppress our humanity.

Other than the letters, activist posters are the main form of visual communication on the online platform. The bold typography of the black-and-white agitprop-style posters take cues from nineteenth-century engravings. The posters twist common phrases or clichés so that we both recognize the statements but also, at the same time, are disturbed by their strange modification. For instance, "Don't know ... your place" or "The Sky ... Has Fallen." Or, they work with the form of the joke—for instance, "How many Tsunamis does it take to change a lightbulb?" The tacit acceptance of climate change as the new normal is displaced by the poster reading "Normal ... Isn't" (Dear Climate, n.d.). The group instructs the viewer to freely download and distribute these posters to circulate their ideas widely.

The spoken word podcasts are poetic compositions, rather than direct appropriations of activist tropes. *Make Arrangements* elides the natural and technological, using collective nouns such as a flock of birds, a flight of airplanes, a fleet of trucks, a cluster of bombs, a constellation of stars, and so on. The electronic sound and the recorded sound merge into a reflective space, oriented toward an uncertain future. This work invites speculation on the new networks and collectives that have emerged in the postindustrial world as we make arrangements—perhaps to leave, to escape, or to endure the coming dark days ahead. Another podcast, entitled *The Hydrosphere Incantation*, offers a steady recitation spoken by a male voice and a female voice in turn. A rhythm made of drips and recorded sounds of water forms the beat. The voices recite words connected to water, such as thunder, springs, sources, puddles, brooks, canals, streams, rivers, swamps, marshes, fens, ponds, lakes, creeks, washes, currents, locks, kettles, damns, reservoirs, lagoons, firths, fjords, estuaries, deltas, sounds … glaciers, ice fields, oceans, and so on. The words have a cumulative weight. There is an innocence in evoking the rhythms of words that access recognition patterns deeply embedded in our subconscious. The appeal to the aural sense reconnects our bodies with the weather world and its soundscape.

The *Dear Climate* project includes an element of willful naïveté by inviting letters to the climate. Logically, there is no way we can communicate with climate through human language. The proposition is absurd. Many of the posters actively jab at our anthropocentric tendencies. One slogan reads, "The Climate … Doesn't care about Me," with the jilted hurt of the failed preeminent species, no longer the master over nature. Artist Kayla Anderson (2015) finds that *Dear Climate*'s dark undercurrent, which refuses to submit easy solutions, is a critical mode for furthering our sense of the enormity of the climate crisis. *Dear Climate* has developed a means to continue to speak about climate change in public, without drumming home a message everyone already knows. Adorno warns against uncritical utopianism in art initiatives, arguing instead that platforms that stimulate thinking have the greatest potential to be effective. For Adorno, "The obviousness of disaster becomes an asset to its apologists—what everyone knows, no-one need say—and under cover of silence is allowed to proceed unopposed" ([1951] 2002, 233). Art has the capacity to do something else, to break the silence through words and acts.

The *Dear Climate* sound pieces, letters, and posters operate at an affective level beyond the call to arms of political activism, although activism too is necessary to this struggle. The invitation to "become climate change" is to actively engage with our bodies and our thought processes as modifiers of climate. Unlike *homo faber*, some artists have a capacity for the long view, beyond survivalist, self-interested solutions, to recharge the sensory processes that condition our thinking. For Adorno, "committed art" is not intended to generate ameliorative measures, legislative acts, or practical institutions, like early propagandist plays. Rather, he argues that committed art must "work at the fundamental level of attitudes" ([1977] 2007, 180). The *Dear Climate* project is committed to shifting human attitudes and to connect these to positive behaviors. One poster, for instance, instructs us to "Travel … Mentally," inviting us to enlarge our horizons imaginatively, without burning fossil fuels. Arendt's suggestion to "train one's imagination to go visiting" (1982, 43) is apt. For Arendt, an ethical politics makes present "the standpoints of those who are absent" (1982, 65–67). The space of the visiting imagination is "open to all sides" and allows our conditions to stand next to those of our hosts—never becoming the same, though, and always maintaining their distance. This double movement of the imagination produces both distance from the familiar (a space for thinking and seeing something anew) and connectivity with the strange through stories told from a plurality of perspectives—or in this case, in aural and textual forms (Engels-Schwarzpaul 2015, 167). For artists engaged in critical art practices, distancing and bridging reaches both inside our communities and beyond to new audiences and imagined futures.

Committed Art: The Maldives Exodus Caravan Show

The *Maldives Exodus Caravan Show* is a form of "committed art" in the humble form of the caravan, free to visit locations outside of fixed institutional structures. The concept was initiated by artist Søren Dahlgaard with climate activist and former president Mohamed Nasheed, who presided over the Maldivian Democratic Party's brief democratic regime from 2008 to 2012. I first encountered the caravan-based exhibition when it arrived at Auckland's harborside, hosted by Te Tuhi Centre for the Arts, in 2014. A floppy island with inflatable palm trees rested on top of an archetypal 1970s caravan, threatening to slip off at any moment. The caravan's interior housed video screens and iPads and acted as a base for performances profiling the work of more than thirty artists. International artists were invited by Dahlgaard to engage discursively with the precarious environmental and political situation in the Maldives, including the rising Indian Ocean and internal ecological damage. For Aucklanders, also perched on a low-lying Pacific island, the situation in the Maldives was easy to empathize with. While in Auckland, the caravan traveled to several schools and public events to offer its creative wares.

The *Maldives Exodus Caravan Show* first appeared in the Fifty-Fifth Venice Biennale (2013), in conjunction with the Museum of Everything, as a splinter event from the official Maldives National Pavilion. Since then, different caravans have hosted the exhibition in Melbourne, New York, Mallorca, Gdansk, and more. A dramatic turn in the political situation in the Maldives caused a splintering from the national pavilion in Venice. In February 2012, members of the police and military forced President Nasheed (a former dissident journalist) to resign. Since the coup, many art organizations in the Maldives have been forced to close, and there were reports of creative practitioners being violently suppressed, along with political opponents of the regime. Artists were becoming unfree to move or even made stateless in this shift in political relations (Oliver 2016, 93). To the curator and participating artists, it became unacceptable to be part of an official event that required a high level of government influence. Instead, the *Maldives Exodus Caravan Show* became an official but independent collateral event for the Venice Biennial (2013) and later a politically mobile forum to continue outside the elitism of this event.

The caravan signals a condition of movement and is commonly associated with a temporary home or the headquarters of temporary activist activity. Dahlgaard comments on the term *exodus* in his title: "Exodus refers to the majority of the Maldivian population that wishes to escape the unprecedented events in the Maldives of unbelievable acts of brutality, polarized discourse, and repression of human rights. Exodus also refers to the climate change issue in the Maldives, which can lead to the entire Maldivian population becoming climate refugees due to the country's status as the first country to be underwater due to global warming" (Te Tuhi Centre for the Arts 2014). Rather than to produce physical art objects for art-world consumption, Dahlgaard's brief to the participating artists, including ten artists from the Maldives, was to produce digital and mobile media artworks, games, music and song, performances, or other ephemera. In 2013, Amani Naseem, Ida Marie Toft, Patrick Jarnfelt, and Sidsel Hermansen traveled to stage the series of game-based social events *Play around Nature* in the Maldives capital city of Malé. Other well-known artists also sent work to the caravan. Danish group SUPERFLEX presented its video *Flooded McDonald's* (2009), and Rirkrit Tiravanija wrote a text for the caravan called *On the Land*. The selection of predominantly performance-based works for the caravan, including Harvey's *Political Climate Wrestle*, takes cues from President Nasheed's own performative sense of the political sphere. In a radical event to highlight the imminent threat of sea-level rise in the Maldives, Nasheed held an underwater cabinet meeting in October 2009, during which the government committed through hand signals to ambitious carbon-reduction goals. Nasheed's recognition of the power of such countervisual spectacle to create social change made collaboration with curator Dahlgaard a natural next step.

Political commentator Christian Parenti writes on the "catastrophic convergence" of poverty, violence, and climate change that arises often in the wake of a colonial legacy (2011, 5). The Maldives is a site of such a convergence. One of the intentions of the *Play around Nature* events in Malé that formed part of the *Maldives Exodus Caravan* project was to ward off political tensions by creating moments of sociality as reprieve from a politically repressive regime, combined with the encroaching sea. *Jelly Stomp* (played on knee-high water), *Jelly Plop* (played in belly-deep water), and *Poisoned Sea* (played in shoulder-deep water or deeper) are fast games played in the water that allow us to face our climate change fears, including the rise of species of jellyfish in warmer waters. The real possibility of exodus due to loss of habitable land or political expulsion is a serious threat, yet the homely figure of the caravan itself is a place of refuge and a joyful escape from the mundane. Haraway encourages a playful mode as an effective

Figure 6.4
Mark Harvey. *Political Climate Wrestle*. 2013. Part of *The Maldives Exodus Caravan Show*, Fifty-Fifth Venice Biennale. Live performance and installation. Photograph: Paolo Rosso.

means to communicate: "Because play is one of those activities through which critters make with each other that which didn't exist before, it's never merely functional; it's propositional. Play makes possible futures out of joyful but dangerous presents. … Play proposes new abstractions, new lures" (Haraway and Kenney 2015, 260–261). Playfulness in art destabilizes normative rules and opens possibilities. By generating participatory moments during which we "mess around," artists promote independent ways to encounter the issues that worry us. Ethical decisions made in jest contravene our expected behaviors, and we can surprise ourselves.

At most of the venues where the *Maldives Exodus Caravan Show* made an appearance, New Zealand artist Mark Harvey has shown up to wrestle for one day. *Political Climate Wrestle* is a performance artwork in which the artist literally wrestles with people over their ecological commitments. Harvey goads participants to debate with him about their climate change–mitigating practices. Verbal arguments escalate into a physical offer to wrestle. I came across Harvey hovering eagerly in a doorway at ST PAUL St Gallery in Auckland in 2015. With a jovial demeanor, Harvey began to question me about my mode of transportation to the gallery. I admitted that I had driven my car to the bus stop to then catch the bus for the major part of the journey, at which point I was offered a wrestling match over the issue of my carbon footprint. Harvey challenges us

to face up to what Zylinska has described as "easy solutionism" and an associated scalar distortion between a small climate-mitigating action and a large-scale global crisis:
"whereby filling in half a kettle is perceived as 'doing one's bit' for the environment"
(Zylinska 2014, 20)—or in my case, using public transport for three-quarters of my trip.

The length of the wrestle will depend on how long Harvey can keep a dialogue
going. Some people last for up to twenty minutes, others for three or four minutes.
Harvey describes the moment of initiating the wrestle as follows: "So if I feel that
someone is ready for it, I will keep the dialogue going—talking at the same time. The
person could say 'Look I rode my bike here.' And I could reply 'so what does that make
you feel like? But where did your rubber come from?' Then usually people will say
when they are ready to wrestle or I ask them 'what do you think? OK, let's wrestle? OK,
let's do it'" (Horsley 2013, 17). In Venice in 2013 Harvey performed this work for eight
hours each day for a week, keeping regular office hours. Harvey describes himself as
combining endurance performance with idiocy and deadpan humor. He asks questions
directly that we are afraid to ask: "Many of us are very romantic about the environmental issue—but what difference are we really making?" (ibid., 16). Yet at the same time,
Harvey acknowledges the fuel-consuming hypocrisy of the activist-artist clocking up
frequent-flyer miles to join the caravan around the world.

Harvey works from a principle of showing, persuading, and inspiring people to join
in, so they themselves become active advocates for a sustainable world. In the 2017
video work and participatory performance *Weed Wrestle*, Harvey wrestles with an Australian wattle plant, now an invasive weed in the subtropical bush in the Waitakere
ranges in Aotearoa New Zealand. In his statement for the work Harvey writes: "In *Weed
Wrestle*, Mark Harvey will attempt to obsessive-compulsively pull invasive weed trees
out of the ground along the edges of native forest in Titirangi. Employing physical
endurance, the work not only intends to generate a sense of somatic heat, but reacts
to the efforts many of us are all taking to combat the effects of climate change" (Harvey 2017). The warmer, frost-free conditions under the new climactic regime support
the growth of weeds, while Indigenous species are coping less well with the warmer
world. There are over fifty thousand species of flora in Aotearoa New Zealand that are
found nowhere else in the world (Salinger 2016), and new species of weeds change the
composition of the soil or take up more water than the local plant life. The remaining Kauri trees (New Zealand white pine) that were extensively milled for ship masts
in the nineteenth and early twentieth centuries now are threatened by a soil-borne
disease called *Kauri die-back* that has been linked to the warmer climate. As part of the
Heat: Solar Revolutions exhibition (2017), Harvey encouraged locals to join him in wrestling the weeds from their neighborhoods. I also joined the shared activity of wrestling

Australian wattle trees from the ground over several hours in the Titirangi bush in the hot sun. The wattle is a particularly tough plant with a long, hook-like root that takes many hands together to wrench from the ground. We collaborated in a group tug-of-war for the larger, more obstinate weeds, tumbling over backward as they finally pulled free. The scattered wattle seedpods needed to be painstakingly collected so as not to disperse the plant further. Bemused bystanders appeared and asked what we were doing, spreading the news of our activity through the neighborhood.

This kind of hosted performance art shakes up the model of the isolated individual property owner weeding his solitary patch. For Adorno, dialectical thought refuses to affirm individual things in their isolation and separateness. This form of thinking "acts as a corrective … to manic fixity," yet it risks being seen by others as unreasonable (2002, 71). As with the *Dear Climate* letters, there is an illogic to *Weed Wrestle* and *Political Climate Wrestle* (How can weeding be art? How is this really helping?), yet at the same time it forges new forms of sociality. Conversation crops up between participants and onlookers. The *Weed Wrestle* event is a situated, local action, rather than an attempt to solve problems on a planetary scale. This is another form of "lingering with the particular" rather than falling into the hyperbolic mode sometimes found in art, ecoactivism, and the environmental humanities. Artworks can both operate at a community scale and unfold at a larger scale through international networks. A small caravan disperses ideas wherever it travels.

When artists enter the fray of climate politics, they often move in with poetics, humor, and aesthetic forms that refuse to accept ecological injustice. The artworks surveyed in this chapter shake us from the inertia associated with the escalation of climate change. Harvey's *Political Climate Wrestle* is confounding, Waerea's *Chasing Fog Club* is a humorous approach to Indigenous understandings of air and water, and *Dear Climate* seduces and subverts through language. Discursive formations about global warming, climate change, and the Anthropocene are constructed in IPCC reports, in news media, and in visualizations and UN conventions, with art practice moving among them in unlikely coalitions. Stengers, drawing on Spinoza, argues for joyful modes of experience that emerge from experimental acts, rather than fear for our future climate. She explains that joy increases the "the power of acting, that is to say too, of thinking and imagining, and it has something to do with a knowledge, but with a knowledge that is not of a theoretical order" (Stengers 2015, 156). When art occupies an imaginative, knowledge-producing space, outside a theoretical order, we affectively lobby our cause.

The performing arts in particular have a strong affinity with politics, Arendt suggests. Like politicians, performance artists need an audience and a publicly organized space for their work. In ancient Greek polis life, "which to an incredibly large extent consisted of citizens talking with one another," the Greeks in their "incessant talk … discovered that the world we have in common is usually regarded from an infinite number of different standpoints, to which correspond the most diverse points of view" (Arendt 2006, 51–52). We learn how to look upon the same world from another's standpoint by talking and acting in public. In Waerea's *Chasing Fog Club* and in *The Distance Plan*, forums are created for diverse worldviews to meet, from Indigenous standpoints to those of urban planners. Yet to avoid instrumentalizing art's role in politics, Arendt finds that artwork prepares the terrain for political action, rather than shouldering the weight of becoming politics itself. What is evident in works such as Howden-Chapman's *Uncertainty Italicized* and Balkin's *Public Smog* is that the actions we take now will have repercussions that stretch out into the future, beyond the life cycle of any one human being. Arendt reminds us that "courage is indispensable because in politics not life but the world is at stake" (2006, 155). Courage in political art practice is being for and with the world, outlasting the self-interest of our limited human lifespan.

Yet Aotearoa New Zealand climate scientist and long-time contributor to the IPCC reports Jim Salinger observes wryly that most of us cannot escape from being "today people" (Salinger 2016). As I write this from a position of immanent critique, I want to believe that committed art can make a difference under the conditions of late capitalism, but doubt remains. At present, many governments are swinging to the right globally, the president of the United States has withdrawn support for the 2015 Paris Agreement and eliminated climate change from the discourse of federal agencies, and the British prime minister has abolished the Department for Energy and Climate Change. For scientists, any sense of a climate change "debate" was over by the early 1990s, so clear was the evidence; yet in the sphere of politics, the combined efforts across the arts, science, activism and many other fields appears to have little effect. Yet, as Adorno reflected ([1951] 2002), perhaps from the vantage of our already damaged lives can intimations of a possible, more sustainable way of living come to light. Intimations of what may be possible emerge in models of collectivity and connection forged through art practice.

7   Weather Materialized: Ice as Medium

Ice as a sculptural medium first appeared in process based art in the 1960s. Today, given the fast-diminishing cryosphere, ice in contemporary art carries a potent material politics. Melting ice readily signals not only the loss of our natural heritage of glaciers, polar ice sheets, and their nonhuman inhabitants, but also the rising seas encroaching on habitable coastal land and small islands around the planet. Ice refracts light to produce intense colors, and it directly engages our sense of temperature on the skin. In specific artworks I will argue, the qualities of ice give the medium an agential power to foster ecological *response-ability* (Haraway 2016). Tongan/Australian artist Latai Taumoepeau's body performances *i-Land X-ile* (2012–2013) and *Repatriate I* and *Repatriate II* (2015), and British Liberate Tate's *Floe Piece* (2012) harness blocks of ice as co-performers; Icelandic artist Bjarki Bragason works with ice as an ephemeral archive; and in Danish-Icelandic artist Olafur Eliasson and geologist Minik Rosing's collaboration *Ice Watch* (2015), twelve large fragments of icebergs occupied center stage in the Place du Panthéon in Paris during COP21. Eliasson intended *Ice Watch* to "make the climate challenges we are facing tangible" and to "inspire shared commitment to taking climate action" (Eliasson and Rosing 2015). As a way of coming to grips with these artworks, I retrieve Arendt's "inspiring principle" to frame the sometimes-beleaguered notion that art can inspire us to act.

The physical form of ice in public art stands in for the threat of sea-level rise. The Sea Ice Index indicates that the ice is diminishing more rapidly than previously thought at both the earth's poles. In the Arctic, by the end of January 2018, ice extent was tracking at a record low; scientists warned that drifting ice builds up in ridges that are dangerous to marine activities. In the Antarctic, sea ice was at the second lowest extent on record, with the greatest disappearances in the Ross Sea and the West Amundsen Seas (NSIDC 2018). The dramatic reduction of polar ice in the Arctic in recent summers and record lows of sea ice around Antarctica causes sea-level rise, along with the warming of the climate that causes seawater to expand. Yet the people and species worst affected by sea-level rise do not necessarily live near poles, due to uneven geological effects of warming. Greenland and Antarctica's massive ice sheets exert a strong gravitational pull on the waters around them, but as they melt, the attraction weakens, causing nearby sea levels to fall. The effect diminishes with distance, so the warmer countries further away from the Arctic encounter the rise in sea level soonest. An unfair burden is placed on low-lying countries in the tropics that are less economically equipped to deal with sea level rise, including Bangladesh, the Maldives, and the islands of Te Moana nui a Kiwa (the Pacific diaspora), rather than those in the developed north that are the biggest carbon spenders.

Rates of rising waters in the Western Pacific over the past two decades are among the highest globally, averaging three millimeters yearly since 1950 and seven to ten millimeters yearly since 1994. In the Solomon Islands, two villages have been relocated and six islands have disappeared completely (Albert et al. 2016, 2; Becker et al. 2012). The unprecedented rate of sea-level rise is exacerbated by the increasing storminess that accelerates the erosion of the shoreline. Artist Latai Taumoepeau's homeland of Tonga is affected by the encroaching seas and the increase in frequency and severity of cyclones. As I write, schools across Aotearoa New Zealand, including my daughter's school, are fund-raising to donate money to Tonga in the aftermath of 2018's Cyclone Gita. The limited alternatives for the islanders in the long term bluntly put is "to adapt or to migrate" (Kautoke 2012). Aotearoa New Zealand and Australia are accepting rising numbers of migrants from smaller islands in the Pacific. By taking extraordinary risks to suspend her body beneath a melting block of ice, Taumoepeau's performance practice calls urgent attention to the effects of the warming climate for inhabitants of Te Moana nui a Kiwa.

In science, we rely on disparate measurements; patterns are pieced together from far-flung monitoring stations. The melting ice caps, the glaciers, the receding lakes and acidifying coral reefs each have their own set of scientific experts. But the problem with only seeing in parts is that the implications for the whole recedes. Hawaiian scholar Manulani Aluli-Meyer writes, "We have looked at parts for so long that we perhaps believe that the gestalt of our knowing is not possible" (2006, 267). To think the whole again, according to Aluli-Meyer, is to confront entrenched patterns of fragmented thinking. A sense of wholeness of mind, body, and spirit can lead to the desire to work on behalf of lands, water, and air. Ancient renditions of the world encourage harmony with place, although Aluli-Meyer (2006, 275–276) speculates that the path to wholeness often starts with culturally specific formations that, in turn, lead to a concern for the collective. When Indigenous artists take public climate action, they encourage others to engage in prosocial behaviors on issues too often dismissed as exclusive to the realm of do-gooders and moralists.

A vital task for art, I believe, is to stir up an affective response to the rapidly shifting ecological conditions. An "inspiring principle," as described by Arendt, must exist beyond the self. As distinct from a motive, a principle is universal and not bound to an individual or group. For Arendt, "The inspiring principle becomes fully manifest only in the performing act itself" (2006, 151). This requires movement beyond human exceptionalism, to connect materially with our internal and exterior natures. Through action in the polis, we inspire and become inspired to act otherwise, whether through political acts, activism, or art as politics by other means. Inspiration connects to the concept of response-ability, in Donna Haraway's lexicon, to describe our potential to awaken each other to political realities. According to Haraway: "Response-ability is that cultivation through which we render each other capable, that cultivation of the capacity to respond" (Haraway and Kenney 2015, 257). This capacity differs from a demand to follow an ethical system or make a formal political commitment; instead, collective actions are made with and for others. These "others" extend beyond human cultures to biotic life, abiotic life, and nonlife, particularly when we admit that we are no less endangered in the long term than the polar caps and creatures of the ice.

In artworks that bring our bodies into relation with cryospheric phenomena, I find an ethos of responsivity. In Eliasson's *Ice Watch* (2015), eighty tons of ice from a fjord outside Nuuk, Greenland, were laid in a clock formation to be touched freely, climbed on, and grieved for at a scale that made them difficult to be overlooked. Climatic timescales are buried in the ice-core archives that Bjarki Bragason investigates in his art practice, in which human and nonhuman coexistences are evident in soot in the ice from the Industrial Revolution. From a feminist materialist position, Astrida Neimanis and Rachel Loewen Walker argue that temporal narratives of climate are stored in our bodies, as well as externally in ice archives. We are continuously making bodily exchanges with climate, as Out-of-Sync's breath collection revealed in chapter 5. If we locate our bodies as climate archives, "we are not masters of the climate, nor are we just spatially 'in' it. As weather-bodies, we are thick with climatic intra-actions; we are makers of climate-time. Together we are weathering the world" (Neimanis and Walker 2014, 558). Responsivity, response-ability, and inspiration have in common an affective and prosocial ethos against a discourse of crisis, catastrophe, and moral obligation.

Ice as Performer

The physical presence of ice as an art material has an historical precedent in the process-based works of Hans Haacke and the Puerto Rican artist Rafael Ferrer. In chapter 1, I introduced Haacke's experiments with live weather materials. Haacke's artwork *Ice Stick* (1964–1966), made at a similar time as *Condensation Cube*, was a seventy-inch rod consisting of a long, copper freezing coil pointing directly out of a stainless steel–clad base containing a refrigeration unit and transformer connected to a power supply. *Ice Stick* would absorb moisture out of the air of the gallery, quickly freezing the vapor to form a live shield of frost as an archive of the system inside. In general, Ferrer (working in the 1960s and 1970s) and other contemporary artists considered in this chapter leave ice to transform its state in the opposite direction: from ice to water. Haacke's operation of freezing involves a host of energetic operations that, if made today, would run counter to the need to reduce energy usage, in light of the ecological crisis. Recent ecological thinking about art practice has favored low-impact materials and efficient power sources. Haacke's works made shortly after *Ice Stick*, *Grass Cube* (1967) and *Bowery Seeds* (1970), pioneered attention to ecological cycles.

The melting of ice is a physical phase transition of a substance from a solid form to a liquid (water). When exposed to the heat of the sun, the internal energy of ice increases, resulting in its temperature rising to the melting point, at which point the ordering of ionic or molecular entities in the solid breaks down to a less ordered state and the solid liquefies. Weather itself is a dissipative system: dissipative structures in physics were once considered waste, but dissipation now is often considered capable of producing energy or a higher form of order (Prigogine and Stengers 1984). In art, the dissipative quality of ice becomes a potent analogue for a new kind of system or energy, just as Alÿs found with *Tornado* (chapter 5), and in his earlier performance *Paradox of Praxis 1 (Sometimes Making Something Leads to Nothing)* (1997), in which he pushed a block of ice around the dusty streets of Mexico City until his object-of-effort simply dissolved into the earth.

Ferrer explored ephemeral materials in his early practice as a rejection of the fetish of the enduring art object. In 1968 in New York, Ferrer dumped piles of dead leaves into the elevators of the Dwan and Fischbach Galleries, in the front room of Castelli Gallery, and at the Castelli Warehouse during the *Anti-form* exhibition curated by Robert Morris, to which he was not invited. The following year Ferrer was asked by Whitney curators Marcia Tucker and James Monte to participate in *Anti-Illusion: Procedures/Materials* (1969). This time, he deposited leaves and blocks of ice on the entrance ramp of the museum to dissipate over the course of the exhibition. By 1970 his practice was established to the extent that he was invited to make a work for the *Information* exhibition for MoMA's sculpture garden in New York. For this work, entitled *50 Cakes of Ice* (1970), Ferrer placed fifty large blocks of ice on a stone-tiled architectural bridge in the sculpture garden. As the ice melted in the summer heat, the ice blocks slid off the bridge, some floating temporarily like ice bergs in the stream below, most turning to water in an open system. The duration of the melting determined the exhibition period of the artwork. Whitney curator Marcia Tucker was powerfully affected by his artworks. In 1971 she wrote, "The allegiance in Ferrer's work is to real things and situations, to a sensory and physical world rather than to an abstract one. There is consequently no way to distance oneself physically or emotionally from his pieces, and their energy, honesty and humor makes them, for me, intensely moving" (Ferrer and Tucker 1971). We empathize with performing blocks of ice as they dissolve in the heat, erasing all evidence of their existence.

Although the ice blocks and leaves were temporary materials, they were strategically placed at prominent thresholds in galleries and institutions to amplify the artist's politics. Ferrer unleashed forces of entropy and decay against the institutional desire for permanence, as a political corrective to accepted structures of the art world. Although this work was made long before the climate crisis, Ferrer's material politics foregrounded ice as a transient element that could resist commodification. In the 1950s and 1960s, Ferrer's homeland of Puerto Rico was experiencing rapid industrialization under Operation Bootstrap, and many aspects of labor relations were legislated by the United States. In 1962, Ferrer's contemporary Raphael Montañez Ortiz, founder of El Museo Del Barrio, wrote the following in *Destructivism: A Manifesto*: "The artist's sense of destruction will no longer be turned inwards in fear. The art that utilizes the destructive processes will purge, for as it gives death, so it will give to life" (Camnitzer 2007, 233). An artwork made of ice has the political capacity to destroy itself, evading entry into a system of exchange value.

Fifty years later in *Floe Piece* (January 2012), the Liberate Tate collective used guerilla performance tactics to bring to catharsis the hidden relationship between the Tate Modern Gallery and British Petroleum (BP). The artists engaged in their democratic right to protest in the public realm, with ice as a co-participant. *Floe Piece* is a human-scale block of Arctic ice brought back to London from a scientific expedition. Liberate Tate activated the fragment of ice by first positioning it on the steps of St. Paul's Cathedral as part of the Occupy London movement. In the second phase of the performance, the ice was carried on a stretcher through the night—in the artists' words, "like a dying patient"—to Tate Modern's Turbine Hall. At the hall, the assembled audience "ritually watched over the ice before leaving it there to melt" (Liberate Tate et al. 2013, 145). The artists were dressed in black clothes of mourning, and their faces were veiled with black cloth. By performing the rituals associated with a funeral and the ritual of protest, the audience is placed in a position from which to empathize, perhaps to grieve, perhaps to act. In the context of the Tate's funding by BP, the event was a call to action squarely directed at the Tate institution itself.

Liberate Tate commented that "seeing this type of Arctic ice for the first time was an emotional experience for us all as the performance enabled us to express the grief and loss felt at that viewing. The people and natural habitats currently affected by climate change are often so far away—the Arctic, the Maldives, Bangladesh—and it felt incredibly significant to bring something tangible from one of those sites into the gallery and to say to Tate, 'Here is some melting Arctic ice, deal with it'" (Liberate Tate et al. 2013, 145). *Floe Piece* is activated by the weather conditions that accelerate melting or freezing. Outdoors (on the steps of St. Paul's Cathedral), the block stayed intact, but when the ice was carried into the gallery the artificially warm climate began to change its state rapidly. Like Haacke's *Ice Stick*, the ice performs to the conditions of the gallery atmospheres both physically and as an analogue for political change.

Performance artists depend on others when their performances take place in the polis, a space of appearances where we can "act." Liberate Tate chose St. Paul's Cathedral and the cathedral of art that the Tate has become to stage *Floe Piece* as an unequivocal activist statement designed to be comprehensible to a large audience. In chapter 6 I noted Arendt's contention that the performing arts have a strong affinity with politics as collective activities and as a space of freedom (2006, 152). We are free in our performative processes—as long as we act with *virtù*, the excellence with which we answer the public opportunities the world opens up before us (Arendt 2006, 151–152). In Eliasson and Rosing's *Ice Watch* (2015), the physical transportation of ice to a potent forum of the Place du Panthéon also "performs" our climate response-abilities in the public realm. The audience-performer is implicated more deeply into this art event through the physical touching of the ice.

Ice at COP21: Olufur Eliasson and Minik Rosing

Ice Watch is a collaboration between artist Olafur Eliasson and geologist Minik Rosing as part of the initiative *Artists4ParisClimate* (2015). Over eighty tons of sea ice was installed in the Place du Panthéon in Paris to draw attention to the fragility and rapid decay of Arctic ice. Twelve colossal bluish icebergs were arranged in a circular formation in the square on Thursday, December 3, 2015, as world leaders and government teams met in Le Bourget for COP21. The fragments of ice conveyed an unequivocal message

Figure 7.1
Olafur Eliasson. *Ice Watch*. 2015. Installation view at Place du Panthéon, Paris, 2015. Photograph:
Martin Argyroglo. © Olafur Eliasson.

about climate change to the large numbers of people who were drawn to the melting
forms. The figure of the doomsday clock as a countdown to finitude hovers over the
twelve blocks of ice; more immediately, the deadly ISIS terrorist attacks shortly before
COP21 became part of the reading of *Ice Watch* as a claiming of free, democratic space
in the symbolic location of the Place du Panthéon. The matter-material of Arctic ice
itself becomes a matter of care through its obdurate presence and the public gathering around it. The duration of the work was dependent on weather conditions; in the
northern winter, the ice melted slowly over eleven days from December 3 to December
14. When lobbying at this historical moment was restricted at COP15 in Paris by the
threat of terrorism, millions of protestors marched throughout the world, as I did in
Aotearoa New Zealand, to pressure governments to take initiative on curbing greenhouse gas emissions.

Eliasson and Rosing assembled a huge network to gather the ice from free-floating
blocks from the Nuup Kangerlua fjord outside Nuuk, Greenland, as the key actors
in the *Ice Watch* event. The project required the financial support of the Bloomberg

Philanthropies charity and collaboration with Julie's Bicycle, the collection of ice by divers and dockworkers from the Royal Arctic Line, transportation in six refrigerated containers from Nuuk to Aalborg by Group Greenland and Greenland Glacier Ice by container ship, and finally transport to Paris by truck. The website for the project publicly declares the carbon footprint as thirty tons of CO_2 to forestall any criticism around the lurking question: Can we justify this expense of energy for a gesture for art? The criticism of art-making as expensive, politically ineffective, or elitist by mainstream media becomes more acute when artists' material decisions are scrutinized. At crisis points, a criticism of art-making as politically ineffective or sensationalizing becomes more acute. In reaction to such criticisms, as Mirzoeff (2011) reminds us, activist artwork and media representations of climate sometimes leap into action with melting ice sculptures and stranded polar bears in a way that can reduce the problem's complexity.

Yet photographs of *Ice Watch*, as a durational event, testify to its affective power; people touch, caress, grieve for the ice. Writer Rebecca Solnit reported, "It's a beautiful, disturbing, dying monument to where we are right now ... People are coming by fascinated, most needing to touch the ice" (Palmer 2015). The material qualities of refraction and the glassy quality of melting ice engages us; we understand melting at an emotional level, forging a sense connection to an issue that until then had been remote, or where logic has failed to convince.

The extensive website for the *Ice Watch* project includes the following comment from Laurent Fabius, French minister of foreign affairs and international development, and president of COP21: "From my visit to the Arctic last year, I have a very lively memory of the horrifying noise and sight of huge ice blocks cracking and breaking away from the pack ... The Arctic is indeed the gatekeeper of climate disorder: for years, this region has been sending us signals that we cannot neglect anymore. The international community must hear them and turn them into acts" (Eliasson and Rosing 2015). Urging politicians to act through the vehicle of an artwork and online lobbying was a strategic move to hold them to their public expressions of commitment to climate change mitigation. There was hope that the powerful symbolism and aesthetics of the ice as "magic glass," in Eliasson's words, might spill into political will (Jones 2015). Yet the lack of strong binding outcomes after COP21, and subsequent withdrawal of the United States, reflected the intractability of nationalist interests. Politicians at COP23 (2017–2018) in Bonn, where Fiji held the presidency, made progress on creating a "Local Communities and Indigenous Peoples Platform" to give greater voice to Indigenous peoples in climate negotiations. Participants followed the Pacifika principle of *Talanoa* or dialogue that opened the forum to non-Party stakeholders. A

Figure 7.2
Bjarki Bragason. *That in Which It*. 2013. Part of *Infinite Next*, Ilulissat, Greenland, 2015.

"Gender Action Plan" was launched to ensure the participation of women increased in the convention, as well as the "Ocean Pathway Partnership" to focus on the relations between climate change and the seas (COP23). As an ephemeral monument to this critical nature-culture balance, *Ice Watch* resonates with Adorno's view that where nature and history meet "is in the fact of transience." Human history is always part of a natural history, Adorno reminds us, in which our collective fate is a mutual conditioning between ourselves and the environment (2006, 122–124). When we stand before the bodies of stranded, wasting-away icebergs, we can no longer cordon off nature in an "insulated sphere" that is somehow separate from the social dynamics that are increasingly addressed in the UN conventions on climate change.

Bjarki Bragason: Ice Archives

On a much more intimate scale, the poetic-sensory qualities of ice play out in Icelandic artist Bjarki Bragason's artworks. The ethical treatment of the cryosphere and its inhabitants, human and nonhuman, in the face of the hurtling pace of technoscientific innovation is foregrounded in Bragason's practice. As well as operating a studio-based practice, he collaborates with scientists in Iceland and Greenland to draw attention to the politics of ice in the diminishing glacier-scapes and the thorny issue of carbon sequestration. In Bragason's photographic series *That in Which It* (2013), more than just the final part of the title sentence is missing. The images document empty molds that are made from the gently absurd process of casting a found piece of glacial ice. In the exhibited photographs of the empty molds, Bragason gives material form to the negative shape of vanishing.

The story of Bragason's chance discovery of a large ice block in his hometown of Reykjavik is recorded in *The Distance Plan* no. 3 (Cunnane and Howden-Chapman). While cycling home from the cinema, the artist noticed a lump of ice melting on the pavement. The same piece of ice had been on display at a climate conference he had visited earlier in the day. He notes how this once precious object was now discarded: "The glaciologists at the university had used it to explain carbon and how time is read from information stored in the ice. Now it was standing on the pavement, melting onto the street" (Cunnane and Howden-Chapman 2015, 33–37). Bragason took the ice home and stored it in the freezer until the next spring, when he cut the block of ice in two with a hot knife. He melted one half of the ice block with a hot-air gun onto a pile of black paper to catch the sediment; the other half he sank into wet drywall concrete set into a cardboard box. During the chemical reaction, the concrete mixture heated up and melted the half-block of ice, leaving behind its exact shape.

These studio experiments became a two-channel video work, and the residue of the meltwater from the ice on the black paper was also exhibited. One of the two channels was an extreme close-up shot, showing only the rapidly melting ice. The close-up seems to be a time-lapse video, because the melting of the ice is so rapid in the heat. On the other channel, we see the artist's hand with the heat gun moving across the piece of ice. The two channels were played on monitors at either side of a long box, so the audience had to move from one end to the other to see the whole. Bragason was interested in causal relationships in a paradoxical process that involved both disposing of and keeping the ice at the same time. The temporary interruption of the decaying ice through the casting process echoes the ritual of a death mask that preserves a decaying body as an aid to memory. Bragason (2017) comments that the rapidly receding glacial topography in Iceland is preserved and measured against his own memories from childhood to adulthood. The attempt to cast the ice is a futile gesture to hold on to a disappearing natural heritage.

The empty molds became studio-style photographs, bereft of ice; the shape is preserved, but the substance has gone. The photographs were first exhibited as part of a research project with artist Anna Líndal and developed into the exhibition *Infinite Next* (2015) in Ilulissat, Greenland. The exhibition was held in a former colonial administration office, which is now a museum in part dedicated to the paintings of the region by Danish artist Emanuel A. Petersen (1894–1948). The site activates Bragason's concern with the colonial legacy that negatively impacted the Indigenous people—and their future interests, now that oil prospecting is beginning in Greenland. The inhabitants are left with little alternative but to support development. In 2016, the photographs of *That in Which It* (2013) appeared in the group show *Imagine the Present* at ST PAUL St Gallery in Auckland. Bragason made a shelf to lean unframed, photographs of molds, laid out like scientific samples against a midnight-blue wall. The objective nature of his photography is devoid of the melancholy of preloss harnessed to dramatic effect by Liberate Tate in *Floe Piece.*

During a residency in Greenland in 2015, Bragason engaged in research alongside scientists taking ice cores for analysis. Bragason found that he was able to see changes in the density of particles in the ice cores, pulled up by portable core drillers. In the cores, fragments could be glimpsed of a time long past, from the paleoclimatology of dusts and other biota to the dense layer of carbon impurities from soot created during the Industrial Revolution. Some of the scientists Bragason spoke to in Ilulissat were concerned that the focus of the natural sciences on identifying trends in numbers meant that their research was taking place in a vacuum, divorced from social and political questions. As a researcher concerned with community understandings of climate

Figure 7.3
Bjarki Bragason. *Ten Thousand and One Years (One Year of Emissions at 449, 5 Metres)*. 2016. Part of
Imagine the Present, ST PAUL St Gallery, AUT, Auckland. Photo: Sam Hartnett.

change, Bragason felt able to augment this side of the science through his freedom to explore how art might situate the glaciologists' research historically and politically. He raised questions of social and environmental justice in formal situations with scientists and politicians at the Ilulissat Climate Days conference, (June 2–5, 2015) and through his artwork itself. Líndal and Bragason further developed the Greenland project, *Infinite Next*, at the Living Art Museum in Reykjavik, curating other artists with similar future-orientated concerns.

Pre- and posthuman temporalities converge in Bragason's study of the scientific practice of testing basalt cores in the Arctic for their capacity for carbon sequestration as long-term storage of atmospheric carbon dioxide. On the one hand, carbon sequestration may be the answer to our survival on the planet as mitigation of warming, but on the other, the wider implications of injecting cores into the sensitive system—the potential danger of leaks and the financial costs—need to be interrogated. Carbon sequestration is also presented as an alternative to less commercially palatable methods of mitigating carbon emissions in the first place, rather than trying to capture carbon in retrospect. In Bragason's artwork *Ten Thousand and One Years* (2016), also exhibited in *Infinite Next* in Reykjavik, an oversized photographic print of a basalt core is draped over a delicate pinewood stand, stained with graphite.

The image was made following a conversation with geologist Sandra Snæbjörnsdóttir, a scientist in the CarbFix project, during observation work by Bragason in Iceland in spring 2016. In this project, scientists work with industry to mineralize CO_2 into calcite by pumping it into subterranean basaltic rock at the Hellisheiði geothermal power plant in Iceland—thus accelerating carbon fossilization to simulate a natural process that would otherwise take ten thousand years. Bragason photographed the basalt core that proved that carbon can be captured; the fossilized emissions in this particular core were produced over the course of one year. Bragason's large-scale photography allows for intensified looking, mimicking a form of scientific scrutiny. The cracks and holes in the basalt cores are analogues for the collision of human and planetary timescales as "ambivalent monuments to the nightmarish speculative reach of the 'tech-x'" (Cunnane 2016). The accelerated time of injected CO_2 sits uncomfortably against the incremental accumulations of climate evident in the ice cores. Engagement with the cryosphere as part of the larger picture of a warming world generates an ecosocial sense of urgency (Haraway 2016) through alternate processes to the positivist approach of technoscience.

Bragason rethinks the pace of technoscientific innovation in the context of more-than-human or planetary temporalities. The pace of "care time" is an alternative to the current accelerated mode of action into nature that María Puig de la Bellacasa describes

Figure 7.4
Latai Taumoepeau, *i-Land X-isle*. 2012. Performance part of *Local Positioning Systems*, Museum of Contemporary Art (MCA), Circular Quay, Sydney. Curated by Performance Space and presented by MCA Australia.

as the "temporal orientation of techno-scientific intervention: driven by an inherently progressivist, productionist and restless mode of futurity." Soil, Puig de la Bellacasa argues, is an important natural sink for carbon and needs to be cared for over time. Attention to more-than-human temporalities through a slower pace of care can disrupt the desire for progress at any cost. The exhaustion of soil quality in "peak soil" can be ameliorated with permaculture approaches that require thoughtful and protracted observation of the land and its local interactions before acting into it (Puig de la Bellacasa 2014, 692–693). The progressivist ethos inherent in technological research into carbon sequestration turns away from the slower pace of environmental care, or redirecting world markets away from the thirst for resources. The legacy of extractivism in the Global North continues in speculation for oil in the new fields in Greenland uncovered by the receding ice, doing little to address the uneven effects on the inhabitants of the Global South, as *i-Land X-ile* underlines.

Latai Taumoepeau: Ice and Rising Oceans

In *i-Land X-ile*, Australian/Tongan artist Latai Taumoepeau uses her body to perform across the gap between the distant cryosphere and the rising levels of the Southern Ocean. The following invitation (Taumoepeau 2012) was circulated by the Museum of Contemporary Art in Sydney prior to her performance:

My name is Latai Taumoepeau, I am a performance artist with a new performance installation campaign called i-Land X-isle. It is about the impact of climate change on vulnerable indigenous communities from the arctic to coastal low lying islands. My body will be bound by rope to a 2 tonne block of ice to parallel the experience of already impacted people of human induced climate change to a form of water torture, that is imposed by developing countries. It will be live and a durational performance over 2 days.

I humbly invite you ... to use my public art spectacle as a platform to raise wider awareness of communities already impacted by human induced climate change and instructions of how ordinary citizens can change to minimise and cease harm to Australia's nearest coastal neighbours all the way to the Arctic.

Faka'apa'apa Atu (with respect), Latai Taumoepeau (MCA, May 26–27, 2012)

On Circular Quay in Sydney in late autumn, the city was at a tolerable heat, but the ice melted quickly nevertheless. Taumoepeau offered her body to a slow drip of water while suspended under a large block of ice in the first public performance of *i-Land X-ile*. The ice block was bound in white cords to a four-posted shelter using Tongan techniques of architectural lashing. In earlier works, Taumoepeau rubbed her body in coconut oil as the traditional way to prepare the Tongan body for performance, but in this two-day durational performance she was clad in an orange wet suit as well as the oil. The long duration of the performance created concern for the artist's well-being; the suspension and the dripping of the ice was painful. Taumoepeau sometimes cried out through the ordeal from intense discomfort. Taumoepeau's sister Seini Taumoepeau broke down out of anxiety about the pain that the cold, dripping water caused her sister. Even for those who did not know her, there was an emotionally intense identification with the risks to her body and many audience members expressed deep concern for the suffering of a body that is usually kept out of public view (Reto and Taumoepeau 2013). In this open performance, passersby had to choose between confronting her, absorbing the pain vicariously, and avoiding looking at all by hurrying past.

Taumoepeau's body, as representative of the biosphere, is trapped in the climate system as it responds to the interactions between the hydrosphere, the cryosphere, and atmosphere. She positions her performance practice as a politicized "campaign" activating a sense of response-ability to act. The performance is firmly situated as a political act in the public sphere, where the constant presence of others provides the raison d'être of the artwork (Arendt 1958, 23). The publicness of this political theater, as Arendt puts it, "signifies the world itself, in so far as it is common to all of us and distinguished from our privately owned place in it" (1958, 52). There is limited potential to intervene in this self-elected act of suffering, yet the act is completely dependent on others in the polis for the campaign to be worthwhile. The forward-facing action is on behalf of all the islanders who are compromised by climate change and have no choice about their future environment.

As a Tongan within a white Australian majority, Taumoepeau's ecological concerns are stitched into wider questions of race, gender, and the Indigenous body politic. Taumoepeau refers to herself as a *Punake*, a Tongan word that she uses to describe a body-centered performance artist. *i-Land X-ile* (2012–2013), along with *Repatriate I and II* (2015) and *Refuge* (2016), explicitly addresses the ecological effects of climate change through an intense material engagement with ice and water. In 2007, Taumoepeau was a delegate for the COP13 United Nations Climate Change conference in Bali, Indonesia (December 3–14), during which she became conversant with the sobering reality of Southern Hemisphere sea-level rise. As the largest per capita contributor to greenhouse gas emissions in the Pacific region, Australia's lack of state initiative on the issue of climate change remains unchanged in the years since this performance. While the Pacific Islands lobby heavily on climate-change issues, the governments in Australasia and mainstream media channels seldom connect mining of fossil fuels, coal-fired energy, and the building of roads to greenhouse gas emissions and climate warming. Taumoepeau's performances make regimes of biopolitical power visible through public spectacle. For Taumoepeau (2013), the work is an attempt to shake off public complacency over the conditions for marginalized communities along with our ecosystem within the mainstream demographic.

In the European tradition, social control mechanisms over the body were inaugurated in the age of kings through sovereign power. Foucault (2003) describes a new form of "biopolitical power" that emerged in the eighteenth and nineteenth centuries and became consolidated in the 1970s through techniques to subjugate the body and control populations. Under the current conditions of neoliberalism, these mechanisms have only become more pervasive and tied in to geontological power (Povinelli 2016), discussed in more detail in the next chapter. Formerly, royal sovereign power included the spectacular, public performance of the right to kill, to take life away, and, "in moments of regal generosity, to let live" (Povinelli 2016, 1). Taumoepeau appropriates this voyeuristic form of spectacular public performance via controlled attention on her own body. In the public realm, there is the possibility of acting in concert, and a certain reality comes from being seen and heard by others (Arendt 1958, 57–58). On the contrary, Canadian Métis/otipemisiw scholar Zoe Todd describes the sense of simultaneous belonging/not belonging, which is part of the Indigenous experience in "white public space" in relation to the discourse about the Anthropocene, dominated by the white academy (Todd 2015, 243).

Todd describes how Indigenous artists often engage directly with materials (water, pollutants, corn)—in Taumoepeau's case, ice—to foreground urgent politics. Bec Dean, a director of Sydney's Performance Space and a strong supporter of Taumoepeau's practice, describes the work of binding the body to a block of ice as a literal representation of a chain of cause and effect (Reto and Taumoepeau 2013). This raises questions about the value of the literal deployment of ice as an analogue for warming, for all the artists discussed in this chapter, and returns to Adorno's gripe with realism. Yet Todd, citing Horton and Berlo, argues that such real materials "act like a bridge—between people and non-human agents," where Indigenous artists in particular draw attention to the compromised conditions of the Anthropocene through real things. Rather than deeming materials to be "mere actants," as Todd argues Latour does, for Indigenous art practitioners they are enlivened with spirit, sentience, will, and knowing (Todd 2015, 248). In the same vein, Mohawk and Anishnaabe academic Vanessa Watts asserts that "our cosmologies (and the theories within them) are righteously different and cannot be separated from the stuff of nature" (2013, 32). In Taumoepeau's performance, Tongan methods of binding the body to the raw stuff of ice signify relations to community, the environment, and a sacred ancestral connection to Tangaloa (the ancestor-spirits in Tongan cosmology).

The *i-Land X-ile* performance recalls historical durational performances such as Serbian artist Marina Abramovich's performance and video installation *Dragon Heads* (1990), in which she endures writhing pythons around her face and neck, surrounded by a circle of ice. Australian artist Stelarc's suspensions also quickly come to mind (1980–2002), including *Seaside Suspension: Event for Wind and Waves* (1981) in Japan. In this work, "the body" was suspended from a wooden scaffold structure in the rocks for twenty minutes by hooks as the tide was drawing closer, in blustery weather conditions. Stelarc's performances have been found to deconstruct the human through exposure of the nonhuman nature of the body as suspended flesh (Kershaw 2007, 231). The universality of Stelarc's own objectifying reference to "the body" is implicitly countered from an Indigenous standpoint in *i-Land X-ile*, in which Taumoepeau binds her body to a raw material to signify a connection to a specific eco-political issue. Her body also enacts the spiritual and ritualistic dimensions of her Tongan cosmology.

Taumoepeau's *i-Land X-ile* circulated rapidly through online media, and the performance has a long afterlife in digital form. In the production and free dissemination of the artist's own body spectacle, the majority culture's representational schemas no longer appear all-determining and coherent. The complex relationship between performance and its subsequent documentation sustains art campaigns long past the event itself. Disseminated images of the performance pierce the spectacular visual material that documents environmental degradation. In the era of the Anthropocene, phenomena are transformed into images under the conditions of constant visuality, as we discussed in chapter 4. Accelerated images of weather-borne disasters and the sublime effects of air pollution allow us to experience the vicarious thrill of disaster from a safe distance. Under such conditions, the images of *i-Land X-ile* perform a present and insistent activation of a specific Indigenous body each time they are encountered. For Adorno, the circulation sphere is the last refuge, "at the very moment when refuge really no longer exists" (2002, 68).

In a review of *i-Land X-isle*, reperformed at Campbelltown Art Gallery in Western Sydney in *Toward the Morning Sun* in 2013, Art Asia Pacific journalist Michael Young wrote the following: "On opening night, Taumopeau was suspended for several hours below blocks of melting ice in a performance described by curator Keren Ruki as 'hauntingly disturbing.' Now, in her absence, a ghostly *trompe-l'oeil* video of the performance with the artist's projected shadow is all that remains, perhaps predicting the fate of the Pacific Islands' culture itself" (2013). Buried in this comment is the fatalist notion that Pacific Island culture and peoples might disappear altogether, to be remembered only through images. Neocolonial narratives about the precarity of Indigenous peoples are reinforced through discursive formations around the effects of climate change on vulnerable, small island nations. There is little reflection on the large global forces that are shaping the current plight of Pacifika peoples, and still less on their own agency in addressing this situation.

Cultural difference and cultural knowing often is overlooked in scientific approaches to the mitigation of climate change. Threats to islanders' lives include increasing groundwater salinization and wave wash-over from increasingly strong cyclones, yet solutions often are taken out of the hands of islanders themselves. In the rhetoric of scientific journals, any long-awaited certainty about the future of low-lying islands will ultimately be delivered by the findings of scientists. Barnett and Campbell (2010) argue that there tends to be a one-dimensional representation of the issues that renders climate change "as an environmental fact against which actors can do little but suffer. They deny the agency of people at risk: to define the problem in their terms; to apply their own systems of knowledge." The denial of agency to the people most affected by climate change is redressed in part by recent Pacific ecologists who assert the value of Indigenous knowledge. For instance, Penehuro Fatu Lefale observes, "The Samoans knowledge of cloud formation, conditions conducive to the formation and onset of severe weather systems and seasonal changes in climate, helped them anticipate, plan and adapt to extreme weather and climate events" (2010, 317). Lefale counters the scientific treatment of small island states as objects that are essentially alike, along with their human populations, if they mention them at all.

The performance of a specific Tongan body to convey a narrative of climate vulnerability is Taumoepeau's uncompromising affirmation of presence in the sphere of art. The performance shifts the frame from a far-away problem of low-lying islands in the Pacific to the event of one person locked in a struggle of endurance with ice in the here and now of a commercial center in Sydney's Circular Quay. Visual authority is a power over the right to look. Seeing and looking are more than perceptual processes for viewers; they are "claims to relations of what is culturally and politically visible and sayable," according to Mirzoeff. Sea-level rise in the Pacific, he argues, is not "visible," and its causality by climate change therefore is not "sayable" (Mirzoeff 2011, 1192). Taumoepeau's performance is a statement that there *is* something we can do if we face the crisis, rather than give in to the fatalism of the already too late. Through her body, she makes visible the conditions that politicians and large corporate stakeholders attempt to suppress.

Taumoepeau describes her practice as connecting to the "intangible cultural heritage of the Moana" (2016). The endurance of the icy meltwater signals courage, resilience, and even the sacrifice required to permeate the dominant political regime. Martineau and Ritskes argue that "the task of decolonial artists, scholars and activists is not simply to offer amendments or edits to the current world, but to display the mutual sacrifice and relationality needed to sabotage colonial systems of thought and power for the purpose of liberatory alternatives" (Todd 2015, 244). The twin imperative to decolonize and to propose viable alternatives is apparent in many Indigenous artists' capacity to activate others. In Taumoepeau's performance, we are mutually affected by her act. When we last met in 2016, Taumoepeau was working on an event at North Melbourne's town hall, one of the City of Melbourne's designated relief centers, to perform a twenty-four hour disaster drill called *Refuge* (2016). The project included six artists who investigated the question of how existing cultural spaces might respond to catastrophic emergencies. In Taumoepeau's performance, participants' bodies were conducted through the "Human Generator 57" to generate an alternative supply of power. Taumoepeau's states: "One person is energetic—a collective body is a power station" (University of Melbourne 2016).

When Taumoepeau endures the freezing meltwater from a block of ice, we do more than intellectually encounter the ungraspable nonidentical of the natural world (Adorno [1973] 2004). When feeling the ice—vicariously through another body, or by touching it ourselves in Eliasson's *Ice Watch*—an embodied sense experience of the otherwise disembodied fact of a warming climate occurs. In the Judeo-Christian tradition, the apostle Thomas needed to see and feel the wounds of Christ to believe in his resurrection. In many Indigenous belief systems, haptic experience also reinforces concept-based understanding of phenomena.* Watts describes how the Sky Woman is present when we walk on the land and through the air "in the relationships between humans and humans, humans and nonhumans, and non-humans and non-humans" (2013, 23). Yet at the same time, in Haudenosaunee worldings, ahuman things are laden with ethical structures, interspecies treaties and agreements, and localized meanings (27).

The stuff of ice and water in the meteorological art and performance discussed in this chapter become viable agitators within climate politics. We experience an excess of refracted colors, sensations, and the chaotic in unexpected meetings with the live melting, freezing, and condensing of cryospheric materials. The capacity of art to move us signals a shift from the conceptual/critical and linguistic turns in art and philosophy (sometimes linked with an aversion to science), toward active sensory encounters. A return to physical reality surfaces in such contemporary art, which according to Quentin Meillassoux (2008) has been "cordoned off" from human thought in the post-Kantian paradigm. Encounters with ice in public art gives us unexpected inspiration, delight, and the opportunity to grieve: affectively channeling what climate science overwhelming detects, reinforcing a shared ecopolitics across these fields. The specificity of a real fragment of an iceberg stands in for the whole cryosphere: our weather world in flux.

8 Speculative Weathers: Cosmic Clouds and Solar Winds

From climate engineering to stratospheric launches, this final chapter follows artworks that collide with and critique Big Science interventions into the climate. We speculatively foray into cosmic weathers and grand designs for a new climatic regime amongst the cloud-making machines of Karolina Sobecka, the stratospheric instrument launches of Joyce Hinterding and David Haines, the jet-stream propelled flights of Tomás Saraceno, the solar weathers of Sarah and Joseph Belknap, and Ursula Biemann's cosmic clouds and galactic winds. These art machines act on us, probing the risks of meddling in nature as well as the uncanny possibilities. The creativity of scientists and geoengineers leads to proposals no less imaginative than artworks to repel the sun's heat: giant mirrors, the production of false clouds, or sun shields made of multitudes of tiny robots among them. Arendt speculates on our future techno-sphere, the seeds of which are clear in the present we inhabit, questioning whether technologies will "serve the world and its things" or whether we are "strangely led astray" by the service they render to human beings (1958, 151). I argue that artworks bring to light the power dynamics in state and multinational agendas that treat climate change as a purely technological problem.

Arendt once mused, "Future technology may yet consist of channeling the universal forces of the cosmos around us into the nature of the earth" (1958, 150). Now that future is upon us, yet plans for climate-altering feats perpetuate the unsustainable pursuit of progress, a troubling state for many artists and our communities. Research on the feasibility of geoengineering projects, such as the Stratospheric Particle Injection for Climate Engineering (SPICE) in Britain, continues despite the postponement of field tests. The SPICE plan proposes to deploy a fleet of up to twenty giant balloons, each the size of a stadium, to inject millions of tons of small particles into the stratosphere to form clouds. The layer of particulate would reflect sunlight back into space to simulate the cooling effect of a volcanic eruption. This project is impressive in scale, yet the potential to cause unintentional harm is real. For many scientists, the risks of geoengineering outweigh the benefits in a delicate and sensitive atmospheric system. Such fantasies of weather and climate control are out of step with long time-scales of biotic evolution and with Indigenous temporalities, in which the present is tied up with the obligation to future generations.

Much of the dialogue about climate modification treats climate change as a techno-logical problem with a technological solution forged by a small elite. In this chapter, I adopt Elizabeth Povinelli's concept of *meteorontological power* (2016, 5), a passing refer-ence within her broader sketch of *geontological power*, a late liberal condition of con-trol. Strategies of climate modification are proposed in the name of climate security, or meteoro-security, in a collision of political and ontological questions around our shared atmosphere. Geoengineering is a third option beside the unpopular choices between reduction of emissions for consumers and multinationals alike, and the economically and socially costly "let-it-go-but-mitigate-it" option (Schrogl and Summerer 2016). Cli-mate modification promises to let us off the hook to carry on extracting and burning until fuel is exhausted. The late settler-liberal agenda that is altering the entire climate, Povinelli argues, depends on dramatic oppositions of life (bios) and death (thanatos) and of "Life (bios) and Nonlife (geos, meteoros)." Yet these enclosures have never been adequate; governance based on separation of life and nonlife has become increasingly untenable—or is "trembling," in Povinelli's view (2016, 16). The delusion that we can control the weather is a manifestation of the continued will to govern nonlife by humans.

Throughout this chapter, I make a case that artists are attuned to this trembling, meteorontological moment. Artist Karolina Sobecka (n.d) describes a "meteorologi-cal turn and an "atmospheric worldview" in aesthetics, critical theory, and design, in which the body and cloud-based infospheres collide. The breathtaking ventures of art-ists into future weathers emerge from certain technoscientific and atmospheric condi-tions. Big Science is characterized by large-scale instruments, ambitious projects, and state- or corporate-funded facilities with large teams of researchers. The vast expense and bureaucratic nature of the scaling up of science was first described by physicist and Oak Ridge National Laboratory director Alvin Weinberg in *Science* in 1961. Weinberg expressed a nostalgia for "little science," via which individual researchers could inde-pendently pursue new knowledge (Dennis 2017). By 1982, during the Cold War, the term Big Science had entered the cultural sphere, not least through the album of that title by Laurie Anderson. In the current era of a technocapitalist "war" against global warming, Stengers warns, the attitude is this: "It's us your saviors or its [sic] the end of the world" (2015, 9). Big Science geoengineering solutions require the mobilization of public finance, leading to private profit. The apparent collusion of Big Science projects and capital is part of the milieu in which artists now operate.

Although some artworks debunk the scientific positivism that augments late liberal capitalist drives, a fascination with the cosmic scope of contemporary science is also apparent in the artworks considered here. When the Belknaps animate sunspots, we are reminded of the telescopic augmentation of our senses and the discovery that the sun and the cosmos do not in fact revolve around us. Video essayist Ursula Biemann speculates on a time before thought, anterior to the emergence of humans, and the ulterior temporalities after our extinction: the milieu of speculative philosophy and the new sciences. The capacity of art to register Quentin Meillassoux's abyssal vision of the cosmos, blithely unaffected by our existence or inexistence, both reflects and spurs imaginative activity. Meteorological art in this chapter expands outwards into the cosmos itself, "indifferent to its own givenness to be what it is, existing in itself regardless of whether we are thinking of it or not" (Meillassoux 2008, 7). Meillassoux traces the decentering of the terrestrial observer within the solar system back to Copernicus, Galileo, and the mathematization of nature to remind us again of the delusion of human exceptionalism within the vastness of the cosmos.

Speculative feminists and posthumanists have called for an ethic of care and response-ability, whereas speculative realists show us a world awaiting inevitable extinction by cosmic event. At the far edge of speculative thought, humans are negatively positioned as inorganic exteriority left behind after capitalism's destruction of planetary resources. The speculative realists seldom consider the alarming rate of species extinction that is already occurring in the current ecopolitical context, as Demos (2016) has persuasively argued. Climate change is signaled indirectly as an accelerant of the world-without-us. For Brassier, solar extinction, or the end of the world via meteor strike, is a thought experiment for human displacement, rather than a fast-approaching reality for many species and biota as our climate warms. He recalls a nihilist fable of Nietzsche as a disquieting revelation of human insignificance in relation to the cosmos. Nietzsche wrote in 1873, "There were eternities during which it did not exist. And when it is all over with the human intellect, nothing will have happened" (cited in Brassier 2007, 205). For Brassier, extinction is not to be understood as the termination of a biological species, but rather "as that which levels the transcendence ascribed to the human" (2007, 224). Speculative thought, nevertheless, operates across this chapter as an intensive threshold that places, or displaces, each human at an ethical crossroads.

The practice of artists is more hopeful; the stratospheric perspective opened up by Sobecka, and Hinterding and Haines camera-instrument launches, take us beyond our terrestrial world to new horizons of fieldwork. These artists often work with small, interdisciplinary teams of researchers to realize artwork on a larger scale than an individual artist can achieve. Art in the speculative mode confronts Big Science, I will argue, by drawing together the ungraspable future with a situated political ecology. Artists collaborate with environmental and citizen science to lift us from the known and perceivable world into the unknown of cosmic weathers. Contemporary art speculations, for curator Lizzie Muller, open "alternative perspectives—whether temporal, spatial, political, interspecies or intergalactic—from which we can see and interrogate our own situation in a new light" (2014, 46). Saraceno's *Aerocene* project deploys solar technology to suspend human passengers above the fragile earth, bringing about a shift in popular perceptions about flight. Artists socialize and play provocateur to new science and technologies, offering a lay audience a glimpse into the cosmos while contesting the negative creative impulses of Big Science. The speculative mode in art helps to draw attention to and to "tremble" meteorontological regimes that resort to the technical fix.

Subatlantic: Underwater Laboratories

Swiss artist Ursula Beimann's video oeuvre centers on our strange atmospheric relations after the meteorological or meteorontological turn. Her art practice involves intensive fieldwork in remote locations, oil fields or oceans, where the effects of environmental change are clear. She often works collaboratively with *World of Matter*, a group of artists, theorists, and social justice activists that includes Paulo Taveres and Emily Eliza Scott. Biemann writes that our posthuman condition, with its volatile atmospheric climate, is no longer placed firmly in absolute matter. Instead, we "flow along formless virtual planes arising from unmeasurable, exhalable and constantly recomposing qualities" (Biemann 2015c). A weather-like experience of drifts and rushes suffuses my experience as audience to Biemann's works. *Deep Weather* (2013) reflects on the present crisis through a mixture of documentary images and poetic narrative, while *Subatlantic* (2015), *Twenty One Percent* (2016), and *Acoustic Ocean* (2018) center on fictional female scientists, in an apparent postclimate change apocalypse. The collaged, science fictional scenarios depart from the documentary form of *Deep Weather*.

The video essay *Subatlantic* (2015a) is set in a remote, unnamed North Atlantic island. The main protagonist, known only through her whispered voiceover, is a female scientist undertaking instrumental observations of a changing environment around the time of the last glacial melts, twelve thousand years ago. The video opens on the steep rocky cliffs of an island, with a mass of sea birds circling on the air currents. Images of waves running backward off the rocks signal that something is amiss. The voiceover (transcribed here from Biemann's video) narrates:

Figure 8.1
Ursula Biemann. *Subatlantic*. 2015. Video still. Image courtesy of the artist. [See color plate 15]

She is in charge of measuring fluctuations and sending the data to a lab on the coast / She inventories the freezing and melting / minutely recording her encounters with difference / All seems to follow a dynamic order, the winds, the streams, the birds, the sky.

The faintness of change made it hard to detect / but the rocks witnessed the steady rise of the sea / until one day all technical equipment had to be moved further inland.

The coast sank into the ocean for 1000 years / The lab now lies under the ocean 100 yards deep / To do her science she had to become a diver, measuring a sinking, contracting world. (Biemann 2015a)

The camera descends into the fluid underwater world of fish and kelp. The narrator describes how warm winds plunge Europe into mild winters. The camera then shifts underneath the ice, descending into the sea, where fragments of ice floes are depicted from a reverse angle. A reflection of the sun glints across a thick, syrupy looking ocean of meltwater. The narration continues: "The massive influx of arctic melt water impedes the sink to the sea floor / The ocean streams are slowing down before they stop altogether" (Biemann 2015a). The thick liquid images allow us to viscerally feel this interruption to the flow, transmuting our viewing conditions into liquid along with the world of the protagonist.

Over the course of the video images of the Arctic sea ice are replaced with a warm, tropical environment in a heavy rainstorm. A boat passes slowly along the overgrown banks of a river. The narration speeds up with the faster pace of the images:

Ideas rush by like weather events / (pause) The art is not to freeze them / She practices a science of intensities / Out in the weather she studies the self-organising flows of matter and energy and the threshold at which sudden phase transitions occur. (Biemann 2015a)

The latter part of the video catches up some time later with the scientist-narrator on a mission with the bioprospecting team of the "international seabed authority," in search of marine genetic resources. She seeks "extreme methane-eating organisms" extracted from the deep. As the arctic sheet ice dissolves, masses of microorganisms are released. The scientist is now in charge of bringing in "the directive for inter-species communication" (Biemann 2015a). *Subatlantic* ends with a note of hope for the new species hybrids that might emerge from the altered climatic regime.

The video essay form allows the scientist character's musings to seep into the icy water that is changing state together with the speed of the narration. The video is set in the Subatlantic climatic phase, which started twenty-five hundred years ago, following the Subboreal phase. For Biemann (2015c), this period is "quickly evolving towards another phase yet to be determined." She observes that the climate crisis brings creative workers into domains of knowledge where they often lack ready competency including "maritime genetics, carbon economics, atmospheric chemistry" (ibid.). Yet in moving image form, atmospheric processes, or maritime warming can be "felt" in a way that they often cannot in scientific communication.

Figure 8.2
Ursula Biemann and Mo Diener. *Twenty One Percent.* 2016. Video still.

Twenty One Percent: The Carbon Imaginary

In *Twenty One Percent* (2016), Biemann and her performance collaborator Mo Diener inhabit the time of the accretion of earth, when cosmic weathers and other accumulations of matter gave rise to life on our planet. The video commences with the sound of Nik Emch's loud electric guitar and a slow track in on the swirling nebula that represents an extraplanetary perspective—like a space-obsessed teenager's dream. Particles of cloud obscure our view as we enter the nebula. An American male voice (Clifford Owens) intones rhythmically over this atmospheric swirl:

Cosmic rays convert the interstellar clouds into complex organic matter initiating new form; generating new purpose / Deep space sugars and hydro-carbons are the building blocks for the genetic materials for life on earth. (Biemann and Diener 2016)

Using cloud animation techniques commonly found in scientific visualization, Biemann sets up a feeling for deep-time phenomena, from the mundane things we know to the remnants of cosmic clouds in Iceland. The near abstract opening scene suggests solar winds streaming outward, pushing against the plasma and fields of the interstellar medium, forming a bubble of heliosphere. On the inside of this bubble is the interplanetary medium; beyond is the interstellar medium. The heliosphere is determined by a balance among the solar wind pressure and the unknown pressures from interstellar gas, magnetic fields, small dust grains, and low-energy cosmic rays. Biemann seeks to connect us to "infinitely larger, untameable forces that animate extra-historical dimensions" (Biemann 2015c). Natural scientists generate such anterior hypotheses about the formation of planets, which Meillassoux (2008) calls "ancestral statements" about the time before us. The "arche-fossil," in Meillassoux's terms, is a material trace "indicating the existence of an ancestral reality or event; one that is anterior to terrestrial life" (2008, 10). A typical museological fossil indicates life, whereas the arche-fossil predates life itself. *Twenty One Percent* reveals a sense of these ancestral temporalities and intra-worldly existences.

The second scene changes to show a female scientific experimenter, Mo Diener, deep in a Northern Hemisphere, carbon-absorbing forest. A table holds a beaker, blue vials, elements and jars of fruit and berries, and other scientific apparatuses. Sporting a silver bandana and silver cuffs, the performer-scientist is fed by tubes of liquid in her suit. Fruit is crushed using pestle and mortar, sieved, and shaken in a beaker. These organic materials are ordinary, yet they are now defamiliarized as cosmic matter. The table layout is reminiscent of Martha Rosler's *Semiotics of the Kitchen* (1975), in which she turns mundane kitchen implements into feminist weapons of critique. But in this case, each implement is approached with the slow, sure hand of the scientist. The experimenter inhales the gas from a beaker through a pipette and shoots it into a pot boiling on an element. Biemann adds to Barad's insight when she writes that "it is the questions, choices, movements, equipment, and directed observations that generate a specific material reality which the artist/scientist co-produces, and of which she is a part" (Biemann 2015b, 121). The sci-fi scientist may be cooking up a new version of the world.

In a later sequence, we find a figure tramping through a snowy landscape in Iceland in a long coat, battling through a howling wind. A female voice (Julia Riedel) narrates:

Interstellar ice stays suspended in the hills / the air thick with water molecules, the winds full of gas particles, inhaling, exhaling / Before humans carbon dioxide was abundant / Catastrophic oxygen pollution caused only creatures who could breathe oxygen to survive / When oxygen reached twenty-one percent life changed / High oxygen made creatures fly and it drove the evolution of thinking minds / Now, rising carbon in the air sucks the oxygen we breathe / In lesser air our minds will fade, without it we have empty skies. (Biemann and Diener 2016)

This narration invites diachronic thinking back to the beginnings of the earth and forward to after we have left it. The human figure is dwarfed in scale in relation to the cosmic perspective. Our imagination goes visiting—in this case, in space and time. Biemann proposes a hybrid of scientist–performance artist, tramping purposefully through the snow in a whirl of cloud, into the unknown. A final scene in *Twenty One Percent* highlights a British voice (Adrian Lucas) chanting the names of carbon compounds against a starry, nighttime sky. The raw recitation of the carbon compounds is a form of concrete poetry that exemplifies Biemann's posthuman concern for transactions of phenomena, traditionally the realm of the natural sciences.

Carbon is an element critical to all life: it is the second-most common element in the human body and a major proportion of all the molecules from which organisms are formed. Living organisms are intimately involved in the carbon cycle, and the rise of carbon in the atmosphere over time will effect a change in our bodies themselves. The *carbon imaginary* is also a symbolic figure in Povinelli's geontological proposition. The carbon imaginary transposes biological concepts such as metabolism, including "birth, growth-reproduction, [and] death," with "ontological concepts, such as event, conatus/affectus and finitude." I find a form of cinematic "carbon imaginary" in *Twenty One Percent*, a place of exchange where conceptual intensities operate, and where can be found, as Povinelli writes, "thrills, wonders, anxieties, perhaps terrors, of the other of Life, namely the Inert, Inanimate, Barren. In this scarred space, the ontological is revealed to be biontology"(2016, 17).

The cinematic carbon imaginary suffuses *Twenty One Percent*, from the biological evolution from high oxygen to the finitude of "empty skies," from metabolizing processes to vast nothingness. In the third great age of carbon, we find destruction of resources and carbon release at unprecedented scales. The rebalance of carbon will happen despite human efforts, if we consider climactic timescales. Humans will have to "index ourselves anew," as Biemann (2015c) writes. Any metabolic indexing of life in a runaway climate change scenario will be outside our human control. In Biemann's recent video installation *Acoustic Ocean* (2018), Indigenous Sami singer, musician, and climate activist Sofia Jannok performs as a biologist-diver who relies on hydrophones, parabolic microphones, and other recording devices to communicate from and with the deep sea. In Biemann's quasi-science fictions, we are thrown back and forth in the interval between earth and cosmos, between historical periods and geographic displacements. Yet far from being disconcerting, these leaps reveal a pattern of interactions and possibilities, both present and yet to come. The work ultimately connects the ancestral, speculative realm to current ecopolitical realities of the changing climate.

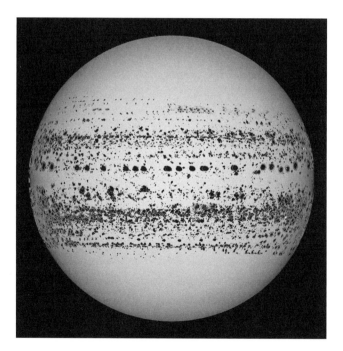

Figure 8.3
Sarah and Joseph Belknap. *Four Months of Sun Spots*. 2014. Digital archival print, 7" × 7". Courtesy of the NASA/SDO and AIA, EVE, and HMI science teams.

Sarah and Joseph Belknap: Solar Weather

Just as Beimann's work reprocesses current scientific and philosophical understand-ings of the climate and cosmos, so are we brought closer to solar weather in Sarah and Joseph Belknap's artwork. The Chicago-based partnership uses consumer technology for easy access to the solar images that become its art materials. The multichannel installation *12 Months of the Sun* (2014), exhibited at the Museum of Contemporary Art, Chicago (2014–2015), is composed of free images from NASA's Space Weather Media Viewer mobile app (2011). The artists animated still files of remote satellite images from the app, in an everyday consumer encounter with the changing face of the sun. The intricate patterns of the sunspots that indicate magnetic energy on the sun drive the mutable aesthetic of the animations. The darker, cooler sunspots are storms on the sun's surface, marked by intense magnetic solar flares and gassy loops from the sun's corona. Solar wind, according to the Space Weather Media Viewer website, (NASA, n.d.) consists of magnetized plasma flares and, in some cases, is linked to sunspots. These heliotropic winds produce galactic rays that may in turn affect atmospheric phenom-ena on earth, such as our clouds.

The solar images are accompanied by science-fictional objects, such as saggy moon skins and pebble-sized models of meteors in the Belknaps' practice. Extraterrestrial bod-ies are drawn into the human range of perception, so we can see and touch cosmic remnants. From a broad range of image renderings offered by the Space Weather Media Viewer mobile app, the Belknaps selected a black-and-white coronagraph, described in scientific terms as a Helioseismic and Magnetic Imager (HMI) intensitygram, for *4 Months of Sun Spots* (2014). They placed this monochrome photograph composite near the entrance to the exhibition entrance. The softly lit image of the solar storms, although a composited image, holds the seductive realism of both a black-and-white photograph and a scientific communication. Unlike the colorful and fast-moving visu-alizations produced by NASA's Goddard Space Flight Center Scientific Visualization Studio, featured on the Space Weather Media Viewer, the artists' *4 Months of Sun Spots* (2014) is a formally restrained and resonant image.

The installation *12 Months of the Sun* in the same exhibition appears much more hap-hazard; a stack of five anachronistic box-television objects were installed with an array of multihued, animated sun images. The Space Weather Media Viewer offers data from a variety of NASA instruments, such as X-ray telescopes and extreme ultraviolet images, are delivered to a terrestrial observatory in Austria as numerical data from orbital satel-lites. The sun images aggregate transient phenomena and are "color quoted" with false colors so that scientists can quickly distinguish them in vibrant greens, purples, and

reds. In the installation, the Belknaps highlighted the aesthetic decisions of the visualization scientists by giving each screen a false-color image of the sun; from the yellows
of atmospheric-assembly images to the red, large-angle spectrometric coronograph
images. Unlike the careful process of the data-producing scientist, however, a random
element of interior psychology is brought into the artists' selection of images in this
case. The Belknaps' chance-based moment of image gathering is described by curator
Karsten Lund as follows: "From May 2013 to May 2014, whenever Joseph thought
about the sun, even casually, he and Sarah would take screen shots of five of the filtered
satellite views. The resulting regimen of screen grabs—irregular and idiosyncratic—was
dictated by their thought patterns and passing conversations" (2014, 2). After a year
the artists had enough images (and had enough conversations) to generate the stack of
animations that includes magnetic storms and other solar weather events.

The work *12 Months of the Sun* signals our precarious position within the broader
cosmos. The artists invite a slowed-down view of plural suns, decentering the singular
encounter with the earth's only sun. Unlike the custom-made instruments of Hinterding and Haines's *Earthstar* (see chapter 2), the artists work with readily available software to reconsider the modes of visualization of scientists. The Belknaps state, "We are
extremely interested in filtered seeing … It [the Media Viewer] allows us to see things
that the human eye cannot see. It is both real and faked/mediated. The enhancement
and modification is not done to deceive but rather to show what we cannot see" (Picard
2014). This filtered seeing, by implication, extends to the filtered view of our physical
reality in an epoch of alternative facts and questionable "truthiness" of images and
models. Sunspots and solar winds have been linked to terrestrial climate change, but
the majority of climate scientists view the sun's influence as minimal compared to
human industrial activity (Scientific American 2017). Some of science's meteorontological power to explain is co-opted when artists create alter images, highlighting the
subjectivity of all scientific processes of visualization.

Cloud-Making

From compositing new weather in animation software to the physical making of
clouds in the troposphere, artists speculate on a possible, even probable future in which
the weather is deliberately remade. Sobecka describes her *Nephology 1: Cloud Maker*
(2012–2013) project as "a personal device" for weather modification. The artwork was
commissioned for the *Speculative Realities* exhibition, held December 15–22, 2013, at
V2 Lab for Unstable Media in Rotterdam. When her custom cloud-making instrument,
carried by a weather balloon, reaches a specific altitude, it releases cloud condensation

Figure 8.4
Karolina Sobecka. *Cloud Machine*. 2013. Commissioned as part of the *Amateur Human and Nephologies* exhibit at the V2 Institute for Unstable Media, Rotterdam. Image courtesy of the artist. [See color plate 16]

nuclei (CCN). A puff of cloud forms from this heat and water vapor when moisture in the air condenses into cloud droplets. The tiny cloud that is emitted gives this grand-sounding scheme a gentle humor. Despite their familiarity, clouds are some of the least understood elements in our atmospheric system; they are shifting moments of condensation and in constant mutation with the winds. Tim Ingold observes that to view the clouds "is to catch a glimpse of the sky-in-formation, never the same from one moment to the next" (2007, 28). Clouds are not objects, but processes.

The whimsical politics of Sobecka's diminutive cloud project implies that simply because we have the means to generate clouds doesn't necessarily mean that we should, on a much larger, climate-altering scale. The formation of clouds from particulate matter features prominently in future projects to protect the warming world from the sun's heat. Dreams of meteorontological power over the weather system have entered a third major phase. In the controversial field of climate engineering, also called *geoengineering*, technical interventions to create brighter, more reflective clouds that shield earth from the sun's radiation are proposed. The World Meteorological Organization (WMO), however, has restricted weather modification programs in member countries, as many scientists agree that the sensitive feedback effects of weather modification are yet to be understood.

A neopositivist optimism pervades the rhetoric of restoring global temperatures to "normal" by increasing cloud reflectivity to compensate for some of the effects of greenhouse gas concentrations. Certain scientists state that their models indicate that their chosen cloud-seeding strategy "can restore global averages of temperature, precipitation and sea ice to present day values" (Rasch, Latham, and Chen 2009, 1). Paul Crutzen, well-known for giving us the term *Anthropocene*, argues for geoengineering as the most effective way to stop global warming. In 2002, Crutzen proposed that "scientists and engineers [must] guide society towards environmentally sustainable management during the era of the Anthropocene. This will require appropriate human behavior at all scales, and may well involve internationally accepted, large-scale geoengineering projects, for instance to 'optimize' climate" (Moore 2016, 140). This language likens climate to a computer system that just needs to be properly managed. Further, Stengers notes the irony inherent in the fact that just as the campaign to deny climate change is running out of steam, new voices advocating geoengineering as the only solution are on the rise. She predicts that the radical uncertainty about the effectiveness of geoengineering—or worse, the catastrophe it might cause—"won't make the capitalist machine hesitate, because it is incapable of hesitating: it can't do anything other" (Stengers 2015, 9). Big Science is beholden to market forces.

At a much smaller scale, Sobecka's cloud machines familiarize us with the grand intent of programs such as SPICE, inviting us to reassess the values we have and the risks that we are prepared to take. A provocation underscores the project: Do we know enough about natural systems in the troposphere to interfere with them? The cloud-making machines give us a sense of what climate engineering really means. For science commentator Robert Russell Sassor (2015), Sobecka's machines are "a way for people to shape their own understanding about a topic or issue and, in some cases, to participate in and influence its discourse." He observes that though measuring parts per million of greenhouse gases makes for compelling science, it has largely failed to inspire the public to any kind of mitigating action. The online *Matter of Air* weblog of Sobecka's research-based practice is important to document the citizen and scientific contexts for her projects. The blog provides detailed, often humorous accounts of the artist's attempts to understand the Big Science pursuit of geoengineering. She speculates on the ethics of further intervention in the troposphere in the following catalog statement: "The absurdity of trying to make a cloud is [instead] linked to the fact that clouds are just tiny 'footprints'—temporary local manifestations—of the giant 'hyper-object,' the climate, so massively distributed in time and space that it is invisible to us, … It towers above human comprehension and makes attempts such as commercial or military weather modification either laughable or horrible" (Kasprzak 2013, 21). Yet a public workshop hosted by Sobecka is more ambivalent when she invites artists, technologists, and scientists to discuss "low environmental impact climate engineering." The question of whether artists or designers play a role in our atmospheric future is raised in this event, designed as a mirror event for the Low Environmental Impact Climate Engineering Experiments held at the Institute for Advanced Sustainability Studies in Potsdam on September 7–8, 2016. The goal of the open workshop was to create a possible list of alternative climate-engineering experiments. The workshop title, *A Machine for Making the Future* (2016), derives from Hans-Jorg Rheinberger's description of future machines that could function as both "technical objects" and "epistemic things." Art objects are situated as vehicles for materializing questions. The workshop encourages reflection, yet the territory is slippery; could climate-modifying art projects develop into risky atmospheric interventions rather than mere thought experiments? We are always part of that nature that we seek to understand, where even artists' instruments have a tangible impact on our skies.

Imbibing Clouds

Sobecka joins a host of other cloud-making artists: Dennis Oppenheim's *Whirlpool (Eye of the Storm)* (1973) traced a spiral tornado in the sky using the white smoke discharged by an aircraft; Andrea Polli's *Cloud Car* emits a cloud of pseudotoxins in reaction to passersby (2009 to present); Dutch artist Berndnaut Smilde's indoor cloud photographs and recent moving image video *Nimbus Atlas* (2015) document a self-made cloud emerging and decomposing in slow motion HD video. However, the invitation to imbibe cloud vapor in liquid form takes Sobecka into uncharted territory. For the project *Thinking Like a Cloud* (2013–2015) Sobecka has designed another cloud machine to collect cloud vapor and offer it for us to drink. The design of her cloud-collecting instrument is inspired by agricultural fog-collecting meshes. Rashel polypropylene wings are fixed to a weather balloon payload that extracts up to 30 percent of the humidity from a cloud into water droplets that flow into a container. The liquid contents, complete with pollutants and microbiomes, are then ingested by volunteers.

Stations for cloud-tasting from test tube–like vessels selected from a "cloud-tasting menu" have been set up at both art and scientific events, such as the Climate Engineering conference in Berlin in 2014. In the cloud-tasting events, Sobecka shares information about the microbiology of each specimen of cloud vapor and asks participants to reflect on how the experience of drinking cloud has shaped their understanding of human effects on the weather system. The cloud-liquid offering at a science conference is a radical intrusion within the established conference stock-in-trade of delivering climate information through presentations and numerical data. The frisson of disgust at consuming the brackish cloud water is revealed in a video of volunteers in Fei Ngo Shan, Hong Kong, in 2013 on Sobecka's website. Although they are not coerced by the artist, the volunteers seem to force themselves to drink from their city's polluted air, the same air that they constantly breathe. The project is designed to promote interconnectedness, yet there is also an element of the childhood dare. We ingest the clouds as the dirty laundry of the skies produced by our own species.

On another level, *Thinking Like a Cloud* returns us to our meteorological beginnings in the cosmic clouds that contain the microbial matter of life. The upper troposphere has historically been beyond our reach, a place of nonidentical otherness. The process of ingesting cloud confronts the separations between cloud object and human subject in the realm of the alter-Anthropocene imaginary (Äsberg, Neimanis, and Hayes 2015, 485). A new kind of transcorporeal engagement with climate emerges in Sobecka's practice. Through taste, we "cultivate an imaginary where our bodies are makers, transfer points, and sensors of climate change" (Neimanis and Walker 2014, 560). To drink the cloud liquid in Sobecka's event registers the effects of climate change intimately inside our bodies.

Cloudbusting: Hinterding and Haines

Rather than cloud-making, as Sobecka does, for Hinterding and Haines the search for a means to puncture the clouds to make rain becomes urgent as drought continues to threaten the Australian continent. *Proposal for Cloud Busting Machines* (2007) first appeared as a series of A3, hand-drawn, ink diagrams exhibited by Hinterding in *The Trouble with the Weather* (UTS gallery, Sydney, 2008). The drawings contain an ethical code for the practice of cloud-busting, written by Austrian psychoanalyst and inventor Wilhelm Reich in the 1950s. Reich's fifteen "Rules to Follow in Cloud Engineering" are inscribed in deep-purple ink next to the cloud-busting-machine diagrams. Rule 9 reads, "Never 'drill a hole' into the sky right above you unless you aim for a long drawn rain." The aerated ink splatters of cloud recall the ink-blown winds in the cloud paintings of Chinese Tang painters. In 2008, when Hinterding sketched the *Proposal for Cloud Busting Machines*, Australia was in severe drought. In China that same year, officials were paying farmers to clear the atmosphere before the Beijing Olympics by firing silver iodide pellets into the clouds.

Figure 8.5
Joyce Hinterding and David Haines. *The Black Ray: Cloudbuster Number Three: Orgone Energy Cloud Engineering Device*. 2012. Installation view in *Orgasm*, Breenspace, Sydney. Anodized aluminum, irrigation piping, and a water pump.

Later in 2008, two practical versions of cloud-busters were developed by Hinterding and Haines in Kellerberren on a residency in the midst of the wheat belt in Western Australia in the ongoing drought. The cloud-busters were built from irrigation materials used in the farming district. The artists chopped up the pipes normally used for misters and sprinklers from the local hardware store and developed the works in the studio. To functionalize the machines, high-pressure water moving through the pipe needs to be connected to running water in both directions or, according to Reich, the users may become ill as the orgone energy required for cloud-busting will be amplified. By 2012,

Haines and Hinterding exhibited the finished cloud-busters at Breenspace. *The Black Ray: Cloudbuster Number Three: Orgone Energy Cloud Engineering Device* and the *Starlight Driver: Cloudbuster Number Four: Orgone Energy Cloud Engineering Device* (2011–2012) are made from anodized aluminum, irrigation piping, and a water pump.

Hinterding and Haines's cloud-busters reflect on the history of our vain attempts to control the weather through atmospheric energies. Pluvicultural weather-modification programs were trialed in Australia as early as 1902, when meteorologist Clement Wragge invented a canon-shaped rainmaker gun for the Queensland government. The large rainmaker gun is still remembered by current Australian meteorologists as entirely dysfunctional (Day 2007, 36). In the era of the Cold War and the Vietnam War, cloud-seeding for weather modification in warfare was attempted by the United States government—at great cost, but with little effectiveness. Although Wilhelm Reich was not an engineer, he won a prize in the 1950s when he broke the drought in the United States with his claim to manipulate orgone energy, a libidinal, bioorganic energy that is attracted to itself—a productive, coalescing energy. Water vaporizers and metal pipes connected to running water draw energy from the atmosphere. This has the intended effect of either creating clouds or producing holes in clouds. Whether or not Reich's practice of Cosmic Orgone Engineering (CORE) is verifiably effective, for Hinterding and Haines, Reich models a holistic relationship across art and science through his efforts to understand the energetic environment.

Hinterding and Haines observe that the current diabolical propositions for weather modification lack accounting for environmental feedback loops of a sensitive system. Kahn (2015) positions *Cloudbusters* in relation to the new exchanges between body and environment now that the "Cold War has morphed to the Warm War." He writes: "Humans have modified the weather by default ever since large-scale agriculture began, but recent proposals to geo-engineer the sky to stave off an increasingly hotter hot-house effect are the mutant spawn of a marriage between managerialism and cane toads let loose at the largest possible scale. This is a militarised response that does nothing to address the amorphous political and economic forces responsible for their own default weather modification" (Davis and Kahn 2015, 33). The cloud-busters are an ethical counterpoint to the knowledge that we now can intervene in the weather. They remain "functional yet disabled" (Haines and Hinterding 2017), stopping short of altering the weather as Sobecka does with her *Nephology 1: Cloud Maker.*

Although the artists confirm that the cloud-busters do indeed seem to work, there is an implicit politics in their choice not to use cloud-seeding apparatuses in any actual environmental system. Hinterding adheres to Reich's Rule 1 from "Rules to Follow in Cloud Engineering": "Shed all ambition to impress anyone" (Reich 1954). Hinterding

Figure 8.6
Joyce Hinterding and David Haines. *Soundship (descender 1)*. 2016. Video still.

observes, "You don't have to turn them on to speculate about what they are," while for Haines there is a provocative role for aesthetics in holding up art-science possibilities for modifying the atmosphere, but not necessarily enacting them (Haines and Hinterding 2017). The cloud-busters are analogues for Hinterding and Haines's concern with energy observation, sensation, and how this becomes evident in the atmosphere through instruments. While the cloud-busters tilt up to the clouds, *Soundship (descender 1)* (2016) is a double video and sound work recorded from an operational data-recording vessel, custom-made by the artists, that broke through the clouds and into the stratosphere.

Stratospheric Weather

Soundship (descender 1) may well be the first artist-launched, site-specific artwork in the stratosphere. In 2016, an unmanned craft was sent into space from a launch site in a field in northwestern New South Wales in Australia. Sobecka's weather balloon gathered or made clouds in the troposphere, whereas Hinterding and Haines collect sounds, video, and other data through the ascent of a helium weather balloon into the uppermost reaches of the atmosphere. This event is exhibited as a double video projection, commissioned by the Museum of Applied Arts and Sciences and shown for the first time at *Gravity (and Wonder)*, hosted by Penrith Regional Gallery from September 30, 2016, to February 28, 2017. The technical cargo of the craft included three GoPro cameras, microphones and GPS trackers, and an invented Aeolian instrument based on a Japanese *unari*, or kite bow.

Soundship (descender 1) returns to the skies as a new frontier for a systems-based art, continuing German artist Otto Piene's speculative explorations. Piene's *Olympic Rainbow* (1972) unleashed five different-colored helium-filled lengths of polythene tubes across the sky for the closing of the 1972 Summer Olympics in Munich. Like Piene, Hinterding and Haines strive for the airstreams, astronomic and cosmonautic realms, assisted by the most recent developments in science and technology. The artists worked with a team that included high-altitude balloon experts Robert and Jason Brand. The left projection of the double-screen installation is the view from a camera looking back at the earth, from which we glimpse the shadow of the balloon itself against the fields of the launch site. Gradually, the blue-green crust of the land fades, and the balloon is clearly adrift in space, rocking very gently in the darkness of the stratosphere. The curve of the earth below is glimpsed through the blueish orb of atmosphere. This sight stirs the melancholy imagining for me that we might one day occupy this vantage point, looking down on the remains of earth. The stratospheric weather is calm and more stable than the gusts of tropospheric wind. The right projection is the camera view up to the balloon and beyond to space with the sun flaming in the corner of the lens.

The sound at first is a soft thrum like the buzz of insects, modulated at intervals by a lower sound as the balloon rises gently. These are the Aeolian sounds of wind across taut ribbons. Higher notes emerge as the balloon rises. Eventually, the balloon floats noiselessly in the darkness of space at zero gravity. Crystalline lights fringe the lens. When the balloon reaches 33, 722 meters and zero pressure, the peaceful motion is disrupted when the weather balloon bursts, as predicted by the launch team. The camera swivels, revealing shattered shards of rubber balloon, and the sun is glimpsed rotating through the blackness of space as the craft tries to right itself. The cords and fragments of equipment twist wildly in the recording; fortunately, a parachute is deployed to carry the payload of equipment back down to earth, where it stops suddenly. Given this hurtling, unruly descent, the retrieval of the unscathed recordings is an accomplishment itself. The craft landed 150 kilometers from where it was launched; a dip in the jet stream meant that it traveled further than expected. An animated weather map on the project's website points to how attuned the team was to the weather conditions surrounding the balloon launch to ensure they retrieved their treasure trove of sound and video data.

The sight of the fragile layer of atmosphere on which our brief existence depends recalls William Nordhaus's warning: "If we do not know how human activities will affect the thin layer of life-supporting activities that gave birth to and nurture human civilisation … should we not be ultra-conservative and tilt towards preserving the natural world at the expense of economic growth and development?" (Flannery [2005] 2010, 267). Yet this floating, omniscient perspective didn't just awaken the consciousness of ecological connectedness that the early astronauts report, the *overview effect*.

Technically assisted vision from space is instrumental to a whole new range of social and scientific agendas. Google Earth, military surveillance systems, and corporate maps have all evolved from the remote perspective from the stratosphere. The prosaic mappings of Google Earth serve economic and military purposes of identification and mapping, whereas *Soundship (descender 1)* gives us back the astounding beauty of the earth viewed gradually from space, with the sensory experience of uncanny space music. Immense scalar perceptions are brought into the orbit of a layperson. We experience an intimate connection to atmosphere, despite the epic scale of this ascending and descending "shot-reverse-shot," from earth to cosmos and back again.

Jet-Streaming through the Sky

Argentinian artist Tomás Saraceno's recent project *Aerocene* is a series of air-fueled and weather-borne sculptures intended to achieve the longest emission-free journey

Figure 8.7
Tomás Saraceno. *Aerocene*. 2015. Pilot launch at the White Sands Desert. Courtesy of the artist; Pinksummer Contemporary Art, Genoa; Tanya Bonakdar, New York; Andersen's Contemporary, Copenhagen; Esther Schipper, Berlin. Photograph © Tomás Saraceno. [See color plate 17]

around the world. The aerated sculptures rise and remain buoyant with the heat of the sun and infrared radiation from the surface of the earth. Some of the airy sculptures float independently; in others, a human participant hangs precariously underneath the forms, utterly dependent on the vagaries of weather. Saraceno often has used atmospheric materials of air and water within his installations. Prior to the *Aerocene* project, his gallery-based, habitable modules were still tethered to the ground, suggesting that we cannot yet escape our dependence on the earth. In *Aerocene*, they ascend toward the stratosphere, targeting the jet streams. "There are highways in the sky; the jet stream moves at a speed of 300 km per hour," Saraceno points out, "but first, you need to know where the jet stream is" (cited in Lacey 2016). To understand how to find the ribbons of very strong winds that move flows of weather around the earth, Saraceno collaborated with scientists and engineers to propel his mobile sculpture.

The *Aerocene* assemblages float through the air, sometimes with their suspended passenger below, without burning fossil fuels, without using solar panels and batteries, and without helium, hydrogen, or other rare gases. For Saraceno, the air is free space, unconstrained by terrestrial limits. Various iterations of the *Aerocene* sculptures have been launched from the Solomon Islands, New Mexico, Cambridge, Paris, Germany, and the United States. On Saraceno's project website, there is an open invitation to participate in Museo Aero Solar via workshops and social gatherings that have already taken place in over twenty-one locations worldwide. In an early experiment in the Solomon Islands, the *Aerocene* crafts were made from biodegradable materials that would dissolve into the earth where they came to rest. The *#fly for change* hashtag keeps us informed about the latest locations of launches. Online participation is invited in the form of hacking the flight path to reset the proposed journey of the aerosolar crafts, with the incentive of winning an aereosolar flight. Saraceno boldly wagers on the "Aerocene epoch" (Aerocene 2017) to supersede the Anthropocene. This ambitious intent to "hack the Anthropocene" destabilizes regimes of meteorontological power. The drifting artwork seems impervious to the geopolitics of tightening national borders on the earth below.

Saraceno models renewable energy sources in his aerosolar inflatables to signal future directions for the aeronautical industry. The artist is a long-term collaborator with MIT's Center for Art, Science, and Technology (CAST) and Leila Wheatley Kinney, as well as Ludovica Illari and Bill McKenna of the Earth, Atmospheric, and Planetary Science Department (EAPS). McKenna describes how Saraceno was intrigued by the potential of global circulation flows to assist flight in his first visits to his lab, during which McKenna was mapping global circulations in a tank. Saraceno's prior experiments with the scientists at France's Centre National d'études Spatiales (CNES) used aerosolar forces to lift him into the air by sun. The next step was to stay airborne throughout the night as well as the day, using the Earth's radiation and thermodynamic gradients. Saraceno and his science collaborators assembled a set of visualizations of fundamental phenomena in the atmosphere, including fronts and jet streams, trade winds, and turbulent weather systems, to coordinate the flight path (Lacey 2016). The scientific expertise involved in designing the flight was made freely available as part of *Aerocene*'s public education program.

Saraceno was intrigued by the so-called overview effect as a phenomenological experience of orbital consciousness. In earlier gallery-based works, Saraceno made spherical sculptures to be inhabited by participants, such as *In Orbit* (2013) and *Cloud Cities* (2011–2016). The formal designs of the spheres are based on observations of natural phenomena like cloud formations, foam, and spider webs. The *Cloud Cities* sculptures (2012–2017) are inflatable acrylic spheres, some filled with living plant organisms, and fed by water suspended around the gallery space in one iteration in Hamburger Bahnhoff. Their ropey tendrils attach to the gallery architecture in a temporary synthesis of industrial materials and organic matter. When we crawl inside the suspended bubble, drawing on the protected air inside, we are experientially propelled into a fragile interaction with the bios, growing in the brightly lit smoothness of the gallery, where we would least expect to find tangled growths of life. We are all implicitly and literally reliant on each other in this cosseted environment; when one person moves, the other must move as well, so there is an ethic of cooperation between people. The spheres have interrelated effects in a complex system.

On Space Time Foam (2012) hosted high-flying participants on billowing pressurized layers of transparent spheres at the HangarBicocca in Milan. Latour (2016) comments on his own experience of reciprocity inside this work: "You cannot move without becoming sensitive to the medium." For Latour, Saraceno offers a powerful view of how networks, spheres, and tensors fit together and are codependent on distributed action "through a complex ecology of tributaries, allies, accomplices, and helpers" (Latour 2016). Saraceno's sense of symbiotic relation with atmosphere recalls designer Buckminster Fuller's geodesic domes, first proposed in a public forum in 1954. The dome-shaped dwelling machines were envisioned to be discrete controlled environments, self-sustaining, dust-free, and climate-controlled, in sites from the Arctic circle to Siberia to the Amazon to the Sahara. Fuller sought a model of reality based on moveable elements and flows of physical, psychosocial, and environmental elements that interconnect in patterned structures. The airborne passenger harnessed to Saraceno's floating sculptural assemblages is even more dependent on a fine balance of weather-driven patterns, relinquishing control over the flight path to the jet stream.

Saraceno's speculative approach to phenomena reveals a bold faith in our creative energies. He observes, "Hydrogen, helium, humans, plants, animals, everything is dark energy. Everything we know, everything that we can name is only four percent of what is out there. ... But, without being negative, curiosity is something that might keep us alive" (Saraceno 2011). There is no place for cynicism in the *Aerocene* (2017) project's message "of simplicity, creativity and cooperation for a world of tumultuous geopolitical relations, reminding us of our symbiotic relationship with the Earth and all its species." Now more than ever, a new ethics of engagement is needed to see ourselves as part of our atmosphere. For Sanford Kwinter, the weather is replacing the former model of "world-as-clock" as a speculative model of the universe. Reflecting on *Aerocene*, Kwinter (2016) writes that "sky has become a place, a plenum, a place to move and think differently, indeed it is becoming both a mode of thought itself and the foundation of an emerging ethos or system of ethoi." Yet to consider the practical ethics of how to best care for the atmosphere crisscrossed by jet contrails, space debris, and climate-modifying compounds is urgent; the sky can no longer be simply a free space for human endeavor, materially or allegorically.

Amid increasing calls for "degrowth," can artists afford to make anything much at all while espousing an ecopolitical agenda? In the contentious essay "Love Your Monsters: Why We Must Care for Technologies as We Do for Our Children," Latour opposes "a principle of abstention" from action or invention, offering instead "a change in the way any action is considered, a deep tidal change in the linkage modernism established between science and politics" (2011, 25). Latour has been criticized for his use of the term *postenvironmentalism* and his faith in technological solutions that might coincide with neoliberal agendas (Demos 2016, 21). Along with Demos, I am as uncomfortable with the term *postenvironmentalism* as I am with *postfeminism*; both imply that the political goals of these movements have been achieved. But Latour's argument is that there is an obligation for technologists to care for their creations and the processes they unleash, rather than to abandon them like Frankenstein's monster. For artists, by implication, any unintended technical malfunctions in the atmosphere are on the heads of their initiators. Artists such as Sobecka, Saraceno, and Hinterding and Haines who experiment in air space are as ethically beholden as geoengineers to take care of our present and future weathers. By my count, this responsibility is being taken seriously, even while artists' material decisions are increasingly scrutinized.

We have never been able to depend on the weather, yet the more weather usurps *homo faber*'s sense of order, the stronger the meteorontological desire for control becomes. An emerging discourse of geosecurity and meteoro-security is overtaking the concern for biosecurity (Povinelli 2016, 19). Climate insecurity has been identified as posing a threat to the sovereignty of countries by exacerbating existing threats to peaceful prosperity. For instance, the American Security Project notes: "Climate change alone will not cause wars, but it serves as an 'Accelerant of Instability' or a 'Threat Multiplier' that makes already existing threats worse" (ASP, n.d.). Rather than position the weather as a threat, Hinterding and Haines's and Saraceno's air instruments move *with* the vagaries of meteorological currents. Ontological questions about how we coexist with nature, along with the physical flux of the stratospheric winds, are negotiated in artworks that relinquish control to the weather itself.

Rapid short-term solutions to climate change would alter our atmospheric future while still maintaining lifestyles of consumption with as little change from their present state as possible. I have argued that artists expose the untenable extreme edge of climate-modification schemes. The transgression of planetary boundaries is offered as a technological solution to late modernity's problems. Yet the process of extracting, dumping, and externalizing the effect of greenhouse gas emissions shatters the "purposefulness of the world" and the cosmos, in Arendtian terms. Arendt traces nature back to its origins in the Latin word *nasci*, to be born, and the Greek origin of *physis*, from *phyein*, to grow out of or to appear by itself. Natural systems should be "whatever they become" (Arendt 1958, 150). Arendt coaxes us toward a noninstrumentalist "letting be" that might slow down our destructive trajectory. The purpose of things exists immanently rather than through instrumental design. Much of an earlier sense of letting things—the weather—*be* is lost in the current bureaucratization of the environment, reframed as in need of rational, evidence-based management. The artworks charted in this chapter share an ethic of meteorontological engagement, rather than abandoning climate warming to scientists and engineers alone.

Meteorological art resists grand schemes like climate modification in favor of working alongside environmental scientists at a modest scale. Hinterding and Haines collaborated with weather balloon experts Robert and Jason Brand to detect the airflows that *Soundship (descender 1)* needed to reach the stratosphere. Saraceno's aerosolar sculptures move beyond the fossil-fuel norms of aviation together with many meteorologists and engineers. Biemann's cinematic imaginary hinges upon the figure of the environmental scientist. The Belknaps redistribute remote solar phenomena through available software, and Sobecka's cloud-makers are "personal devices" that neither demystify nor sensationalize science. Artists open technologies for us to comprehend and debate ecological threats and opportunities otherwise out of our grasp. Meteorontological art is oriented toward an unknown future, tentatively testing out aesthetic forms that could even contribute to our survival. Far from a sense of desolation and abandonment in the face of a world without us, such artworks provoke us to think and act on our hopes for future weathers.

Conclusion

In cities, we can almost be convinced by the living conditions of our internal artificial atmospheres, with electric lights instead of the sun and air conditioning to control the temperature. Substituted air releases us from the limits that once dictated a closer relationship with the weather. Now, even a substituted external environment is proposed. But the ecological cost of making artificial climates, and our mistreatment of the atmosphere as a whole, is becoming devastatingly apparent. We continue to treat our weather and climate as objects when we turn away from Indigenous, activist, and artist voices that establish the human as part of nature and nature as part of ourselves. In this book, I have traced a genealogy of meteorological art practices that are weather-like: from Indigenous cosmovisions to the speculative weathers of the final chapter. Taken together, the rogue weathers of these artworks release our imagination from the controlled weather-as-data set, or televisual spectacle.

The weather, once considered threatening and all-powerful over humanity—as painted in William Hodges's *A View of Cape Stephens with Water Spouts* (1776)—is now often positioned as controllable or alterable. It is spoken of, rather than listened to. Environmentalist notions of stewardship of the atmosphere generally situate humans as acting on behalf of the nonhuman. Instead, in this book, I have treated weather as a political force in a "*res*-publica" of things, or *res*, that "act" or resonate with human and nonhuman senses other than the rational-cognitive (Latour 2005). Contemporary meteorological art exceeds the painted frame of weatherscape through its chaotic appearances. When we raise a kite or a sail to the winds, the weather as an energetic force transcends exchange value in human economies. A postanthropocentric orientation surfaces in meteorological art, at its most apparent in F4's *O-Tū-Kapua (What Clouds See)* and Sobecka's *Thinking Like a Cloud*. Artworks such as these exist of and for the weather. The oscillating pole in Lye's *Wind Wand* (2000) and the waves that crash on the groynes beneath it are made for the energetic transfer of winds, as much as they are made for "us." *Wind Wand* tells the story of the increasingly storm-afflicted shores of Aotearoa New Zealand, along with the suffering of inhabitants of other small islands in higher latitudes in Te Moana nui a Kiwa.

In 2016, Tongan performance artist Kalisolaite 'Uhila used his body as a human sundial in *Oku 'ikai tatali 'a e taimi mo e tahi ki ha taha* (Time and Tide Waits for No Man). In a performance made of tides, weather, and time, he stands motionless in the sunlight by the Wellington foreshore, facing the sea. By becoming still, 'Uhila's body absorbs the seas and weather, and we attune to the elements as we watch the artist and his lengthening shadow. The performance evokes the thirteenth-century Tongan gateway Ha'amonga 'a Maui (the burden of Maui), an ancient stone threshold once used as a sundial for the shadows it casts. 'Uhila's durational performances are slight incursions into everyday life, like a shifting weather front that connects a sacred history to the contemporary moment. He engages with the sun as a divine ancestor, yet his performance practice foregrounds issues of homelessness and cultural disjunction for the Tongan migrant in Aotearoa New Zealand.

By adopting a meteorological mode of being, from the systems-based art in the 1960s to contemporary generative art, former separations among nature, science, technology, and art evaporate. Meteorological media in the 1960s challenged the fixity of the art object and the authority of art, and state, institutions. Haacke's weather systems and Lye's wind sculptures were animated by the weather, yet they also attend to systemic politics. Medalla's cloud sculptures drew together experiences of war with the free sky-space of potential as an absurdist, frothing machine, whereas Shiomi's event-scores and Nakaya's fog gardens reach for our weathers without and within. *Cloud Music* unleashed its collaborators from the constraints of the television and space-science industries with all the delight in weather's liveness and ungraspability that persists today in contemporary art.

Meteorological art projects operate in a moving fabric of social-scientific imbroglios, including art audiences, gallery systems, and science organizations. Scientific visualization once seemed to directly communicate the weather to us, but the work of artists makes evident that the former obviousness of "matters of fact" through a lens of scientific objectivity are in fact precarious and value-laden. Artworks not only draw on scientific concepts and data sets to deepen understanding of cultural and informational processes—in Corby and Bailey's *Cyclone.Soc*, for instance—but also produce cultural debates about atmosphere in which science and politics are implicated. Contemporary artists infiltrate the environment of unpredictable and continuous circulation of weather data. Weather delivers sensory signals through activations of temperature, sounds, movements, or light that are turned into numbers through sensors. In digital forms of art, weather dynamics and information dynamics are indistinguishable in their qualities of openness, resonance, contagion, and emergence.

Meteorological instruments are often unacknowledged actants in weather or climate research. Weather balloons, sonic anemometers, hydrographs, or satellite sensors mediate between social and natural weather systems; they have their own affordances, their own agency. Whether they are automatically programmed or human-operated, artists' redeployment of instruments inflects the scientific practices in which they are conventionally used. When meteorological instruments function unexpectedly, through tactile sensations or perceptual shifts, hidden mechanisms are transposed into affects. Hinterding and Haines's *Earthstar* affords us sound, the sun's aromas, and a vision so intense that we come to intimately sense the gaseous sun. In Polli's sonification of climate data, we can hear change over time. Such creative encounters offer a shift in feeling about a physical or social process. The affective quality of sonification, Polli proposes, allows sound to resonate across disciplinary boundaries. When conceived as quasi instrument-objects, the implicit social processes within weather instrumentation are highlighted, rather than their role as message-bearers. Art projects such as *Makrolab* pry open restricted technologies and play a critical role as intermediaries within an open system.

Meteorological art-makers give us atmospheres that enfold our senses in unexpected unions of the chaotic and the ordered. Affect is generated in the reception of meteorological artworks, in a similar way to the noise, heat, and waste that is produced in making new artworks. Affect, so often understood as eliminable noise in the scientific rationalist tradition, has been found to be unavoidable and generative in this book. Machinic glitches or noise is eliminated by scientists in the satellite map to naturalize and create consistency, but in art, noise is recognized as an active component through which affect flows relationally. Both the weather itself and the instruments that mediate it create noise that is unpredictable, productive of change, and implicit in all systems. For Serres, noisy interruptions are an initiator of change in systems. When artists introduce weather dynamics such as variability and reactivity into their machines of perception, they create a feeling of chaotic forces.

Meteorological art connects a polity that assembles very different interest groups around the problems facing our atmosphere. I have argued that weather, perceived not only through media but *as* media, produces new kinds of sociality. Meteorological art undoes traditional separations between science and social life in the slow work of collective, political composition (Latour 2004b). By recognizing cultural and interphylum differences, art can return some of the passions that have been "cleaned up" or eliminated from the scientific account. If scientific facts are constructed by the dropping of the modalities that qualify a given statement, then meteorological art can return some of the missing qualifiers by admitting multiple social realities. Our atmosphere is addressed as a contingent assemblage of biophysical and social matters of care and as a home to spirits.

To access a greater polity, contemporary artists use social media to extend the scope of gallery-based practices to a wider community. The temporary social forums convened by theweathergroup_U and Out-of-Sync maintain climate on the agenda by forging collective passions. Social media itself is a public barometer of opinions and affects that artists often co-opt. As an aggregative type of instrument, social media is often treated statistically, or biopolitically, by the state or corporations. But even within vast social networks, smaller nodes thrive. Saraceno's *Aerocene* blog, for instance, is a site on which like-minded groups can join the programming of his solar sculpture, or make one themselves from biodegradable materials in a workshop. When artists engage with the warming climate, they subvert the mantras in ecopolitics that cause climate-change fatigue. Apolitical art "sleeps through the deluge," while committed art risks a hurtling descent into "blind praxis," to borrow Adorno's (2005) distinction; artists tread these two extremes with care. Waerea's fog-chasing and Harvey's weed-wrestling unsettle legally enforced or arbitrary protocols of social behavior via wry forms of activism. Meteorological art is taken to be a productive and open-admission forum for the mesh of anxieties, hopes, and indifference that surrounds atmospheric politics.

Art takes the form of a cultural processing of a deluge of information in Balkin and Howden-Chapman's artworks that delve into the IPCC reports. They interrogate accepted channels of disseminating information about climate change and reorient the contexts in which this term is mobilized. We may aspire to keep track of scientific developments, but the layperson needs strategies to combat the facticity and often-impenetrable nature of this discourse. Art can hold and distill new scientific findings on sensory and conceptual registers. Yet art does not attempt to order or control the chaos of weather as digital information, discourse, or physical force, rather, we cling to disparate fragments for only a moment. Artists have never left the weather to the supervision of scientists alone, so I have argued less for a "meteorological turn" than for a continuum of collaborative practices over time. In light of the war on science, environmental scientists and meteorologists now more than ever are cared for as crucial partners in art practice, along with our audience-participants.

Both the arts and the sciences are early warning systems in the social environment, as Marshall McLuhan (1997b) once said. Media focus often wanders away from the slower-burning issue of climate outside times of drought, devastating floods, or cyclones. Meteoric weather events, such the heavy rains of Cyclone Gita (2018) that has caused massive slips in Aotearoa New Zealand and full-scale destruction in Tonga, have a compelling power to galvanize immediate action on climate change that is absent from government policy at times of benevolent weather. The long-term changes needed in consumer, state, and corporate behavior to mitigate the increased storminess and drought are sidelined by policymakers all too often. The micropolitical yet globally implicated work of artists and activists maintains climate on the political agenda in the face of suppression of scientific and community cries for action.

The medium of ice has become a prime figure for generating Arendtian "inspiring principles" in the polis. Artists join forces with a host of scientific, and community partners to activate ice as a co-performer. The work of Bragason in Iceland highlights the complexity of the technical fix of carbon sequestration. In the South, Taumoepeau's *i-Land X-ile* draws attention to her own performing body to stand in for the melting cryosphere and the rising sea-level that threaten small islands in Te Moana nui a Kiwa. As environmentalist Rachel Carson presciently observed in 1951, a decade before she wrote *Silent Spring*, it is curious that although we have altered the sea in a "sinister way," it will continue to exist; the threat is to life itself, the human beings who cannot recognize how deeply we are endangered (1951, 3). The warming atmospheric system and seas will persist though the oceans have been dangerously altered for life. Carson warned that to dispose nuclear waste first in the sea and investigate later would lead to disaster, just as proposals to deposit carbon into the earth could also have disastrous consequences in our own age.

In his commentary on Hinterding and Haines's *Earthstar*, Douglas Kahn finds three weathers: the weather on the sun's surface that is obscured by the white visible light of the sun from the human eye; the weather we experience that fosters our "heliotropic plants and circadian mammals"; and "the solar winds the sun throws out that creates the space weather that the earth moves and rotates through" (2015, 33). Like Kahn, I have found multiple conditions in meteorological art, from the external vistas of space and time via satellite meteorology to our immersion in daily weather patterns. This book has oriented inward, into our bodies suffused with atmospheres and chemical compounds produced by sunlight, and spun outward again to explore art's meteorontological horizons under late liberal conditions.

Artists take us on stratospheric missions in which we experience weatherscapes beyond the earth. They give us a "reverse shot" of our world when we are imaginatively or literally propelled into the upper reaches of space, or a paleoclimatic glimpse into the world before us. As the writing of this book progressed, meteorontological concerns shifted to the foreground, as a questioning of the "manic fixity" in many human systems observed by Adorno. Our living conditions today are inflected by the knowledge that human activity has a radical effect on the climate. This condition is not a given because our relations with the atmosphere may yet be ameliorated through alterations in our patterns of consumption. Adorno's nonidentarian standpoint on nature not only orients itself toward understanding how things came to be what they are, as injured or damaged in ethical terms, but anticipates a different future. Beyond this, meteorological art constructs the grounds of possibility for a mediated politics of climate—one in which humans are neither helpless spectators of an oncoming apocalypse nor the unique species with the power to mitigate climate change.

I expected to find art projects that confront the potential harm of climate modification, but I was surprised to find artists flying close to the sun of geoengineers in manufactured weather derangements. The speculative release from regimes of control offered by art invites us to imagine a less instrumentalist way forward, even while provoking us with minor weather modifications, as Sobecka does. The ethics of collective action in art contests the intentions of Big Science and neoliberal corporate mandates, controlled by the few. Kwinter's (2016) ethos of sky as a mode of thinking about ecological relations differently can be detected in Constable's early process of "skying," through to Sobecka's cloud-tasting, and Saraceno's *Aerocene* project. A weather ethos is found in art in the form of *response-ability* or sensitivity that draws us into alignment with the weather's temporal rhythms. We feel ourselves adrift with the balloons in Haacke's *Sky Line*. By allowing this drift, art invites the slowed-down reasoning that Stengers advocates, increasing receptivity to the causes that mobilize us.

Like the ceaseless flux of cloud forms, human beings are *initium*, according to Arendt—newcomers by birth, prompted to create regardless of the political climate. As a great many of the world's political regimes lapse into a conservatism, I take heart from Arendt's observation: "What usually remains intact in the epochs of petrification and foreordained doom is the faculty of freedom itself, the sheer capacity to begin, which animates and inspires all human activities and is the hidden source of production of all great and beautiful things" (2006, 167). She is less concerned with the agent of a miraculous act, whether it be a human act or an act of nature, than with the "process in whose framework it occurs and whose automatism it interrupts" (168). Meteorological art performs extraordinary leverages of the weather imaginary as a vital counterpoint to regimes of the quantitative and to crippling institutional and governmental stasis around climate change.

Throughout the book, I have implied that the practice of meteorological art inflects how we participate in political life and how we take account of Indigenous cosmologies in global politics. A multipolar worldview undermines the claim of liberal democracy to provide a rational, universal model that all societies should adopt. I have described a kind of cultural and political pluralism that differs from a "well meaning cosmopolitan assertion of individual liberty" (Mouffe 2005, 115). The *cosmos* in *cosmopolitics*, for Stengers, is an operator of "putting into equality" rather than a search for equivalence or universality. A truly cosmopolitical world is open to noncitizens and admits nonhuman stakeholders into politics. Kant's high humanist version of the cosmopolitical right is a condition of global hospitality for strangers, beyond the bounds of nation-states, that he uses to criticize slavery. Yet in Kant's account, nonhumans are relegated to an ancillary position in which "the sea, the ships and camels that carry humans across the desert" facilitate all humanity in "profiting in common from its surface" (Kant [1796] 1939, 25). In this book, the political realm of climate politics as exclusively the right of the human citizen is challenged by a renewed attention to nonhuman agency, Indigenous cosmologies, and excluded people, including refugees and migrants.

Indigenous weather knowledge embedded in meteorological art—in particular, Māori knowledge—has been positioned as resistant to science's purported universality, with a capacity for global resonance. The Indigenous ontologies of Huhana Smith, Zoe Todd, Vanessa Watts, and others both trouble and expand the field of Euro-American postanthropocentric thought. I acknowledge Todd's view that "all of us involved in the business of art and academia need to question existing relationships in intellectual and/or art contexts that privilege white voices speaking Indigenous stories" (2015, 251). This book has attempted to heed this principle by pointing to Indigenous authors for further research. In Robertson's lens-based art and Shearer's solar-powered audio compositions, the atmosphere is invested with the significance of a living ancestor, rather than a resource to manage or a technoscientific problem. Māori communal practices and values, such as mauri (life force) and katitiakitanga (gaurdianship), have long conjoined the human and nonhuman worlds, as opposed to the often-protectionist conservation lobby that would fence off the human from the environment. My broader argument is that all modes of meteorological knowing and being should be inflected with respect for the mauri of visible and invisible matter. An Indigenous ethic of care is signaled in *dadirri*, a deep and attentive listening to the earth's biota, air, and winds and inward to ourselves.

Artists play a vital part in reorientating future relations with our shared atmosphere. The post-Kantian cosmopolis is open to more than one species, more than one identity, and more than one set of ecological values. To position the weather *as* media situates meteorological art as a political practice for a more than human benefit. Artists perturb narratives of control over the atmosphere when they intuitively seek counter-patterns and resist identifying processes. Instead, meteorological art dwells in a place of uncertainty, where we relinquish agency to a host of others. The weather, on the other hand, asserts itself as a force that acts, whether in a storm as in Alÿs's *Tornado* or as an air particle in Polli's *Particle Falls* or as a tohu, a sign of rain, in Robertson's weatherscapes. The interwoven eddies and flows that constitute the atmospheric system are simultaneously vast and smaller than we can see, inside and outside our bodies. In meteorological art, we can sense the nonidentical other in the aroma of the sun's heat on the earth after rain, the winds that lash the shores in a heavy storm, or the chance shower that alters the minutiae of our daily rhythms.

References

Abraham, Itty. 2000. "Postcolonial Science, Big Science, and Landscape." In *Doing Science + Culture*, edited by Roddey Reid and Sharon Traweek, 49–70. London: Routledge.

Abrams, Janet, and Peter Hall. 2006. *Else/where: Mapping New Cartographies of Networks and Territories*. Minneapolis: University of Minnesota Press.

Adam, Barbara. 1998. *Timescapes of Modernity: The Environment and Invisible Hazards*. London: Routledge.

Adamson, Joni, and Salma Monani, eds. 2016. *Ecocriticism and Indigenous Studies*. New York: Routledge.

Adorno, Theodor. [1951] 2002. *Minima Moralia: Reflections from a Damaged Life*. Translated by E. F. N. Jephcott. London: Verso.

Adorno, Theodor. [1973] 2004. *Negative Dialectics*. Translated by E. B. Ashton. New York: Continuum.

Adorno, Theodor. [1969] 2005. "Marginalia to Theory and Praxis." In *Critical Models: Interventions and Catchwords*, translated by H. W. Pickford, 273–276. New York: Columbia University Press.

Adorno, Theodor. 2006a. "The History of Nature (I)." Translated by R. Livingstone. In *History and Freedom: Lectures 1964–1965*, edited by Rolf Tiedemann, 115–119. Cambridge: Polity Press.

Adorno, Theodor. 2006b. "The History of Nature (II)." Translated by R. Livingstone. In *History and Freedom: Lectures 1964–1965*, edited by Rolf Tiedemann, 120–131. Cambridge: Polity Press.

Adorno, Theodor. [1977] 2007. "Commitment." In *Aesthetics and Politics*, edited by Ronald Taylor, 177–195. New York: Verso.

Adorno, Theodor. 2008. *Lectures on Negative Dialectics, Fragments of a Lecture Course 1965/1966*. Translated by R. Livingstone. Cambridge: Polity Press.

Adriaansens, Alex, Lev Manovich, Rafael Lozano-Hemmer, Brian Massumi, and Sher Doruff. 2003. *Making Art of Databases*. Rotterdam: V2 Publishing/NAi Publishers.

Aerocene. 2017. "Aerocene: An Open Artistic Project." http://aerocene.org.

Albert, Simon, Javier X. Leon, Alistair R. Grinham, John A. Church, Badin R. Gibbes, and Colin D. Woodroffe. 2016. "Interactions between Sea-Level Rise and Wave Exposure on Reef Island Dynamics in the Solomon Islands." *Environmental Research Letters* 11 (5) (May): 1–7. http://iopscience.iop.org/article/10.1088/1748-9326/11/5/054011.

Alpers, Svetlana. 2005. *The Vexations of Art: Velazquez and Others*. New Haven, CT: Yale University Press.

Altvater, Elmar. 2016. "The Capitalocene, or, Geoengineering against Capitalism's Planetary Boundaries." In *Capitalocene or Anthropocene? Nature, History, and the Crisis of Capitalism*, edited by Jason Moore, 138–152. Oakland, CA: PM Press/Kairos.

Aluli-Meyer, Manulani. 2006. "Changing the Culture of Research: An Introduction to the Triangulation of Meaning." *HŪLILI* 3 (1): 263–279.

Anderson, Katharine. 2005. *Predicting the Weather: Victorians and the Science of Meteorology*. Chicago: University of Chicago Press.

Anderson, Kyla. 2015. "Ethics, Ecology, and the Future: Art and Design Face the Anthropocene." *Leonardo* 48 (4): 338–347.

Apple, Billy. 2017. Interview by Janine Randerson. Phone interview, Auckland, New Zealand, March 28.

Apple, Billy, Andrew Clifford, Wystan Curnow, and Mary Morrison. 2015. *Severe Tropical Storm 9301 Irma*. Auckland, New Zealand: Te Tuhi Centre for the Arts.

Arends, Bergit, and Davina Thackara. 2003. *Experiment: Conversations in Art and Science*. London: Wellcome Trust.

Arendt, Hannah. 1958. *The Human Condition*. Chicago: University of Chicago Press.

Arendt, Hannah. 1982. *Lectures on Kant's Political Philosophy*. Chicago: University of Chicago Press.

Arendt, Hannah. 2006. *Between Past and Future*. New York: Penguin.

Aristotle. 1952. *Meteorologica*. Translated by Henry D. P. Lee. Cambridge, MA: Harvard University Press.

Armand, Louis. 2008. "Language and the Cybernetic Mind." *Theory, Culture & Society* 25 (2): 127–152.

Arns, Inke. 2004. "Interaction, Participation, Networking: Art and Telecommunication." *Media Art Net*. http://www.medienkunstnetz.de/themes/overview_of_media_art/communication/.

Aronowitz, Stanley. 1996. *Technoscience and Cyberculture*. New York: Routledge.

Äsberg, Cecilia, Astrida Neimanis, and Suzie Hayes. 2015. "Post-humanist Imaginaries." In *Research Handbook on Climate Governance*, edited by Karin Bäckstrand and Eva Lövebrand, 480–490. Cheltenham, MA: Edward Elgar Publishing Limited.

ASP (American Security Project). n.d. "Climate Security." Accessed March 29, 2017. http://www .americansecurityproject.org/issues/climate-security/.

Atkinson, Judy. 2002. *Trauma Trails: Recreating Song Lines: The Transgenerational Effects of Trauma in Indigenous Australia*. Melbourne: Spinifex Press.

Auslander, Phillip. 2005. "David Haines and Joyce Hinterding: Artspace." *Artforum International* 44 (2) (October): 289.

Australian Science and Technology Heritage Centre. n.d. "Federation and Meteorology." Accessed March 30, 2017. http://www.austehc.unimelb.edu.au/fam/fam.html.

Autogena, Lise, and Josh Portway. J. 2011. "Most Blue Skies." Lecture at Data Landscapes Symposium, Arts Catalyst, London, May 20–22. http://www.artscatalyst.org/experiencelearning/detail/ data_landscapes_symposium/.

Bachelard, Gaston. 1988. *Air and Dreams: An Essay on the Imagination of Movement*. Translated by Edith R. Farrell and C. Frederick Farrell. Dallas: Dallas Institute of Humanities and Culture.

Badt, Kurt. 1950. *John Constable's Clouds*. London: Routledge & K. Paul.

Baird, Davis. 2004. *Thing Knowledge: A Philosophy of Scientific Instruments*. Berkeley, CA: University of California Press.

Bancroft, Frederic, ed. 2004. *Constable's Skies*. New York: Salander-O'Reilly Galleries.

Bann, Stephen. 1966. *Four Essays on Kinetic Art*. St. Albans, UK: Motion Books.

Baracchi, Pietro. 1898. "Cloud Observations in Victoria." *Report of the Australasian Association for the Advancement of Science* 7:259–265.

Barad, Karen. 1998. "Getting Real: Technoscientific Practices and the Materialization of Reality." *A Journal of Feminist Cultural Studies* 10 (2): 87–127.

Barad, Karen. 2007. *Meeting the Universe Halfway*. Durham, NC: Duke University Press.

Barad, Karen. 2012. "On Touching—the Inhuman That Therefore I Am." *differences* 23 (3): 206–223.

Barnett, Jon, and John Campbell. 2010. "Introduction." In *Climate Change and Small Island States: Power, Knowledge and the South Pacific*, edited by Jon Barnett and John Campbell, 1–4. London: Earthscan.

Batchen, Geoffrey. 2002. *Each Wild Idea: Writing, Photography, History*. Cambridge, MA: MIT Press.

Bateson, Gregory. 1973. *Steps to an Ecology of Mind: Collected Essays in Anthropology, Psychiatry, Evolution and Epistemology*. St. Albans, UK: Paladin.

Baum, Tina. 2017. *Defying Empire: 3rd National Indigenous Art Triennial*. Exhibition catalogue. Canberra: National Gallery of Australia.

Beardsley, John. 1981. "Art and Authoritarianism: Walter De Maria's 'Lightning Field.'" Edited by Walter De Maria. *October* 16 (Spring): 35–38. doi:10.2307/778373.

Beck, Ulrich. 1995. *Ecological Enlightenment: Essays on the Politics of the Risk Society*. Atlantic Highlands, NJ: Humanities Press.

Becker, Melanie, Benoit Meyssignac, William Llovel, and Thierry Delcroix. 2012. "Sea Level Variations at Tropical Pacific Islands since 1950." *Global and Planetary Change* 80–81 (January): 85–98.

Beech, David. 2014. "To Boycott or Not to Boycott?" *Art Monthly* 380 (October): 11–14.

Beer, Gillian. 1990. "Science and Literature: Boundaries of Explanation." In *Companion to the History of Modern Science*, edited by Robert C. Olby, 783–799. London: Routledge.

Behrman, David, and Bob Diamond. 2013. Interview by Janine Randerson. Skype interview, Auckland, New Zealand–New York–San Jose, May 12.

Behrman, David, Bob Diamond, and Robert Watts. [1976] 1992. "Cloud Music: A Hybrid Audio-Video Installation." In *W. and S. Vasulka, Pioneers of Electronic Art*, 152–153. Linz: Ars Electronica.

Bell, Avril. 2008. "Recognition or Ethics? De/centring the Legacy of Settler Colonialism." *Cultural Studies* 22 (6): 850–869.

Benayoun, Maurice. 2014. *Emotion Winds*. Accessed February 15, 2018. http://benayoun.com/moben/2014/05/29/emotion-winds/.

Bennett, Jane. 2004. "The Force of Things: Steps toward an Ecology of Matter." *Political Theory* 32 (3): 347–372.

Bennett, Jane. 2010. *Vibrant Matter: A Political Ecology of Things*. Durham, NC: Duke University Press.

Bennett, Jane, and William Chaloupka, eds. 1993. *In the Nature of Things: Language, Politics, and the Environment*. Minneapolis: University of Minnesota Press.

Bergson, Henri. 1965. *Duration and Simultaneity, with Reference to Einstein's Theory*. Translated by L. Jacobson. Indianapolis: Bobbs-Merrill.

Bergson, Henry. 2002. "The Idea of Duration." In *Key Writings*, edited by Keith Ansell-Pearson and John Mullarkey, 59–94. New York: Continuum.

Berland, Jody. 1996. "Mapping Space: Imaging Technologies and the Planetary Body." In *Technoscience and Cyberculture*, edited by Stanley Aronowitz, Barbara Martinsons, and Michael Menser, 123–139. New York: Routledge.

Berland, Jody. 2009. *North of Empire: Essays on the Cultural Technologies of Space*. Durham, NC: Duke University Press.

Biemann, Ursula. 2015a. *Subatlantic*. HD video. 00:11:24. Switzerland. http://www.vdb.org/titles/subatlantic.

Biemann, Ursula. 2015b. "Geochemistry and Other Planetary Perspectives." In *Art in the Anthropocene: Encounters among Aesthetics, Politics, Environments and Epistemologies*, edited by Heather Davis and Etienne Turpin, 117–130. London: Open Humanities Press.

Biemann, Ursula. 2015c. "Late Subatlantic: Science Poetry in Times of Global Warming." *L'Internationale Online*. http://www.internationaleonline.org/research/politics_of_life_and_death/45_late_subatlantic_science_poetry_in_times_of_global_warming.

Biemann, Ursula. 2018. *Acoustic Ocean*. Video installation. 00:18:200. Switzerland. https://www.geobodies.org/art-and-videos/acoustic-ocean.

Biemann, Ursula, and Mo Diener. 2016. *Twenty One Percent*. HD video. 00:18:200. Switzerland. https://www.geobodies.org/art-and-videos/21-percent.

Biesta, Gert. 2012. "Becoming Public: Public Pedagogy, Citizenship and the Public Sphere." *Social & Cultural Geography* 13 (7): 684–696.

Bijvoet, Marga. 1997. *Art as Inquiry: Toward New Collaborations between Art, Science, and Technology*. New York: Peter Lang.

Billington, Michael. 2014. "2071 Five-Star Review—Urgent Call for the Greatest Collective Action in History." *Guardian*, November 7. https://www.theguardian.com/stage/2014/nov/07/2071-review-urgent-call-history-royal-court-theatre.

Birringer, Johannes. 1998. "Makrolab: A Heterotopia." *PAJ: A Journal of Performance and Art* 20 (3): 66–75.

Boettger, Suzaan. 2002. *Earthworks: Art and the Landscape of the Sixties*. Berkeley: University of California Press.

Boettger, Suzaan. 2008. "Global Warnings." *Art in America* 96 (6): 154–161.

Bordo, Susan. 1987. *The Flight to Objectivity: Essays on Cartesianism and Culture*. Albany: State University of New York Press.

Bourdieu, Pierre, and Hans Haacke. 1995. *Free Exchange*. Cambridge: Polity Press.

Bourriaud, Nicholas. 2002. *Relational Aesthetics*. Translated by Simon Pleasance, Fronza Woods, and Mathieu Copeland. Paris: les presses du réel.

Bragason, Bjarki. 2015. *Infinite Next*. Exhibition catalogue. http://www.nylo.is/events/infinite-next/.

Bragason, Bjarki. 2017. Interview by Janine Randerson. Skype interview, Auckland, New Zealand–Reykjavik, January 20.

Braidotti, Rosi. 2016. "The Critical Posthumanities; or, Is Medianatures to Naturecultures as Zoe Is to Bios?" *Cultural Politics* 12 (3): 380–390.

Brassier, Ray. 2007. *Nihil Unbound: Enlightenment and Extinction*. London: Palgrave Macmillan.

Brett, Guy. 1995. *Exploding Galaxies: The Art of David Medalla*. London: Kala Press.

Briggs, John. 1992. *The Patterns of Chaos: Discovering a New Aesthetic in Art, Science, and Nature*. New York: Simon & Schuster.

British Broadcasting Corporation. 2009. "Maldives Cabinet Makes a Splash." *BBC News*, October 17. http://news.bbc.co.uk/2/hi/8311838.stm.

Brown, Andrew. 2014. *Art and Ecology Now*. London: Thames and Hudson.

Buchmann, Sabeth. 2005. "From Systems-Oriented Art to Biopolitical Art Practice." Presentation at *Open Systems: Rethinking Art c. 1970*, Tate Modern, London, September 17.

Burnham, Jack. 1968a. *Beyond Modern Sculpture: The Effects of Science and Technology on the Sculpture of This Century*. New York: George Braziller.

Burnham, Jack. 1968b. "Systems Esthetics." *Artforum* 7 (1): 30–35.

Burnham, Jack. 1969. "Real Time Systems." *Artforum* 8 (1): 49–55.

Burnham, Jack, and Hans Haacke. 1967. *Hans Haacke: Wind and Water Sculpture*. Evanston, IL: Northwestern University.

Burnham, Jack, H. S. Becker, Hans Haacke, and J. Walton. 1975. *Hans Haacke: Framing and Being Framed: 7 Works 1970–75*. Halifax: The Press of the Nova Scotia College of Art and Design.

Cage, John. 1961. *Silence: Lectures and Writings*. Middletown, CT: Wesleyan University Press.

Callon, Michel. 1986. "Some Elements of a Sociology of Translation: Domestication of the Scallops and the Fishermen of St Brieuc Bay." In *Power, Action and Belief: A New Sociology of Knowledge*, edited by John Law. London: Routledge & Kegan Paul.

Campbell, Stephen. 2003. "Giorgione's 'Tempest,' 'Studiolo' Culture, and the Renaissance Lucretius." *Renaissance Quarterly* 56 (2): 299–332.

Camnitzer, Luis. 2007. *Conceptualism in Latin American Art: Didactics of Liberation*. Austin: University of Texas Press.

Cann, Tyler. 2005. "Time Is a Man, Space Is a Woman: Empathy and Eros in Len Lye's work." Presentation at *Particles and Pixels: Moving Image Culture after Len Lye*. MIC Toi Rerehiko, Auckland, New Zealand, September 25.

Carroli, Linda. 2005. "New Media Artists Camp: Artists David Haines and Joyce Hinterding in Arnhem Land." *Photofile* 76 (Summer): 46–47.

Carson, Rachel. 1951. *The Sea around Us*. London: Staples Press.

Carus, Titus Lucretius. 1931. *On the Nature of the Universe*. Translated by R. E. Latham. Harmondsworth: Penguin Books.

Chambers, Linda E. 2006. "Associations between Climate Change and Natural Systems in Australia." *Bulletin of the American Meteorological Society* 87 (2): 201–206.

Chakrabarty, Dipesh. 2009. "The Climate of History: Four Theses." *Critical Inquiry* 35 (2): 197–222.

Chun, Wendy. 2011. *Programmed Visions: Software and Memory*. Cambridge, MA: MIT Press.

Cianciotta, Aurelio. 2009. "Andrea Polli: Sonic Antarctica." *Neural*, March 30. http://neural
.it/2009/03/andrea-polli-sonic-antartica/.

Clark, Hazel, and Benny Ding Leong. 2003. "Culture-Based Knowledge Towards New Design
Thinking and Practice: A Dialogue." *Design Issues* 19 (3): 48–58.

Clarke, Bruce, and Linda Dalrymple Henderson. 2002. *From Energy to Information: Representation in
Science and Technology, Art, and Literature*. Stanford, CA: Stanford University Press.

Clayton, Martin. 2004. "A deluge c. 1517–18." In *Holbein to Hockney: Drawings from The Royal
Collection*. London: Royal Collection Enterprises Ltd.

Cmielewski, Leon, and Josephine Starrs. 2011. Interview by Janine Randerson. MIC Toi Rerehiko,
Auckland, New Zealand, March 3.

Coles, Romand. 1993. "Ecotones and Environmental Ethics: Adorno and Lopez." In *The Nature of
Things: Language, Politics, and the Environment*, edited by Jane Bennett and William Chaloupka,
226–249. Minneapolis: University of Minnesota Press.

Collings, Matthew. 1999. *This Is Modern Art*. London: Weidenfeld & Nicolson.

Connor, Simon. 2002. "Michel Serres's Milieux." http://stevenconnor.com/milieux.html.

Connor, Simon. 2006. "Atmospherics: The Weather of Sound." Lecture at *Sounding Out 3*, University of Sunderland, September 8.

Cook, Deborah. 2011. *Adorno on Nature*. Durham, UK: Acumen.

COP23. 2017–2018. "COP23 Fiji." 23rd Conference of the Parties to the United Nations Framework Convention on Climate Change (UNFCCC). November 6–17. https://cop23.com.fj/key
-achievements-cop23/.

Corby, Tom. 2006. *Network Art: Practices and Positions*. London: Routledge.

Corby, Tom. 2008. "Landscapes of Feeling, Arenas of Action: Information Visualisation as Art
Practice." *Leonardo* 41 (5): 460–467.

Cosgrove, Denis E. 2001. *Apollo's Eye: A Cartographic Genealogy of the Earth in the Western Imagination*. Baltimore: Johns Hopkins University Press.

Coupe, Laurence. 2000. *The Green Studies Reader: From Romanticism to Ecocriticism*. London:
Routledge.

Crary, Jonathan. 1992. *Techniques of the Observer: On Vision and Modernity in the Nineteenth Century*. Cambridge, MA: MIT Press.

Crary, Jonathan. 2006. "Spectral." In *Sensorium: Embodied Experience, Technology, and Contemporary Art*, edited by Caroline A. Jones, 207–211. Cambridge, MA: MIT Press.

Crist, Eileen. 2007. "Beyond the Climate Crisis: A Critique of Climate Change Discourse." *Telos*
141 (Winter): 29–55.

Crist, Eileen, and Helen Kopina. 2014. "Unsettling Anthropocentrism." *Dialectical Anthropology* 28 (4): 387–396.

Critchley, Simon. 2007. *Infinitely Demanding: Ethics of Commitment, Politics of Resistance*. London: Verso.

Crosby, Alfred W. 1997. *The Measure of Reality: Quantification and Western Society, 1250–1600*. Cambridge: Cambridge University Press.

Cubitt, Sean. 1998. *Digital Aesthetics*. London: Sage Publications.

Cubitt, Sean. 2005. *Eco Media*. New York: Rodopi.

Cubitt, Sean. 2006. "TV News titles: Picturing the Planet." *Jump Cut: A Review of Contemporary Media* 48 (Winter). http://www.ejumpcut.org/archive/jc48.2006/CubittGlobe/index.html.

Cubitt, Sean. 2008. "Virtual Dialectics and Technological Aesthetics." *Cultural Politics* 4 (2): 133–154.

Cubitt, Sean. 2009. "After Tolerance." In *Digital Labor: The Internet as Playground and Factory*, edited by Trebor Scholz, 58–68. New York: Eugene Lang College, the New School.

Cubitt, Sean. 2017. *Finite Media: Environmental Implications of Digital Technologies*. Durham, NC: Duke University Press.

Cubitt, Sean, Salma Monani, and Stephen Rust. 2016. "Introduction: Ecologies of Media." In *Ecomedia Studies: Key Issues in Environment and Sustainability*, edited by Sean Cubitt, Salma Monani, and Stephen Rust, 1–15. London: Routledge.

Cunnane, Abby. 2016. Interview by Janine Randerson ST PAUL St Gallery, Auckland, New Zealand, November 17.

Cunnane, Abby, and Amy Howden-Chapman, eds. 2015. *The Distance Plan*, no. 3. http://thedistanceplan.org.

Cunnane, Abby, and Amy Howden-Chapman, eds. 2016. *The Distance Plan*, no. 4. http://thedistanceplan.org.

Curry, Patrick. 2006. *Ecological Ethics: An Introduction*. Cambridge: Polity Press.

Curtin, Deane. 2005. *Environmental Ethics for a Postcolonial World*. Lanham, MD: Rowman and Littlefield.

CYLAND. 2018. *Cyfest 11: Weather Forecast: Digital Cloudiness*. Festival catalogue. St. Petersburg: CYLAND International MediaArtLab.

Dadson, Phil. 2005. *Polar Projects*. The Physics Room. http://www.physicsroom.org.nz/gallery/2005/dadson/.

Dadson, Phil. 2017. Interview by Janine Randerson. Northcote, Auckland, New Zealand, January 27.

Damisch, Hubert. 2002. *A Theory Of /Cloud/: Toward a History of Painting*. Stanford, CT: Stanford University Press.

Danto, Arthur Coleman. 2005. *Unnatural Wonders: Essays from the Gap between Art and Life*. New York: Farrar Straus Giroux.

Davis, Anna. 2015. "Energies and Apparitions." In *Energies: Haines & Hinterding*, edited by Anna Davis and Douglas Kahn, 7–21. Exhibition catalogue. Sydney: Museum of Contemporary Art Australia.

Davis, Anna, and Douglas Kahn, eds. 2015. *Energies: Haines & Hinterding*. Sydney: Museum of Contemporary Art Australia.

Davis, Heather, and Etienne Turpin, eds. 2015. *Art in the Anthropocene: Encounters among Aesthetics, Politics, Environments and Epistemologies*. London: Open Humanities Press.

Davison, Isaac. 2017. "New Zealand River Given Legal Status of a Person." *New Zealand Herald*, March 15. http://m.nzherald.co.nz/nz/news/article.cfm?c_id=1&objectid=11818858.

Day, David. 2007. *The Weather Watchers: 100 Years of the Bureau of Meteorology*. Carlton, Australia: Melbourne University Publishing.

Dean, Jodi. 2016. "The Anamorphic Politics of Climate Change." *e-flux*, 69 (January). http://www.e-flux.com/journal/69/60586/the-anamorphic-politics-of-climate-change/.

Dear Climate. n.d. *Dear Climate*. Accessed February 12, 2018. http://www.dearclimate.net/#/homepage.

De Certeau, Michel. 1984. "Walking in the City." In *The Practice of Everyday Life*, translated by Steven F. Rendall, 91–111. Berkeley: University of California Press.

Deleuze, Gilles, and Felix Guattari. 1988. *A Thousand Plateaus: Capitalism and Schizophrenia*. London: Athlone Press.

Deleuze, Gilles, and Felix Guattari. 2000. "Affect, Percept and Concept." In *The Continental Aesthetics Reader*, edited by Clive Cazeaux, 465–489. London: Routledge.

De Lisle, John. 1986. *Sails to Satellites: A History of Meteorology in New Zealand*. Wellington: New Zealand Meteorological Service.

De Maria, Walter. 1980. "The Lightning Field." *Artforum* 18 (80): 52–59.

De Maria, Walter. [1960] 1995. "On the Importance of Natural Disasters." In *Theories and Documents of Contemporary Art: A Sourcebook of Artists' Writings*, ed. Kristine Stiles and Peter Selz, 527. Berkeley: University of California Press.

Demos, T. J. 2009. "The Politics of Sustainability: Contemporary Art and Ecology." In *Radical Nature: Art and Architecture for a Changing Planet 1969–2009*, edited by Francesco Manacorda, 16–30. London: Koenig Books.

Demos, T. J. 2012. "Art after Nature: The Post-Natural Condition." *Artforum* 50 (8): 193.

Demos, T. J. 2013a. "Contemporary Art and the Politics of Ecology: An Introduction." *Third Text* 27 (1): 1–9.

Demos, T. J. 2013b. "The Law of the Land: An Interview with Amy Balkin." *International New Media Gallery* (November): 11–17. http://www.inmg.org/archive/balkin/catalogue/demos/#.WNoSQBhh0dk.

Demos, T. J. 2016. *Decolonizing Nature: Contemporary Art and the Politics of Ecology*. Berlin: Sternberg Press.

Dennis, Michael. 2017. "Big Science." *Encyclopedia Britannica*, May 19. https://www.britannica.com/science/Big-Science-science.

De Santolo, Jason. 2018. "Towards Understanding the Renewal of Ancient Song Traditions through Garrwa Video: An Indigenous Story Research Study." PhD diss., University of Technology Sydney (UTS), Sydney, Australia.

Descartes, Rene. 2001. *Discourse on Method, Optics, Geometry, and Meteorology*. Indianapolis, IN: Hackett Publishing.

Diamond, Bob, David Behr, and Robert Watts. 1974. "Press Release for Cloud Machine." *Experimental Television Centre*. http://experimentaltvcenter.org/cloud-driven-music-description-device-and-installation.

Dieter, Michael. 2009. Processes, Issues, AIR: Toward Reticular Politics. *Australian Humanities Review*, no. 46 (May): 57–68.

Dillon, Grace L., ed. 2012. *Walking the Clouds: An Anthology of Indigenous Science Fiction*. Tucson: University of Arizona Press.

Dimítropouios, Harris. 1985. "Walter De Maria—*The Lightning Field* (Constructing a Causeway)." *Art Papers* 9 (4): 14–16.

Duchamp, Marcel. 1973. *Salt Seller: The Writings of Marcel Duchamp*. Edited by Michel Sanouillet and Elmer Peterson. New York: Oxford University Press.

Dvorak, Vernon F. 1972. *A Technique for the Analysis and Forecasting of Tropical Cyclone Intensities from Satellite Pictures*. Washington, DC: US Department of Commerce, National Oceanic and Atmospheric Administration, National Satellite Service.

EAT (Experiments in Art and Technology). 1998. *Experiments in Art and Technology: A Brief History and Summary of Major Projects 1966–1998*. March 1. http://www.vasulka.org/archive/Writings/EAT.pdf.

Eco, Umberto. [1962] 1989. *The Open Work*. Translated by Anna Cancogni. Cambridge, MA: Harvard University Press.

Ede, Sian. 2000. *Strange and Charmed: Science and the Contemporary Visual Arts*. London: Calouste Gulbenkian Foundation.

Edwards, Paul N. 2010. *A Vast Machine: Computer Models, Climate Data, and the Politics of Global Warming*. Cambridge, MA: MIT Press.

Eglash, Ron, Jennifer L. Croissant, Giovanna di Chiro, and Rayvon Fouché, eds. 2004. *Appropriating Technology: Vernacular Science and Social Power*. Minneapolis: University of Minnesota Press.

Eliasson, Olafur. 2003. *Olafur Eliasson: The Weather Project*. Edited by Susan May. London: Tate Publishing.

Eliasson, Olafur, and Minik Rosing. 2015. *Ice Watch*. Accessed February 24, 2018. http://icewatch paris.com/.

Emanuel, Kerry. 2005a. *Divine Wind: The History and Science of Hurricanes*. New York: Oxford University Press.

Emanuel, Kerry. 2005b. "Increasing Destructiveness of Tropical Cyclones over the Past 30 Years." *Nature* 436 (7051): 686–688.

Emmelhainz, Irmgard. 2015. "Conditions of Visuality under the Anthropocene and the Anthropocene to Come." *e-flux* 63 (March). http://www.e-flux.com/journal/63/60882/conditions-of-visuality-under-the-anthropocene-and-images-of-the-anthropocene-to-come/.

Engels-Schwarzpaul, Tina. 2015. "The Offerings of Fringe Figures and Migrants." *Educational Philosophy and Theory* 27 (11): 1211–1226.

Evening Standard. 2007. "Hayward Gallery Wants you to Get Lost: Anthony Gormley." *Evening Standard*, May 14, 2017. http://www.standard.co.uk/news/hayward-gallery-wants-you-to-get-lost-6582395.html.

Farbotko, Carol, and Heather Lazrus. 2012. "The First Climate Refugees? Contesting Global Narratives of Climate Change in Tuvalu." *Global Environmental Change* 22 (2): 382–390.

Favret, Mary A. 2004. "War in the Air." *Modern Language Quarterly* 65 (4): 531–559.

Feilhauer, Matthias, and Soenke Zehle. 2009. "Ethics of Waste in the Information Society." *International Review of Information Ethics* 11. http://www.i-r-i-e.net/inhalt/011/011-full.pdf.

Ferrer, Raphael, and Marcia Tucker. 1971. "Raphael Ferrer." Exhibition catalogue. New York: Whitney Museum of American Art. https://archive.org/details/rafaelferrer00ferr.

Finley, Gerald. 1997. "The Deluge Pictures: Reflections on Goethe, JMW Turner and Early Nineteenth-Century Science." *Zeitschrift fur Kunstgeschichte* 60 (4): 530–548.

Flannery, Tim. [2005] 2010. *The Weather Makers: The History and Future Impact of Climate Change*. Melbourne: The Text Publishing Company.

Fleming, James Rodger. 2006. "The Pathological History of Weather and Climate Modification: Three Cycles of Promise and Hype." *Historical Studies in the Physical and Biological Sciences* 37 (1): 3–25.

Fleming, James Rodger. 2007. "The Climate Engineers." *Wilson Quarterly* 31 (2): 46–60.

Flusser, Vilém. 1999. *The Shape of Things: A Philosophy of Design*. London: Reaktion.

Flusser, Vilém. 2007. "Crisis of Linearity." Translated by Adelheid Mers. *Boot Print* 1 (1): 18–21.

Flusser, Vilém. [1985] 2011. *Into the Universe of Technical Images*. Minneapolis: University of Minnesota Press.

Flusser, Vilém. 2013. *Towards a Philosophy of Photography*. London: Reaktion Books.

Foucault, Michel. 1979. *Discipline and Punish: The Birth of the Prison*. Translated by A. Sheridan. Harmondsworth, UK: Penguin.

Foucault, Michel. 2003. *Society Must Be Defended: Lectures at the College de France, 1975–76*. Edited by Mauro Bertani and Alessandro Fontana. New York: Picador.

Frankland, Richard. 2016. Keynote presentation at Performance Climates, PSi Performance Studies International #22, University of Melbourne, July 8.

Fraser, Alistair B., and Raymond L. Lee Jr. 2001. *The Rainbow Bridge: Rainbows in Art, Myth, and Science*. University Park, PA: Penn State University Press.

Fried, Michael. [1967] 1998. *Art and Objecthood: Essays and Reviews*. Chicago: University of Chicago Press.

Friedman, Robert M. 1989. *Appropriating the Weather: Vilhelm Bjerknes and the Construction of a Modern Meteorology*. Ithaca, NY: Cornell University Press.

Friedman, Ken, Owen Smith, and Lauren Sawchyn, eds. 2002. *The Fluxus Performance Workbook*. Performance Research. http://www.deluxxe.com/beat/fluxusworkbook.pdf.

Frisinger, H. Howard. 1977. *The History of Meteorology to 1800*. New York: Science History Publications.

Fuller, Mathew. 2005. "Freaks of Number." In *Engineering Culture: On The Author as (Digital) Producer*, edited by Geoff Cox and Joasia Krysa, 161–175. New York: Autonomedia.

Fuller, Mathew. 2007. *Media Ecologies: Materialist Energies in Art and Technoculture*. Cambridge, MA: MIT Press.

Fuller, Mathew. 2008. *Software Studies: A Lexicon*. Cambridge, MA: MIT Press.

Fuller, R. Buckminster. 1969. *Operating Manual for Spaceship Earth*. New York: Simon and Schuster.

Gabrys, Jennifer. 2007. "Automatic Sensation: Environmental Sensors in the Digital City." *Senses and Society* 2 (2): 189–200.

Galilei, Galileo. 1957. *Discoveries and Opinions of Galileo*. Translated by S. Drake. New York: Anchor Books.

Galison, Peter. 1994. "The Ontology of the Enemy: Norbert Wiener and the Cybernetic Vision." *Critical Inquiry* 21 (1): 228–266.

Galison, Peter. 1997. *Image and Logic: A Material Culture of Microphysics*. Chicago: University of Chicago Press.

Galloway, Alexander R. 2004. *Protocol: How Control Exists after Decentralization*. Cambridge, MA: MIT Press.

Garrard, Greg. 2004. *Ecocriticism*. London: Routledge.

Garrett, Richard. 2007. "The Davis Instruments Vantage Pro Weather Station." *Leonardo Music Journal* 17 (1): 90.

Gaviria, Andres Ramirez. 2008. "When Is Information Visualization Art? Determining the Critical Criteria." *Leonardo* 41 (5): 479–482.

Gessert, George. 2007. "Gathered from Coincidence: Reflections on Art in a Time of Global Warming." *Leonardo* 40 (3): 231–236.

Golinski, Jan. 2007. *British Weather and the Climate of Enlightenment*. Chicago: The University of Chicago Press.

Gooding, David, Trevor Pinch, and Simon Schaffer, eds. 1989. *The Uses of Experiment: Studies in the Natural Sciences*. Cambridge: Cambridge University Press.

Gorz, Andre. 1980. *Ecology as Politics*. New York: Black Rose Books.

Grasskamp, Walter, Molly Nesbit, and Jon Bird. 2004. *Hans Haacke*. London: Phaidon.

Graubard, Stephen Richards, ed. 1986. *Art and Science*. Lanham, MD: University Press of America.

Greenberg, Clement. 1962. "After Abstract Expressionism." *Artforum International* 6 (8): 26–30.

Grove, Richard H. 1995. *Green Imperialism: Colonial Expansion, Tropical Island Edens, and the Origins of Environmentalism, 1600–1860*. Cambridge: Cambridge University Press.

Groys, Boris. 2011. "The Border Between Word and Image." *Theory, Culture & Society* 28 (2): 94–108.

Guattari, Felix. 1989. *The Three Ecologies*. New York: The Athlone Press.

Guattari, Felix. 1995. *Chaosmosis: An Ethico-Aesthetic Paradigm*. Sydney: Power Publications.

Haacke, Hans. 2003. "Condensation Cube." *Leonardo* 36 (4): 265.

Haacke, Hans, and Alexander Alberro. 2016. *Working Conditions: The Writings of Hans Haacke*. Cambridge, MA: MIT Press.

Habermas, Jurgen. 1989. *The Structural Transformation of the Public Sphere*. Cambridge: Polity Press.

Hacking, Ian. 1990. *The Taming of Chance*. New York: Cambridge University Press.

Haines, David, and Joyce Hinterding. 2017. Interview by Janine Randerson. Te Uru Gallery, Auckland, New Zealand, February 14.

Hamblyn, Richard. 2002. *The Invention of Clouds: How an Amateur Meteorologist Forged the Language of the Skies*. New York: Picador.

Hamblyn, Richard. 2005. "The Celestial Journey." *Tate Etc.*, no. 5 (Autumn): 84–91.

Hammer, Espen. 2005. *Adorno and the Political*. New York: Routledge.

Hammer, Espen. 2015. *Adorno's Modernism: Art, Experience, and Catastrophe*. Cambridge: Cambridge University Press.

Hara, Rurihiko. 2016. "Nature's Own Performance: Fujiko Nakaya's Fog and Garden." Paper presented at *Performance Climates*, PSi Performance Studies International #22, University of Melbourne, July 7.

Haraway, Donna. 2003. *The Companion Species Manifesto: Dogs, People, and Significant Otherness*. Chicago: Prickly Paradigm Press.

Haraway, Donna. 2008. *When Species Meet*. Minneapolis: University of Minnesota Press.

Haraway, Donna. 2016. *Staying with the Trouble: Making kin in the Chthulucene*. Durham, NC: Duke University Press.

Haraway, Donna, and Martha Kenney. 2015. "Anthropocene, Capitalocene, Chthulhocene." In *Art in the Anthropocene: Encounters among Aesthetics, Politics, Environments and Epistemologies*, edited by Heather Davis and Etienne Turpin, 255–270. London: Open Humanities Press.

Harman, Graham. 2002. *Tool-Being: Heidegger and the Metaphysics of Objects*. Chicago: Open Court.

Harman, Graham. 2007. "The Importance of Bruno Latour for Philosophy." *Cultural Studies Review* 13 (1): 31–49.

Harré, Niki. 2011. *Psychology for a Better World: Strategies to Inspire Sustainability*. Auckland, New Zealand: University of Auckland, Department of Psychology.

Harvey, Mark. 2017. "Weed Wrestle." In *HEAT: Solar Revolutions. Program*, edited by Amanda Yates and Andrew Clifford. Auckland, New Zealand: Te Uru Waitakere Contemporary Gallery.

Haskell, Barbara, and John Handhardt. 1991. *Yoko Ono: Arias and Objects*. Salt Lake City: Peregrine Smith Books.

Hassan, Robert. 2008. *Information Society*. Cambridge: Polity Press.

Hawkins, Gay. 2005. *The Ethics of Waste: How We Relate to Rubbish*. Lanham: Rowman and Littlefield.

Hayes, Michael K., and Dana Miller, eds. 2008. *Buckminster Fuller: Starting with the Universe*. New York: Whitney Museum of American Art.

Hayles, N. Katherine. 1990. *Chaos Bound: Orderly Disorder in Contemporary Literature and Science*. Ithaca: Cornell University Press.

Hayles, N. Katherine. 1999. *How We Became Posthuman: Virtual Bodies in Cybernetics, Literature, and Informatics*. Chicago: University of Chicago Press.

Hegerl, Gabriele C., and Susan Solomon. 2009. "Risks of Climate Engineering." *Science* 325 (5943): 955–956. doi:10.1126/science.1178530.

Heidegger, Martin. 1977. *The Question Concerning Technology and Other Essays*. New York: Garland Pub.

Henderson-Sellers, Ann. 1984. *Satellite Sensing of a Cloudy Atmosphere: Observing the Third Planet*. London: Taylor and Francis.

Henderson-Sellers, Ann, and Kendal McGuffie. 2005. *A Climate Modelling Primer*. Chichester, UK: Wiley.

Henry, John. 2002. *The Scientific Revolution and the Origins of Modern Science*. New York: Palgrave.

Herdeg, Walter. 1973. *The Artist in the Service of Science*. Zurich: Graphic Press.

Hjorth, Larissa, Sarah Pink, and Kristen Sharp. 2014. *Screen Ecologies: Art, Media, and the Environment in the Asia-Pacific Region*. Cambridge, MA: MIT Press.

Holmes, Brian. 2007. "Coded Utopia: Makrolab, or the Art of Transition." *Continental Drift* (blog), March 27, 2007. http://brianholmes.wordpress.com/2007/03/27/coded-utopia/.

Holmes, Brian. 2008. "Swarmachine: Activist Media Tomorrow." *Third Text* 22 (5): 525–534.

Holzaepfel, J. 2001. "David Tudor, John Cage and Comparative Indeterminacy." Paper presented at Getty Research Institute Symposium, Los Angeles, May 17–19.

Horrocks, Roger. 2001. *Len Lye: A Biography*. Auckland, New Zealand: Auckland University Press.

Horsley, Francesca. 2013. "Political Climate Wrestle." *DANZ Quarterly* 33:16–17.

Howden-Chapman, Amy. 2016. Interview by Janine Randerson. Mount Street, Auckland, New Zealand, August 25.

Howearth, Bunty. 2003. *Mists of Time: Ngapuhi Myths and Legends*. Auckland, New Zealand: Reed.

Howes, David. 2005. "Hyperaesthesia, or the Sensual Logic of Late Capitalism." In *Empire of the Senses*, edited by David Howes, 281–304. New York: Berg.

Humboldt, Alexander V., David Livingstone, and John Ruskin. 1880. *The Wonders and Beauties of Creation: As Portrayed by Humboldt, Livingstone, Ruskin, and Other Great Writers*. London: Gall and Inglis.

Hunt, Alex, and Bonnie Roos. 2010. *Postcolonial Green: Environmental Politics and World Narratives*. London: University of Virginia Press.

Hunt, Sarah. 2014. "Ontologies of Indigeneity: The Politics of Embodying a Concept." *Cultural Geographies* 21 (1): 27–32.

Hurrell, John. 2016. "Facing Environmental Breakdown." *EyeContact*, September 7. http://www.eyecontactsite.com/2016/09/facing-environmental-collapse.

Ihde, Don. 1993. *Postphenomenology: Essays in the Postmodern Context*. Evanston, IL: Northwestern University Press.

Ihde, Don. 1998. *Expanding Hermeneutics: Visualism in Science*. Evanston, IL: Northwestern University Press.

Ihde, Don. 2002. *Bodies in Technology*. Minneapolis: University of Minnesota Press.

Iles, Chrissie. 1997. *Yoko Ono: Have You Seen the Horizon Lately?* New York: Museum of Modern Art.

Iles, Chrissie. 2001. *Into the Light: The Projected Image in American Art, 1964–1977*. New York: Whitney Museum of American Art.

Ingold, Tim. 2000. *The Perception of the Environment: Essays on Livelihood, Dwelling and Skill*. New York: Routledge.

Ingold, Tim. 2007. "Earth, Sky, Wind and Weather." *Journal of the Royal Anthropological Institute* 13:19–38.

Ingold, Tim. 2010. "Footsteps through the Weather World: Walking, Breathing, Knowing." *Journal of the Royal Anthropological Institute* 16 (May): 121–139.

Ingold, Tim. 2011. *Being Alive: Essays on Movement, Knowledge and Description*. London: Routledge.

IPCC (Intergovernmental Panel on Climate Change). 2014. "Summary for Policymakers." In *Climate Change 2014: Mitigation of Climate Change. Contribution of Working Group III to the Fifth Assessment Report of the Intergovernmental Panel on Climate Change*, edited by O. Edenhofer, R. Pichs-Madruga, Y. Sokona, E. Farahani, S. Kadner, K. Seyboth, A. Adler, I. Baum, S. Brunner, P. Eickemeier, B. Kriemann, J. Savolainen, S. Schlömer, C. von Stechow, T. Zwickel, and J. C. Minx, 1–30. Cambridge: Cambridge University Press.

Irigaray, Luce. 1999. *The Forgetting of Air in Martin Heidegger*. Translated by M. B. Mader. Austin: University of Texas Press.

James, William. 1912. *Essays in Radical Empiricism*. London: Longmans, Green.

Jankovic, Vladimir. 2000. *Reading the Skies: A Cultural History of English Weather, 1650–1820*. Manchester: Manchester University Press.

Jarvis, Simon. 1998. *Adorno: A Critical Introduction*. Cambridge: Polity Press.

Jarzombek, Mark. 2005. "Haacke's Condensation Cube: The Machine in the Box and the Travails of Architecture." *Thresholds* 30 (Summer): 99–103.

Jay, Martin. 1993. *Downcast Eyes: The Denigration of Vision in Twentieth-Century French Thought*. Berkeley: University of California Press.

Jones, Caroline A., and Bill Arning. 2006. *Sensorium: Embodied Experience, Technology, and Contemporary Art*. Cambridge, MA: MIT Press.

Jones, Jonathan. 2015. "Olafur Eliasson: Why I'm Sailing Arctic Icebergs into Paris." *Guardian*, November 17. http://www.theguardian.com/artanddesign/jonathanjonesblog/2015/nov/17/olufar-eliasson-ice-watch-paris-icebergs-place-de-la-republique.

Joyce, Zita. 2008. "Creating Order in the Ceaseless Flow: The Discursive Constitution of the Radio Spectrum." PhD diss., University of Auckland, Auckland, New Zealand. http://hdl.handle.net/2292/5619.

Kac, Eduardo. 1988. *Satellite Art: An Interview with Nam June Paik*. http://ekac.org/paik.interview.html.

Kahn, Douglas. 2010. "A Natural History of Media." Lecture at Gus Fisher Gallery, Auckland, New Zealand, December 16.

Kahn, Douglas. 2011. *Earth Sound, Earth Signal*. Berkeley: University of California Press.

Kahn, Douglas. 2015. "Haines & Hinterding as Understood through Lightning." In *Energies: Haines & Hinterding*, edited by Anna Davis and Douglas Kahn, 22–33. Exhibition catalogue. Sydney: Museum of Contemporary Art Australia.

Kamm, Rebecca. 2011. "Te Urewera—from the Beginning." *New Zealand Herald*, September 19. http://www.nzherald.co.nz/entertainment/news/article.cfm?c_id=1501119&objectid=10752866.

Kanawa, Lisa. 2010. "Climate Change Implications for Māori." In *Māori and the Environment: Kaitiaki*, edited by Rachael Selby, Pātaka J. G. Moore, and Malcolm Mulholland, 109–122. Wellington, New Zealand: Huia Publishers.

Kant, Immanuel. [1796] 1939. *Perpetual Peace*. New York: Columbia University Press.

Karoly, David. 2007. *"Lies, Damn Lies and Statistics: What Has Caused Recent Global Warming? Dispelling the Myths about Climate Change Science."* Presentation at Climate Adaptation Science and Policy Initiative (CASPI), University of Melbourne.

Kasprzak, Michelle. 2013. "Interview with the Commissioned Artists." In *Speculative Realities*, Blowup Reader #6, 15–22. Rotterdam: V2_ Institute for the Unstable Media. http://v2.nl/files/2013/ebooks/speculative-realities-blowup-reader-6-pdf.

Kautoke, Afuafu. 2012. "Climate Change in Tonga: The Vulnerability of Tongatapu to Climate Change and Sea Level Rise." University of the South Pacific. Accessed March 28, 2017. http://www.usp.ac.fj/?id=10923.

Keane, Basil. 2006. "Tāwhirimātea: The Weather." *Te Ara—The Encyclopedia of New Zealand*. http://www.TeAra.govt.nz/en/tawhirimatea-the-weather/page-online.

Kellein, Thomas, and Tony Stoss, eds. 1993. *Nam June Paik: Video Time—Video Space*. New York: Harry N. Abrams.

Kemp, Martin. 2000. *Visualizations: The Nature Book of Art and Science*. Berkeley: University of California Press.

Kemp, Martin. 2006. *Seen/unseen: Art, Science and Intuition from Leonardo to the Hubble Telescope.* Oxford: Oxford University Press.

Kepes, Gyorgy. 1956. *The New Landscape in Art and Science.* Chicago: Paul Theobald.

Kershaw, Baz. 2007. *Theatre Ecology: Environments and Performance Events.* New York: Cambridge University Press.

Kheradmand, Juan, and Houshang Kheradmand, eds. 2011. *Climate Change: Geophsyical Foundations and Ecological Effects.* Rijeka: InTech.

Kidder, Stanley, and Thomas H. Vonder. 1995. *Satellite Meteorology: An Introduction.* San Diego: Academic Press.

Klein, Naomi. 2014. *This Changes Everything: Capitalism vs. the Climate.* New York: Simon and Schuster.

Kotz, Liz. 2001. "Post Cagean Aesthetics and the 'Event Score.'" *October* 95 (Winter): 54–89.

Kranz, Stewart. 1974. *Science and Technology in the Arts: A Tour through the Realm of Science/Art.* New York: Van Nostrand Reinhold.

Krauss, Rosalind E. 1985. *The Originality of the Avant-Garde and Other Modernist Myths.* Cambridge, MA: MIT Press.

Krauss, Rosalind E. 1977. *Passages in Modern Sculpture.* London: Thames and Hudson.

Krauss, Rosalind E. 1979. "Grids." *October* 9 (Summer): 50–64.

Kristeva, Julia. 1989. *Black Sun: Depression and Melancholia.* Translated by L. S. Roudiez. New York: Columbia University Press.

Kuhn, Thomas S. 1962. *The Structure of Scientific Revolutions.* Chicago: University of Chicago Press.

Kwinter, Sanford. 2016. "Sensing the Aerocene." *sanfordkwinter.com* (blog), December. http://sanfordkwinter.com/Sensing-the-Aerocene.

Lacey, Sharon. 2016. "Behind the Artwork: Tomás Saraceno's Aerocene Project." *Arts at MIT*, March 4. http://arts.mit.edu/behind-artwork-tomas-saracenos-aerocene-project/.

Laird, Tessa. 2006. "Severe Tropical Storm 9301 Irma: Art Review." *New Zealand Listener*, May 13–19.

Landsea, Christopher W. 2005. "Meteorology: Hurricanes and Global Warming." *Nature* 438 (7071): 11–13.

Lash, Scott. 2010. *Intensive Culture: Social Theory, Religion and Contemporary Capitalism.* Los Angeles: Sage Publications.

Latour, Bruno. 1986. "Visualisation and Cognition: Drawing Things Together." In *Knowledge and Society: Studies in the Sociology of Culture Past and Present*, vol. 6, edited by Henricka Kuklick, 1–40. Greenwich, CT: Jai Press.

Latour, Bruno. 1991. "Technology Is Society Made Durable." In *A Sociology of Monsters: Essays on Power, Technology and Domination*. Sociological Review Monograph No. 38, edited by John Law, 103–132. London: Routledge.

Latour, Bruno. 1996. "On Interobjectivity." *Mind, Culture, and Activity* 3 (4): 228.

Latour, Bruno. 1998. "On Recalling ANT." In *Actor Network Theory and After*, edited by John Law and John Hassard, 15–25. Oxford: Blackwell Publishers.

Latour, Bruno. 2002. "Morality and Technology: The End of Means." *Theory, Culture & Society* 19 (5–6): 247–260.

Latour, Bruno. 2004a. "From Realpolitik to Dingpolitik, or How to Make Things Public." In *Making Things Public: Atmospheres of Democracy*, edited by Bruno Latour and Peter Weibel, 3–31. Cambridge, MA: MIT Press.

Latour, Bruno. 2004b. *Politics of Nature: How to Bring the Sciences into Democracy*. Cambridge, MA: Harvard University Press.

Latour, Bruno. 2005. *Reassembling the Social: An Introduction to Actor-Network-Theory*. New York: Oxford University Press.

Latour, Bruno. 2007. "Beware, Your Imagination Leaves Digital Traces." *Times Higher Education Literary Supplement*, April 6. http://www.bruno-latour.fr/node/245.

Latour, Bruno. 2009. "It's Development, Stupid, or How to Modernize Modernization." *Bruno Latour* (blog). http://www.bruno-latour.fr/node/153.

Latour, Bruno. 2011. "Love Your Monsters: Why We Must Care for Technologies as We Do for Our Children." In *Love Your Monsters: Postenvironmentalism and the Anthropocene*, edited by Ted Nordhaus and Michael Shellenberger, 17–25. Oakland, CA: Breakthrough Institute.

Latour, Bruno. 2013. "Telling Friends from Foes in the Time of the Anthropocene." In *The Anthropocene and the Global Environment Crisis: Rethinking Modernity in a New Epoch*, edited by Clive Hamilton, Christophe Bonneuil, and François Gemenne, 145–155. London: Routledge.

Latour, Bruno. 2016. "On Sensitivity: Art, Science and the Politics in the New Climatic Regime." Paper presented at *Performance Climates*, PSi Performance Studies International #22, University of Melbourne, August 1.

Latour, Bruno, and C. Porter. 1993. *We Have Never Been Modern*. New York: Harvester Wheatsheaf.

Latour, Bruno, and P. Weibel. 2005. *Making Things Public: Atmospheres of Democracy*. Cambridge, MA: MIT Press.

Latour, Bruno, and Steve Woolgar. 1986. *Laboratory Life*. Princeton, NJ: Princeton University Press.

Lausten, Thorbjørn. 2008. Interview by Janine Randerson. Copenhagen Central Train Station, Denmark, September 5.

Law, John. 2004. "And If the Global Were Incredibly Small and Non-coherent? Method, Complexity and the Baroque." *Environment and Planning D: Society and Space* 22 (1): 13–26. https://doi.org/10.1068/d316t.

Lee, Pamela. 2004. *Chronophobia: On Time in the Art of the 1960s.* Cambridge, MA: MIT Press.

Lee, Zune. 2011. Interview by Janine Randerson. Audio Foundation, Auckland, New Zealand, September 19.

Lefale, Penehuro Fatu. 2010. "Ua'afa le Aso Stormy Weather Today: Traditional Ecological Knowledge of Weather and Climate. The Samoa Experience." *Climatic Change* 100 (2): 317–335.

LeWitt, Sol. 1967. "Paragraphs on Conceptual Art." *Artforum* 1 (June): 79–83.

Liberate Tate. 2012. "Disobedience as Performance." *Performance Research* 17 (4): 135–140. doi:10.1080/13528165.2012.712343.

Liberate Tate, Steven Lam, Gabi Ngcobo, Jack Persekian, Nato Thompson, and Anne Sophie Witzke. 2013. "Art, Ecology and Institutions: A Conversation with Artists and Curators." *Third Text* 27 (1): 141–150.

Lippard, Lucy, Stephanie Smith, and Andrew Revkin, eds. 2007. *Weather Report: Art and Climate Change.* Boulder, CO: Boulder Museum of Contemporary Art.

List, Roland. 2004. "Weather Modification: A Scenario for the Future." *Bulletin of the American Meteorological Society* 85 (1): 51–63.

Liu, Zhe, and Ying Chen. 2015. "Impacts, Risks, and Governance of Climate Engineering." *Advances in Climate Change Research* 6 (3–4): 197–201. doi:10.1016/j.accre.2015.10.004.

Lochhead, Judy. 2001. "Hearing Chaos." *American Music* 19 (2): 210–246.

Lockhart, Gary. 1988. *The Weather Companion: An Album of Meteorological History, Science, Legend, and Folklore.* New York: Wiley.

Loos, Ted. 2011. "Shifting Sands of Societies and Politics." *New York Times*, April 27. http://www.nytimes.com/2011/05/01/arts/design/francis-alys-a-story-of-deception-to-open-at-moma.html.

Lorenz, Edward N. 1963. "Deterministic Periodic Flow." *Journal of the Atmospheric Sciences* 20 (2): 130–148.

Lorenz, Edward N. 1967. *The Nature and Theory of the General Circulation of the Atmosphere.* Geneva: World Meteorological Organization.

Lorenz, Edward N. 1993. *The Essence of Chaos.* Seattle: University of Washington Press.

Lowry, William P. 1969. *Weather and Life: An Introduction to Biometeorology.* New York: Academic Press.

Luckhurst, R., and J. McDonagh. 2002. *Transactions and Encounters: Science and Culture in the Nineteenth Century.* Manchester: Manchester University Press.

Lund, Karsten. 2014. *Eyes on the Sun, Hands on the Moon*. Exhibition catalogue. Chicago: Museum of Contemporary Art.

Lye, Len. 1961. "Tangible Motion Sculpture." *Art Journal* 20 (4): 226–227.

Lye, Len. 1984. *Figures of Motion: Len Lye, Selected Writings*. Edited by Wystan Curnow and Roger Horrocks. Auckland, New Zealand: Auckland University Press.

MacDonald, Scott. 1989. "Yoko Ono: Ideas on Film: Interviews/Scripts." *Film Quarterly* 43 (1): 2–23.

Mackenzie, Adrian. 2009. "Intensive Movement in Wireless Digital Signal Processing: From Calculation to Envelopment." *Environment & Planning* 41 (6): 1294–1308.

Macunias, George. 1963. *Fluxus Manifesto*. George Macunias Foundation. http://georgemaciunas.com/about/cv/manifesto-i/.

Malina, Roger. 2007. "Lovely Weather: Asking What the Arts Can Do for the Sciences." http://vectors.usc.edu/thoughtmesh/publish/111.php.

Manhire, Bill. 2006. *Are Angels OK? The Parallel Universes of New Zealand Writers and Scientists*. Wellington, New Zealand: Victoria University Press.

Manovich, Lev. 2002. "The Anti-Sublime Ideal in Data Art." meetopia.net/virus/pdf-ps_db/LManovich_data_art.pdf.

Manovich, Lev. 2011. "Trending: The Promises and the Challenges of Big Social Data." http://manovich.net/index.php/projects/trending-the-promises-and-the-challenges-of-big-social-data.

Marcuse, Herbert. 1969. *An Essay on Liberation*. Boston: Beacon Press.

Marcuse, Herbert. 1972. "Ecology and Revolution." *Liberation* 16 (September): 10–12.

Martin, Colin. 2006. "Science in Culture: Artists on a Mission." *Nature* 441 (7093): 578.

Marx, Leo, and Merrott Roe Smith. 1994. *Does Technology Drive History? The Dilemma of Technological Determinism*. Cambridge, MA: MIT Press.

Massey, Doreen. 2003. "Some Times of Space." In *Olafur Eliasson: The Weather Project*, edited by Susan May, 107–118. London: Tate Publishing.

Massumi, Brian. 2000. "Too-Blue: Colour Patch for an Expanded Empiricism." *Cultural Studies* 14 (2): 177–226.

Massumi, Brian. 2002. *Parables for the Virtual: Movement, Affect, Sensation*. Durham, NC: Duke University Press.

Massumi, Brian. 2007. "The Thinking-Feeling of What Happens: A Semblance of a Conversation." In *Interact or Die!*, edited by Joke Brouwer, Arjen Mulder, Brian Massumi, Detlef Mertins, Lars Spuybroek, Moortje Marres, and Christian Hubler, 70–97. Rotterdam: V2_Publishing.

Masters, H. G. 2008. "Yoko Ono: The Artist in Her Unfinished Avant-Garden." *Art AsiaPacific* 58 (May–June): 143–149.

Maysmor, Bob. 2006. "Kites and manu tukutuku—Manu tukutuku—Māori kites." *Te Ara—the Encyclopedia of New Zealand*, June 12. http://teara.govt.nz/en/kites-and-manu-tukutuku/page-1.

McDougall, Marina. 2013. "Learning to Love the Fog." In *Over the Water*, edited by Tim Hawkinson, 9–19. Exhibition catalogue. San Francisco: Exploratorium.

McKim, Kristi.2013. *Cinema as Weather: Stylistic Screens and Atmospheric Change*. New York: Routledge.

McLagen, Meg, and Yates McKee, eds. 2012. *Sensible Politics: The Visual Culture of Nongovernmental Activism*. New York: Zone Books.

McLuhan, Marshall. 1962. *The Gutenberg Galaxy: The Making of Typographic Man*. Toronto: University of Toronto Press.

McLuhan, Marshall. 1997a. "Acoustic Space." In *Marshall McLuhan Essays: Media Research, Technology, Art, Communication*, edited by Michel A. Moos, 39–43. Amsterdam: OPA.

McLuhan, Marshall. 1997b. "The Relation of Environment to Anti-Environment." In *Marshall McLuhan Essays: Media Research, Technology, Art, Communication*, edited by Michel. A. Moos, 110–119. Amsterdam: OPA.

McLuhan, Marshall, and Victor J. Papanek. 1967. *Verbi-Voco-Visual Explorations*. New York: Something Else Press.

McQuire, Scott. 2008. *Media City*. London: Sage Publications.

McQuire, Scott. 2015. "Digital Photography and the Operational Archive." In *Genealogies of Digital Light Project*, edited by Sean Cubitt, Daniel Palmer, and Nathaniel Tkacz, 144–161. London: Open Humanities Press.

Meillassoux, Quentin. 2008. *After Finitude: An Essay on the Necessity of Contingency*. Translated by R. Brassier. London: Bloomsbury Publishing.

Merleau-Ponty, Maurice. 1962. *Phenomenology of Perception*. London: Routledge.

Merleau-Ponty, Maurice. 1964. *Cezanne's Doubt: Sense and Non-sense*. Evanston, IL: Northwestern University Press.

Merleau-Ponty, Maurice, and Claude Lefort. 1968. *The Visible and the Invisible: Followed by Working Notes*. Evanston, IL: Northwestern University Press.

Middleton, William Edgar Knowles. 1969. *The Invention of Meteorological Instruments*. Baltimore: Johns Hopkins Press.

Miles, Malcolm. 2014. *Eco-Aesthetics: Art, Literature and Architecture in a Period of Climate Change*. London: Bloomsbury.

Mills, Jonathon, ed. 2007. *Ethically Challenged: Big Questions for Science*. Melbourne: Melbourne University Publishing.

Mirzoeff, Nicholas. 2011. "The Clash of Visualizations: Counterinsurgency and Climate Change." *Social Research: An International Quarterly* 78 (4) (Winter): 1185–1210.

Mok, Kimberley. 2013. "Artist Creates Cloud Making Machine to Test Geoengineering 'Limits of Knowledge.'" *TreeHugger*, January 26. http://www.treehugger.com/sustainable-product-design/artist-creates-cloud-making-machine-geoengineering.html.

Moore, Jason W., ed. 2016. *Anthropocene or Capitalocene? Nature, History, and the Crisis of Capitalism*. Oakland, CA: Kairos/PM Press.

Morioka, Yuji. n.d. "Interactive Landscape." Translated by Bert Winther. *Process Art*. Accessed November 22, 2016. http://processart.jp/nakaya/e/.

Morton, Timothy. 2007. *Ecology without Nature: Rethinking Environmental Aesthetics*. New York: Harvard University Press.

Morton, Timothy. 2011. "Dark Ecologies." Lecture at Auckland University of Technology (AUT), Auckland, New Zealand, May 25.

Morton, Timothy. 2012. "From Modernity to the Anthropocene: Ecology and Art in the Age of Asymmetry." *International Social Science Journal* 63 (207–208): 39–51.

Morton, Timothy. 2013. *Hyperobjects: Philosophy and Ecology after the End of the World*. Minneapolis: University of Minnesota Press.

Mouffe, Chantal, Rosalyn Deutsche, Branden W. Joseph, and Thomas Keenan. 2001. "Every Form of Art has a Political Dimension." *Grey Room* 2:98–125.

Mouffe, Chantal. 2005. *On the Political*. London: Routledge.

Mouffe, Chantal. 2007. "Artistic Activism and Agonistic Spaces." *Art and Research: A Journal of Ideas, Contexts and Methods* 1 (2). http://www.artandresearch.org.uk/v1n2/mouffe.html.

Mouffe, Chantal. 2008. "Art and Democracy: Art as an Agnostic Intervention in Public Space," in *Art as Public Issue: How Art and Its Institutions Reinvent the Public Dimension*, edited by Jorinde Seijdel, 6–13. Rotterdam: NAi Publishers.

Muller, Lizzie. 2009. "Smelling the Sun, Breathing a River: New Work by Joyce Hinterding and David Haines." *RealTime Arts*, no. 89 (February–March): 27. http://www.realtimearts.net/article/89/9342.

Muller, Lizzie. 2014. "Speculative Objects: Visual Arts and Science Fiction Futures." In *SPECTRA: Images and Data in Art/Science: The Currency of Images in the Studio and the Laboratory*(Proceedings from the Symposium SPECTRA 2012), edited by Mary Rosengren and Cris Kennedy, 46–55. Adelaide: Australian Network for Art and Technology (ANAT), CSIRO Discovery Centre.

Murphie, Andrew. 2012. "Hacking the Aesthetic: David Haines and Joyce Hinterding's New Ecologies of Signal." *Journal of Aesthetics and Culture* 4 (1). www.tandfonline.com/doi/full/10.3402/jac.v4i0.18153.

Mundine, Djon. 2008. "The Spirit Within: North Eastern and Central Arnhem Land." In *They Are Meditating: Bark Paintings from the MCA's Arnott Collection*, edited by Linda Michael, 77–146. Exhibition catalogue. Sydney: Museum of Contemporary Art, Sydney.

Munroe, Alexandra, Yoko Ono, Jon Hendricks, and Bruce Altshuler. 2000. *Yes Yoko Ono*. New York: Japan Society.

Munster, Anna. 2006. *Materializing New Media: Embodiment in Information Aesthetics*. Dartmouth, NH: Dartmouth College Press.

NASA (National Aeronautics and Space Administration). 2012. "Section One: Above the Atmosphere." *Sp-168 Exploring Space with a Camera*. http://history.nasa.gov/SP-168/section1.htm#6.

NASA (National Aeronautics and Space Administration). n.d. *Space Weather Media Viewer*. United States. https://sunearthday.nasa.gov/spaceweather/.

Nash, Madeleine. 2006. "Storm Warnings (Atlantic Hurricanes and Global Warming)." *Smithsonian* 37 (6): 88–96.

National Snow and Ice Data Center (NSIDC). 2018. "Sea Ice Tracking Low in Both Hemispheres." United States. February 6, 2018. http://nsidc.org/arcticseaicenews/.

Naumann, Francis M. 1982. "Affectueusement, Marcel: Ten Letters from Marcel Duchamp to Suzanne Duchamp and Jean Crotti." *Archives of American Art Journal* 22 (4): 2–19.

Neimanis, Astrida, and Rachel Loewen Walker. 2014. "Weathering: Climate Change and the 'Thick Time' of Transcorporeality." *Hypatia* 29 (3): 558–575.

Nicolson, Benedict, and the Paul Mellon Foundation for British Art. 1968. *Joseph Wright of Derby: Painter of Light*. London: Mellon Foundation for British Art; London: Routledge.

Nisbet, James. 2013. "A Brief Moment in the History of Photo-Energy: Walter De Maria's Lightning Field." *Grey Room* 50 (Winter): 66–89.

O'Hara, Frank. 1995. *The Collected Poems of Frank O'Hara*. Edited by Donald Allen. Berkeley: University of California Press.

Oliver, James. 2016. "Soren Dahlgaard: The Maldives Exodus Caravan Show." In *ART+CLIMATE=CHANGE*, edited by Guy Abrahams, Kelly Gellatly, and Bronwyn Johnson, 92–93. Carlton, Australia: MUP Custom.

Ono, Yoko. 1966. "Cut along dotted line and look at the sky through the hole." In *Art and Artists* 1 (5), ed. Mario Amaya, 16. London: Hansom Books.

Ono, Yoko. 1970. *Grapefruit: A Book of Instructions and Drawings by Yoko Ono*. London: Peter Owen Limited.

Out-of-Sync. 2006. "Talking about the Weather." *Out-of-Sync Homepage*. http://www.out-of-sync .com/weatherwebsite2012/project.html.

Out-of-Sync. 2007. Interview by Janine Randerson. SCANZ Symposium, Taranaki, July 19.

Palmer, Lauren. 2015. "Olafur Eliasson Responds to Paris Summit with a Doomsday Clock Made of Glacial Ice: Going, Going … Gone." *Artnet*, December 3. https://news.artnet.com/art-world/ ice-watch-olafur-eliasson-climate-summit-384704.

Parenti, Christian. 2011. *Tropic of Chaos: Climate Change and the New Geography of Violence*. New York: Nation Books.

Park, Geoff. 2006. *Theatre Country: Essays on Landscape and Whenua*. Wellington, New Zealand: Victoria University Press.

Parks, Lisa. 2005. *Cultures in Orbit: Satellites and the Televisual*. Durham, NC: Duke University Press.

Parks, Lisa. 2007. "Orbital Performers and Satellite Translators: Media Art in the Age of Iono-spheric Exchange." *Quarterly Review of Film & Video* 24 (3): 207–216.

Parsons, Glenn. 2008. "Environmental Art: An Affront to Nature?" In *Nature and Aesthetics*, edited by Glenn Parsons. London: Continuum Books.

Parikka, Jussi. 2011a. "Introduction: The Materiality of Media and Waste." In *Medianatures: The Materiality of Information Technology and Electronic Waste*, edited by Jussi Parikka. Ann Arbor, MI: Open Humanities Press. http://www.livingbooksaboutlife.org/books/Medianatures.

Parikka, Jussi. 2011b. "Media Ecologies and Imaginary Media: Transversal Expansions, Contrac-tions, and Foldings." *Fibreculture*, no. 17: 34–50. http://seventeen.fibreculturejournal.org/ fcj-116-media-ecologies-and-imaginary-media.

Parikka, Jussi. 2011c. "New Materialism as Media Theory: Medianatures and Dirty Matter." *Com-munication and Critical/Cultural Studies* 9 (1): 95–100.

Parikka, Jussi. 2015. *A Geology of Media*. Minneapolis: University of Minnesota Press.

Pedrotti, Frank L., and Leno S. Pedrotti. 1993. *Introduction to Optics*. Upper Saddle River, NJ: Pren-tice Hall.

Peljhan, Marko. n.d. "Makrolab Mark II 2000." http://krcf.knowbotiq.net/cfa/hh/makrolab/ makrolab.ljudmila.org/vision/markdva.html.

Peljhan, Marko, Ieva Auzina, Rasa Smite, and Raitis Smits. 2001. "Interview with Marko Peljhan." RIXC Interview. http://www.ladomir.net/filter/citizen-science/2001-rixc-interview.

Peters, John Durham. 2015. *The Marvelous Clouds: Toward a Philosophy of Elemental Media*. Chi-cago: University of Chicago Press.

Picard, Caroline. 2014. "Sarah and Joseph Belknap Translate the Solar System for Earthlings." *Artslant*, December 8. https://www.artslant.com/ny/articles/show/41488.

Pickering, Andrew. 2010. *The Cybernetic Brain: Sketches of Another Future*. Chicago: University of Chicago Press.

Pickles, John. 2004. *A History of Spaces: Cartographic Reason, Mapping, and the Geo-Coded World*. New York: Routledge.

Polli, Andrea. 2004. "Modelling Storms in Sound: The Atmospherics/Weather Works Project." *Organised Sound* 9 (2): 175–180.

Polli, Andrea. 2005. "Atmospherics/Weather Works: A Spatialized Meteorological Data Sonification Project." *Leonardo* 38 (1): 405–411.

Polli, Andrea. 2009a. "Airspace: Antarctic Sound Transmission." Paper presented at *After Media: Embodiment and Context*, Digital Arts and Culture Conference, University of California, Irvine, December 12–15. http://escholarship.org/uc/item/83r992f6.

Polli, Andrea. 2009b. "Listening to the Poles." In *RETHINK: Contemporary Art and Climate Change* (online forum), edited by Anne Sophie Witzke. Aarhus, Denmark: Alexandra Institute.

Polli, Andrea. 2011. Interview by Janine Randerson. Auckland Airport, Auckland, New Zealand, June 25.

Polli, Andrea. 2016. *The Making of Energy Flow on the Rachel Carson Bridge*. Pittsburgh, PA: Carnegie Museum of Art, November 16. https://vimeo.com/193613157.

Popper, Karl. 1965. *Of Clouds and Clocks*. St. Louis: Washington University.

Povinelli, Elizabeth. 2016. *Geontologies: A Requiem to Late Liberalism*. Durham, NC: Duke University Press.

Prade, E. L. 2002. "The Early Days of E.A.T." *IEEE MultiMedia* 9 (2): 4–5. doi:10.1109/93.998040.

Price, Mark. 2016. "Tomás Saraceno." *Sculpture* 35 (6): 78–79.

Prigogine, Ilya, and Isabelle Stengers. 1984. *Order Out of Chaos: Man's New Dialogue with Nature*. Boulder, CO: New Science Library.

Proctor, James D. 2009. *Envisioning Nature, Science and Religion*. West Conshohocken, PA: Templeton Foundation Press.

Proulx, Gerard J., ed. 1971. *The Standard Dictionary of Meteorological Sciences*. Montreal: McGill-Queens University Press.

Puig de la Bellacasa, María. 2014. "Making Time for Soil: Technoscientific Futurity and the Pace of Care." *Social Studies of Science* 45 (5): 691–716.

Puig de la Bellacasa, María. 2017. *Matters of Care: Speculative Ethics in More than Human Worlds*. Minneapolis: University of Minnesota Press.

Qvortrop, Lars. 2003. "Digital Art and Design Poetics: The Poetical Potentials of Projection and Interaction." In *Digital Media Revisited: Theoretical and Conceptual Innovation in Digital Domains*, edited by Andrew Morrison, Terje Rasmussen, and Gunnar Liestol, 239–263. Cambridge, MA: MIT Press.

Rancière, Jacques. 1999. *Disagreement: Politics and Philosophy*. Translated by J. Rose. Minneapolis: University of Minnesota Press.

Rancière, Jacques. 2008. "Aesthetic Separation, Aesthetic Community: Scenes from the Aesthetic Regime of Art." *Art and Research: A Journal of Ideas, Contexts and Methods* 2 (1). http://www.artand research.org.uk/v2n1/ranciere.html.

Rancière, Jacques. 2010. *Dissensus: On Politics and Aesthetics*. Translated by S. Corcoran. London: Continuum.

Randerson, Janine. 2013. "Cloud Music: A Cloud System." In *Proceedings of the 19th International Symposium of Electronic Art*, edited by Kathy Cleland, L. Fisher, and R. Harley. Sydney: ISEA International, the Australian Network for Art & Technology and the University of Sydney. http://hdl .handle.net/10652/2741.

Randerson, Janine, Jennifer Salmond, and Chris Manford. 2015. "Weather as Medium: Art and Meteorological Science." *Leonardo* 48 (1): 16–24.

Randerson, Janine, and Rachel Shearer. 2017. "Dark Sun: Solar Frequencies, Solar Affects." In *Animism in Art and Performance*, edited by Chris Braddock, 67–88. London: Palgrave Macmillan.

Randerson, Janine, and Amanda Yates. 2016. "Negotiating the Ontological Gap: Place, Performance and Media Arts Practices in Aorearoa/New Zealand." In *Ecocriticism and Indigenous Studies: Conversations from Earth to Cosmos*, edited by Joni Adamson and Salma Monani, 23–43. New York: Routledge.

Random International. 2012. *Rain Room*. http://random-international.com/work/rainroom/.

Rasch, Philip J., John Latham, and Chih-Chieh (Jack) Chen. 2009. "Geoengineering by Cloud Seeding: Influence on Sea Ice and Climate System." *Environmental Research Letters* 4 (4). doi:10.1088/1748-9326/4/4/045112.

Reeves, Eileen A. 1997. *Painting the Heavens: Art and Science in the Age of Galileo*. Princeton, NJ: Princeton University Press.

Reich, Wilhelm. 1954. "Rules to Follow in Cloud Engineering." *CORE 7*. [Appendix A.] Orgone Institute 6:1–4. https://archive.org/stream/ContactFromSpaceByWilhelmReich/Contact-from -Space%20by%20Wilhelm%20Reich_djvu.txt.

Reto, Iona (dir.), and Latai Taumoepeau. 2013. *Body of Art*. HD video documentary. 00:14:38. Sydney: Sydney Institute of Film Academy. https://vimeo.com/60363446.

Richards, Ivor A. 1976. *Complementarities: Uncollected Essays*. Cambridge, MA: Harvard University Press.

Robbins, Cameron. 2014. *Wind Section Instrumental*. https://cameronrobbins.com/wind-section -instrumental-sonic-wind-section/.

Robinson, Henry S. 1943. "The Tower of the Winds and the Roman Market-Place." *American Journal of Archaeology* 47 (3): 291–305.

Robertson, Natalie. 2005. "Between Earth and Sky—Ways of Making a Place in a Placeless World." Presentation at *Regaining Ground*.

Robertson, Natalie. 2011. Interview by Janine Randerson. Mt. Albert, Auckland, New Zealand, February 25.

Ross, Andrew. 1991. *Strange Weather: Culture, Science, and Technology in the Age of Limits*. London: Verso.

Ross, Andrew. 1996. *Science Wars*. Durham, NC: Duke University Press.

Ruskin, John. 1846. *Modern Painters*. London: Smith Elder.

Rutsky, Randolph L. 1999. *High Techne: Art and Technology from the Machine Aesthetic to the Posthuman*. Minneapolis: University of Minnesota Press.

Salinger, Jim. 2016. "Climate Change Update: How a Warmer World Is Affecting Us." Paper presented at *TEMP Forum II*, Corban Art Estate, Auckland, New Zealand, November 15.

Saraceno, Tomás. 2011. *Tomás Saraceno: Cloud Cities*. Video documentary. Dornbracht Installation Projects. October 24. https://www.youtube.com/watch?v=J3-bMY76KkU&t=29s.

Sassor, Robert Russell. 2015. "Envisioning a Climate for Change." *Stanford Social Innovation Review* (blog), March 18. https://ssir.org/articles/entry/envisioning_a_climate_for_change.

Schrogl, Kai-Uwe, and Leopold Summerer. 2016. "Climate Engineering and Space." *Acta Astronautica* 129 (December): 121–129. doi:10.1016/j.actaastro.2016.08.033.

Scientific American. n.d. "The Role of Sunspots and Solar Winds in Climate Change." *Earthtalk* (blog). https://www.scientificamerican.com/article/sun-spots-and-climate-change/.

Scott, Jill. 2006. *Artists-in-Labs: Processes of Inquiry*. Vienna: Springer.

Searle, Adrian. 2010. "Francis Alÿs Treads the Thin Green Line." *Guardian*, June 14. https://www.theguardian.com/artanddesign/2010/jun/14/francis-alys-story-of-deception.

Selby, Rachael, Pātaka Moore, and Malcolm Mulholland, eds. 2010. *Māori and the Environment: Kaitiaki*. Wellington, New Zealand: Huia Publishers.

Serres, Michael. 1982a. *Hermes: Literature, Science, Philosophy*. Baltimore, MD: Johns Hopkins University Press.

Serres, Michael. 1982b. *The Parasite*. Baltimore, MD: Johns Hopkins University Press.

Serres, Michael. 1995a. *Genesis*. Ann Arbor: University of Michigan Press.

Serres, Michael. 1995b. *The Natural Contract*. Ann Arbor: University of Michigan Press.

Shanken, Edward. 2002. "Art in the Information Age: Technology and Conceptual Art." *Leonardo* 35 (4): 433–438.

Shearer, Rachel. 2017. "Wiriwiri." In *HEAT: Solar Revolutions*, edited by Amanda Yates and Andrew Clifford. Auckland, New Zealand: Te Uru Waitakere Contemporary Gallery. Accessed February 22, 2018. http://www.teuru.org.nz/teuru/assets/File/HEAT%20Exhibition%20Programme.pdf.

Simondon, Gilbert. 1958. *On the Mode of Existence of Technical Objects*. Paris: Editions Montaigne.

Simondon, Gilbert. 2009. "The Position of the Problem of Ontogenesis." *Parrhesia* 7:4–16.

Skrebowski, Luke. 2005. "All Systems Go: Recovering Hans Haacke's Systems Art." Presentation at the *Open Systems: Rethinking Art c. 1970* conference, Tate Modern, London, September 17.

Skrebowski, Luke. 2008. "All Systems Go: Recovering Hans Haacke's Systems Art." *Grey Room* 30 (Winter): 54–83.

Sloterdijk, Peter. 2009. *Terror from the Air*. Translated by A. Patton and S. Corcoran. Cambridge, MA: MIT Press.

Smith, Huhana. 2012. "Hei Whenua Ora ki Te Hākari: Reinstating the Mauri of Valued Ecosystems: History, Lessons and Experiences from the Hei Whenua Ora ki Te Hākari/Te Hākari Dune Wetland Restoration Project." Ngā Māramatanga-ā-Papa [Iwi Ecosystem Services] Research Monograph Series No. 9. Lincoln, New Zealand: Manaaki Whenua Landcare Research.

Smith, Roberta. 2010. "After Process, a Return to the Tropics." *New York Times*, June 10. http://www.nytimes.com/2010/06/11/arts/design/11ferrer.html.

Snow, Charles P. 1959. *The Two Cultures and the Scientific Revolution*. Cambridge: Cambridge University Press.

Sobecka, Karolina. 2015. "Last Clouds." In *Art in the Anthropocene: Encounters among Aesthetics, Politics, Environments and Epistemologies*, edited by Heather Davis and Etienne Turpin, 213–222. London: Open Humanities Press.

Sobecka, Karolina. 2016. *A Machine for Making the Future*. Accessed February 12, 2018. http://www.flightphase.com/MachineForMakingTheFuture/.

Sobecka, Karolina. n.d. *The Matter of Air*. Accessed March 28, 2017. http://www.amateurhuman.org/.

Stadler, L. 2010. "Air, Light and Air-Conditioning." Translated by Jill Denton. *Grey Room* 40 (Summer): 84–99.

Stengers, Isabelle. 1997. *Power and Invention: Situating Science*. Minneapolis: University of Minnesota Press.

Stengers, Isabelle. 2005. "Introductory Notes on an Ecology of Practices." *Cultural Studies Review* 11 (1): 183–196.

Society* 25 (4): 91–110.

Stengers, Isabelle. 2010. *Cosmopolitics*. Minneapolis: University of Minnesota Press.

Stengers, Isabelle. 2015. *In Catastrophic Times: Resisting the Coming Barbarism*. Translated by A. Goffey. London: Open Humanities Press.

Stengers, Isabelle, and Michael Lissack. 2004. "The Challenge of Complexity: Unfolding the Ethics of Science. In Memoriam Ilya Prigogine." *Emergence* 6 (1–2): 92–99.

Stephens, Graeme. 2005. "Cloud Feedbacks in the Climate System: A Critical Review." *American Meteorological Society* 18:237–273.

Stewart, Garrett. 2011. "Book Quirks." *Critical Inquiry* 37 (2): 355–363.

Stieglitz, Alfred. 2000. *Stieglitz on Photography: His Selected Essays and Notes*. Edited by Sarah Greenough. New York: Aperture Foundation.

Sturken, Marita. 2006. "Weather Media and Homeland Security: Selling Preparedness in a Volatile World." SSRC.org, June 11. http://understandingkatrina.ssrc.org/Sturken/.

Tait, Peta. 2016. "Performing Species Kinship and Strange Emotions." Paper presented at *Performance Climates*, PSi Performance Studies International #22, University of Melbourne, July 7.

Taumoepeau, Latai. 2012. "i-Land X-isle." *Center for Sustainable Practice in the Arts*, May 25. http://www.sustainablepractice.org/2012/05/25/i-land-x-isle-latai-taumoepeau/.

Taumoepeau, Latai. 2016. "Stitching Up the Sea." *Sacred: Homelands Festival*, November 23–27, London. https://sacredhomelandsfestival.wordpress.com/latai-taumoepeau/.

Tate. 2012. "TateShots: David Medalla." *TateShots, Bloomberg*, June 21. https://www.youtube.com/watch?v=2u8VJp4VMcw.

Te Kuwaha. n.d. "NIWA National Institute of Water and Atmospheric Research: Māori Research Unit." NIWA. http://www.niwa.co.nz/our-science/te-kuwaha.

Television New Zealand. 2004. "Erosion Threatens Mt Taranaki." *One Network News*, 8:13 p.m., December 4, New Zealand.

TEMP. n.d. *O-Tū-Kapua (What Clouds See)*. Accessed March 1, 2017. http://www.tempauckland.org.nz/air/.

Terra, Jun. 1995. "David Medalla in London." *Third Text* 95 (30): 93–100. doi:10.1080/09528829508576534.

Terranova, Tiziana. 2004. "Communication beyond Meaning: On the Cultural Politics of Information." *Social Text* 22 (3): 51–73.

Te Tuhi Centre for the Arts. 2014. "The Maldives Exodus Caravan Show." March 8–July 13. http://www.tetuhi.org.nz/whats-on/exhibitiondetails.php?id=142.

Thomson, Jon, and Alison Craighead. 2007. "Thomson & Craighead: Weather Gauge." *Leonardo* 40 (3): 229–229.

Thornes, John E. 1999. *John Constable's Skies: A Fusion of Art and Science*. Birmingham: University of Birmingham Press.

Thornes, John E. 2008. "Cultural Climatology and the Representation of Sky, Atmosphere, Weather and Climate in Selected Art Works of Constable, Monet and Eliasson." *Geoforum* 39 (2): 570–580.

Thrift, Nigel. 2004. "Remembering the Technological Unconscious by Foregrounding Knowledges of Position." *Environment and Planning D: Society & Space* 22 (1): 175–190.

Thrift, Nigel. 2008. *Non-representational Theory: Space, Politics, Affect*. London: Routledge.

Todd, Zoe. 2014. "An Indigenous Feminist's Take on the Ontological Turn: 'Ontology' Is Just Another Word for Colonialism (Urbane Adventurer: Amiskwacî)." *Uma (in)certa antropologia* (blog), October 24. http://umaincertaantropologia.org/2014/10/26/an-indigenous-feminists-take-on-the-ontological-turn-ontology-is-just-another-word-for-colonialism-urbane-adventurer-amiskwaci/.

Todd, Zoe. 2015. "Indigenizing the Anthropocene." In *Art in the Anthropocene: Encounters among Aesthetics, Politics, Environments and Epistemologies*, edited by Heather Davis and Etienne Turpin, 241–254. London: Open Humanities Press.

Tondeur, Anais. 2015. *The Eophone's Whistle*. http://www.anais-tondeur.com/recent-work/eophone/.

Tufte, Edward R. 2001. *The Visual Display of Quantitative Information*. Cheshire, CT: Graphics Press.

Tuhiwai-Smith, Linda. 1999. *Decolonizing Methodologies: Research and Indigenous Peoples*. New York: Zed Books.

Turner, Fred. 2005. "Where the Counterculture Met the New Economy." *Technology and Culture* 46 (3): 485–512.

Tuters, Marc, and Kazys Varnelis. 2006. "Beyond Locative Media: Giving Shape to the Internet of Things." *Leonardo* 39 (4): 357–363.

University of Melbourne. 2011. *Data Assimilation and Bushfire Modelling for Early and Rapid Bushfire Detection*. Melbourne: Institute for a Broadband Enabled Society.

University of Melbourne. 2016. "Refuge: Your Relief Centre." University of Melbourne, July 9. http://sustainable.unimelb.edu.au/refuge-your-relief-centre.

van Kranenburg, Rob. 2006. "When Wireless Dreams Come True." *Mute*, October 5. http://www.metamute.org/editorial/articles/when-wireless-dreams-come-true.

Virilio, Paul. 1994. *The Vision Machine*. Bloomington: Indiana University Press.

Virilio, Paul, and Sylvere Lotringer. 2002. *Crepuscular Dawn*. Los Angeles: Semiotext(e).

Virilio, Paul, and Julie Rose. 2003. *Art and Fear*. London: Continuum.

Vitz, Paul C., and Arnold B. Glimcher. 1984. *Modern Art and Modern Science: The Parallel Analysis of Vision*. New York: Praeger.

Waerea, Layne. 2016. "Free Social Injunctions: Art Interventions as Agency in the Production of Socio-legal Subjectivities Not Yet Imagined or Realised." PhD diss., Auckland University of Technology (AUT), Auckland, New Zealand.

Wallace, Linda. 1994. "2000 Thunderstorms: Joyce Hinterding." *Continuum* 8 (1): 432–435.

Wallis, Brian, and Jeffrey Kastner. 1998. *Land and Environmental Art*. London: Phaidon.

Walsh, K. J. E., K.-C. Nguyen, and J. L. McGregor. 2004. "Fine-Resolution Regional Climate Model Simulations of the Impact of Climate Change on Tropical Cyclones near Australia." *Climate Dynamics* 22 (1): 47–56.

Walton, David. 2011. "Measurement in Science." Presentation at *Data Landscapes Symposium*, The Arts Catalyst, London, May 20–22. https://www.artscatalyst.org/data-landscapes-symposium.

Watson, Matthew. 2011. "SPICE: Stratospheric Particle Injection for Climate Engineering." *SPICE*. Accessed March 30, 2017. http://www.spice.ac.uk.

Watson, Ruth. 2009. "Mapping and Contemporary Art." *Art and Cartography* 46 (4): 293–307.

Wattenberg, Martin, and Fernanda Viégas. 2007. *Artistic Data Visualization: Beyond Visual Analytics*. Cambridge, MA: Visual Communication Lab, IBM Research.

Wattenberg, Martin, and Fernanda Viégas. n.d. *Wind Map*. Accessed December 1, 2009. http://hint.fm/projects/wind/.

Watts, Vanessa. 2013. "Indigenous Place-Thought & Agency amongst Humans and Non-humans (First Woman and Sky Woman Go on a European World Tour!)." *Decolonization* 2 (1): 20–34.

von Bertalanffy, Ludwig. 1968. *General System Theory: Foundations, Development, Applications*. New York: Braziller.

theweathergroup_U. 2008. *THEWEATHERGROUP*. Accessed February 12, 2018. http://www.theweathergroup.org/2008/.

Wechsler, Judith. 1978. *On Aesthetics in Science*. Cambridge, MA: MIT Press.

Weibel, Peter, and Morten Søndergaard. 2008. *Thorbjørn Lausten: Visual Systems*. Heidelberg: Kehrer.

Whatmore, Sarah. 2002. *Hybrid Geographies: Natures, Cultures, Spaces*. London: Sage Publications.

Whatmore, Sarah. 2006. "Materialist Returns: Practising Cultural Geography in and for a More-than-Human World." *Cultural Geographies* 13 (4): 600–609.

Whitehead, Alfred N. 1978. *Process and Reality: An Essay in Cosmology*. Edited by David Griffin and Donald Sherburne. New York: Free Press.

Whitelaw, Mitchell. 2004. *Metacreations: Art and Artificial Life*. Cambridge, MA: MIT Press.

Whitelaw, Mitchell. 2008. "Art against Information: Case Studies in Data Practice." *Fibreculture* 11. http://eleven.fibreculturejournal.org/fcj-067-art-against-information-case-studies-in-data-practice/.

Whitelaw, Mitchell, and Sam Hinton. 2010. "Exploring the Digital Commons: An Approach to the Visualisation of Large Heritage Datasets." Presentation at *Electronic Visualization and the Arts*, London, July 5–7. http://creative.canberra.edu.au/mitchell/.

WHO (World Health Organization). 2011. "Annual Mean PM10 Particulate Matter with Diameter of 10 μm or Less, by Country." *WHO Report*, September. www.who.int/phe/health_topics/outdoorair/databases/OAP_database_8_2011.xls.

Wiener, Norbert. 1948. *Cybernetics: Or Control and Communication in the Animal and the Machine*. Cambridge, MA: MIT Press.

Wiener, Norbert. 1956. "Nonlinear Prediction and Dynamics." In *Proceedings of the Third Berkeley Symposium on Mathematical Statistics and Probability*, Vol. 3: Contributions to Astronomy and Physics, edited by Jerzy Neyman, 247–252. Berkeley: University of California Press.

Wilson, Stephen. 2002. *Information Arts: Intersections of Art, Science, and Technology*. Cambridge, MA: MIT Press.

Wood, Gillen D'Arcy. 2007. "Constable, Clouds, Climate Change." *Wordsworth Circle* 38, no. 1–2 (Winter–Spring): 25–33.

World Meteorological Organization. 2016. "Provisional WMO Statement on the Status of the Global Climate in 2016." World Meteorological Organization, November 14. http://public.wmo.int/en/media/press-release/provisional-wmo-statement-status-of-global-climate-2016.

World Meteorological Organization. n.d. *Meteoterm Database*. Accessed March 27, 2017. https://www.wmo.int/pages/prog/lsp/meteoterm_wmo_en.html.

Wright, Laura. 2010. "Diggers, Strangers and Broken Men." In *Postcolonial Green: Environmental Politics and World Narratives*, edited by Bonnie Roos and Alex Hunt, 64–79. Charlottesville: University of Virginia Press.

Wynne-Jones, Victoria. 2013. *Rainbow Warriors of Light*. Exhibition catalogue. Auckland, New Zealand: McCahon House Trust.

Yoshimoto, Midori. 2005. *Into Performance: Japanese Women Artists in New York*. New Brunswick, NJ: Rutgers University Press.

Young, Michael. 2013. "Towards the Morning Sun." *ArtAsia Pacific*, January. http://artasiapacific.com/Magazine/WebExclusives/TowardsTheMorningSun.

Zielinski, Siegfried. 2006. *Deep Time of the Media: Toward an Archaeology of Hearing and Seeing by Technical Means*. Cambridge, MA: MIT Press.

Zielinski, Siegfried, Gloria Custance, and Silvia M. Wagnermaier. 2005. *Variantology 1: On Deep Time Relations of the Arts, Sciences and Technologies*. Cologne: Verlag der Buchhandlung Walther König.

Zylinska, Joanna. 2014. *Minimal Ethics for the Anthropocene*. Ann Arbor, MI: Open Humanities Press.

Index

Proposal for Cloud Busting Machines
(Hinterding), 171
Public Smog (Balkin), 126, 136
Puig de la Bellacasa, María, 93, 113, 149–150

Rainbows, xxvi, xxxiii–xxxiv
Rain Room (Random International), 42
Rain Tower (Haacke), 14–15
Randomness, 39–40. *See also* Indeterminacy,
projects using
Reading the IPCC Fourth Assessment Report
(Balkin), 116, 126
Reading the IPCC Synthesis Report (Balkin),
125
Recording of Climate in an Art Exhibition
(Haacke), 21
Refuge (Taumoepeau), 155–156
Reich, Wilhelm, 171–173
Renaissance, the European, xxiv–xxvi
Research methods, xv, xvi–xvii
Response-ability (Haraway), 137, 139, 152,
159, 186
Robbins, Cameron, 70–71
Robertson, Natalie, 91, 94, 98–99, 101–104,
187
Romantics, the, xxix
Rosing, Minik, xxxv, xxxix, 137, 142–143
Ross, Andrew, 89, 106
Ruskin, John, xxviii

Saraceno, Tomás, 160, 176–180, 184, 186
Satellites, 47–51, 110–111
Scarce, Yhonnie, 97
Science. *See also* Art-science encounters
Aluli-Meyer's critique, xx
Big Science, xxi, xxxix, 157–158, 160, 169,
186
critiques over military involvement, xxxi
collaboration with artists, 40, 65, 82, 85, 96,
106, 143, 116
and freedom, 41
masculine bias of, 29
and measurement, 56, 138–139

need for, and mutual dependence, xv
scientific positivism, xxi, xxxi, 159
Stengers's critique, xx
"two cultures" (Snow), xxxiii, 14
Scientific visualizations. *See* Data visualization
Scientists, xxiv, xxxv
Sea Ice Index, 137
Seaside Suspension: Event for Wind and Waves
(Stelarc), 153
Second nature, 17–19, 22
Serres, Michel, 20, 22, 67, 183
Severe Tropical Storm 9301 Irma (Apple), xvii,
50, 54, 56–57, 66
Sharples, Pita, 94
Shearer, Rachel, 91, 94, 98–99, 187
Sheehan, Maree, 64
Shiomi, Mieko, 25–26, 28–29, 31, 42, 182
Shitao, xxiv
Signal interceptions, 81
Sky, the, 31, 39, 173, 179, 182, 186. *See also*
Most Blue Skies (Autogena and Portway)
Sky Dispenser (Yoko Ono), 31
Skying (painting technique), xxviii, 186
Sky Line (Haacke), 16–17, 186
Sky TV (Yoko Ono), 25, 30–31
Smith, Huhana, 94, 187
Sobecka, Karolina
cloud machines, generally, 169–170, 173,
180–181, 186
ethical obligations, 179
geoengineering workshop, 170
Matter of Air blog, 169
meteorological turn, 158
Nephology 1: Cloud Maker, 167–168, 173
Thinking Like a Cloud, 170–171
Social media, xxxiv, 59, 62, 184
Social meteorology, 89–90, 93–94, 112
Soil, 134, 150
Solomon Islands, 138, 177
Sonfist, Alan, 17
Sonic Antarctica (Polli), 67, 83–84
Soundship (descender 1) (Hinterding and
Haines), 17, 73, 174–176, 180